CHOSEN

BY FATE

The Story of Detective Thaddeus Carter

Alphonso Williams, Jr.

Crime Fiction
Novel

ISBN: 9781737526933

CONTENTS ————————————

PROLOGUE _____

A week had passed since Tonya Carter's return.

The day he rescued his daughter, Nicholas Carter went missing. He was now a miserable, wanted man who had lost his job and was on the run. Nicholas couldn't even call his wife. There was no doubt she hated him by now. He found little succor in alcohol, which seemed to take up most of his days. Someday, when the dust had settled, he would return. They could even leave Tampa if she wanted. For now, his life was a mess— one he needed to get back together.

Tonya's brother, Thaddeus, thought his sister's return would provide some sort of tranquility for him, but it didn't. Rage swelled in him every time he looked at her. He had wanted to find the bastard who did this to her himself, wishing he was old enough and strong enough to execute his vengeance. The past few days were utter hell for him. He kept thinking of Jacob and Tonya. Surely, he was losing his mind.

Tonya was in a state of mental paralysis. She saw the white light everywhere she looked. Momma would bring in a doctor to check on her twice a week and the doctor reported she was improving. Only, nothing was improving. Nobody said her father was gone, but she knew he was. The depth of loss was overwhelming.

Tonya's mother was going out of her mind but pretending everything was fine, like she had it all together.

And Thaddeus wasn't the boy she used to know. Something in him had changed. Her sister, Shanice, was fine as far as she could tell, but that did not mean something couldn't happen to her soon. Tonya imagined all these things as the burn of tears filled her eyes every night. Momma would come into her room and assure her she would be well soon. That everything was going to be fine.

Tonya had always known once the family portrait had broken, nothing was ever going to be the same.

PART ONE

All of us are products of our childhood.

- Michael Jackson

Chapter One

No one he knew thought of this place as the Garden of Love. It was a beautiful green garden behind his yard, brimming with roses, chrysanthemums, and forget-me-not scenting the air with a heavenly fragrance when dusk fell. Sometimes, when his mother let him, Thaddeus walked to the garden and sat on the bench, watching people walk by in the small neighborhood. He observed the clouds and even the butterflies, which seemed to flutter out of nowhere. To him, it was as though the garden beautified everything around it.

Except the people.

Tonya, his eldest sister, said some of the butterflies flew in from the east coast, while others were shipped in for professors doing experiments with their students. He had no idea how Tonya knew that, but the truth was she knew many things and Thaddeus was in total awe of her wisdom. She was usually right about most things and, although he suspected it had something to do with her age, he didn't think he would ever possess her kind of wisdom.

His mother would be upset if she found him in the garden instead of at home doing his homework or cutting the grass. Thaddeus hated that he was only fourteen and had to do all the *hard* labor.

His friends at school didn't talk about the chores they did at home. They only spoke of playing video games, visiting friends and watching television. Only a few of them bothered doing their homework. While Tonya always told him they were bad examples, not worthy of emulation, Thaddeus wondered what it would be like to live so freely. Instead, his parents were constantly pushing him to grow up faster and do all the things grownups did, as if something were coming he needed to be prepared for. A larger phase of life most kids only heard of.

He would never understand the way his parents thought. More frankly, he would never understand the way most adults thought. It was like they had a whole different mindset which revolved around the constant fear of an incoming evil. His mother insisted the doors be locked. She would get upset when his father returned home a little later than usual.

"Don't you realize how unsafe the streets are?" she would say. "You shouldn't stay out so late. How come you were late? Did something happen?"

And his father would explain how there was a change of plans at the office, or how he was trying to finish up work from the previous day. Thaddeus' mother would continue to ramble inaudible things about how he had to be more careful. How the city wasn't safe.

No one needed a magic mirror to see that—it was a glaring fact. The streets were filled with cigarette butts, empty alcohol bottles, various blood-stained materials and scary-looking men around every corner.

Both his mother and Tonya said those men were dangerous and should be avoided at all cost. They were the kind of people he should never be found associating with and Thaddeus had no intention of that ever happening. On his way home from school, he often saw them leaving trap houses or bars, stumbling from side to side, struggling to keep their balance. Often, he wondered how alcohol and drugs had the power to do that to them, or anyone.

Thaddeus had never been drunk before. Once, he found his father's bottle of whiskey at the back of the fridge when nobody was around. Tonya had gone to her best friend's place, his mother had gone to the salon—she kept complaining about the new development of split ends—and his father was at work, as usual. So, he decided to give it a try.

He carefully took the bottle out of its place, scared the glass would slip from his hand. It looked fragile. Then, he took a small cup which he had often seen his father use when drinking whiskey and filled the cup halfway. He began to drink but barely any content entered his mouth as most of the whiskey poured from the corners of his lips and ended up down the sink. It did not taste anything like he'd thought it would. The raw, unrefined liquid burned his throat. He wondered why people would drink such a thing. Why would they spend so much of their money drinking until they'd had more than they could handle?

For Thaddeus, there was no stumbling. He didn't stagger or slur his words. He wondered how this same thing made men as sturdy as heavyweight champions falter in their steps.

Their staggering wasn't the only thing that made his mother and Tonya believe they were bad guys. It was the way they spoke and dressed. In church, Momma paid heed to every message the preacher taught—except the one that said not to judge people by their appearances. But then, he guessed, she was probably right. New cases of robberies and kidnappings on the rise and little Thaddeus couldn't help but think that if there was anyone behind the cases, it must be the scary-looking guys in the neighborhood.

The Garden of Love was the only beautiful place in the whole city. Destruction had touched every other place, yet the Garden was safely carved out of the carnage as though by a guardian angel. It was beautiful how none of the darkness which shrouded the entire town seemed to exist in the garden. Much of the Garden's light was shed onto their apartment, just a stone's throw away. His mother did all she could to make sure the compound was always neat. As beautiful as the Garden.

Not everyone was allowed to visit them. Thaddeus didn't have many friends of his own. Tonya had her best friend, Emily, who was always welcome; besides her, every other person needed to be introduced beforehand to his mother. After which, she would ask several questions about their family, as though she were interrogating a suspect. He understood she was just being careful and didn't want anyone negatively influencing her children.

Even his father hardly brought any of his friends home. Sometimes, Thaddeus thought his father had no friends and felt pity for him. He wondered what a life without any friends would be like. Later, he understood his father did have friends and he was only respecting his wife's wishes.

As Thaddeus sat on the bench watching a purple butterfly flutter around the fountain, a boy around his age sat down beside him. His attention was buried in an Archie comic book. He knew from glancing at the current page that it was a book he had read before. Thaddeus had read almost every single book in the series and, at some point, had even started a fan spin-off for the character Veronica. He liked Veronica. He thought she was beautiful, even though she was a comic character. She was the kind of girl every boy would want.

The boy looked up and noticed how interested Thaddeus was in the book he was reading. "Do you read Archie, too?"

Thaddeus hadn't realized he had been staring so intently. He smiled proudly. "Yes, I do. Read almost every single one."

"That's good," the boy said without inflection, before returning his gaze to the book in his hands.

Obviously, he didn't appreciate distractions—most people were like that—or maybe, he was just shy. Thaddeus' teacher told him that people who seemed withdrawn, or who stared at the ground more than they did at actual people, were often merely a shy set of folks.

He hadn't seen the boy around before and suspected there was more to do with his quietness than the fact that he was reading. His hair, a bright-but-unusual shade of blond, was thin and a bit straggly. His face was pale, with well-enunciated freckles dotting his cheek. He was as fat as a cow, though he looked healthy enough. Constantly pushing the silver horn-rimmed glasses up his nose to keep them from falling, the boy wiped his eyes each time he took the glasses off to clean them with his handkerchief. He was shaking his head, too, as he read; as though there was a plot point he was trying to stop from happening. Halfway through, he slammed the book shut and took off his glasses again. He turned toward Thaddeus, smiling. It was the first time he had smiled and the act revealed a wide gap in between his teeth.

"My name is Jacob. What's yours?"

"Thaddeus." He held out his hand for a handshake the way most adults did.

The boy glanced down at Thaddeus' outstretched hand, but instead of bringing forth his hand, he smiled and leaned back onto the bench.

Thaddeus returned his hand to his side, eager to make a companion out of the curious little guy. "I haven't seen you around before."

"I haven't been around before."

"Really? Are you new in town?"

"Yes."

"That's cool. Where did you guys move from?"

"Not guys."

"What?"

"Not 'guys.' Just me."

Thaddeus gave him a confused stare. "You moved here on your own?"

"No. My mom lives here. My parents... They just got divorced. And, I don't know how, but my mom won custody. So now I have to start living here with her. I was living in Dallas with my dad before. He plays golf."

"Oh," was all Thaddeus said in response. Then after a minute, "I'm sorry about that. I'm sorry your parents had to separate."

"Don't be." The fat boy shrugged his shoulders and drank water from a bottle Thaddeus hadn't noticed before. "They weren't so good with each other, you know? I think it's better they're not living together anymore. They stay out of each other's hair."

"So, you like your mom more?"

Jacob looked at him, the light quickly disappearing from his eyes. "No. Not a teeny-weeny bit. I don't think there was ever a time that I did. I wish I could live with my dad instead, but Daddy says the police won't let him take care of me instead. And, if he does anything funny, he might get arrested and sent to prison and have to eat horrible food and won't get to see me for an awfully long time."

The horror in his eyes grew as he listed out each possible danger. Jacob looked down at his fingers and began twisting them, sniffing slightly.

There was a bandage around his left thumb, which Thaddeus was going to ask about, only he didn't know if it was alright to. His mother always warned him about being intrusive and breaking into other people's privacy. She said it was wrong, disrespectful, and an uncultured thing to do. When he'd asked Tonya if the reason why she spent hours on the telephone, smiling and laughing at everything her caller said, was because she had a boyfriend, his mother had gone off at him. She told him it was not any concern of his. It was the same, too, when he asked her about the bleeding on her skirts.

Therefore, Thaddeus didn't know if it would be fitting to ask the boy about the bandage on his finger. But then, the boy had already told him a couple of things without him asking, so perhaps he wouldn't mind.

Jacob said, just as Thaddeus was about to ask about the bandage, "I don't think she likes me either." Still looking down at his fingers, he crossed his feet and scratched his leg.

Jacob was timid, Thaddeus thought. He had mistaken the boy's coldness for hostility or dislike, but the truth was he was just shy. Momma told him children who were used to being put down grew up to be more timid than others. She said that it wasn't a good thing to put down or mistreat any child because then the child would grow up to become shallow, withdrawn, self-conscious, or even a victimized adult.

"Why would you say that?" Thaddeus asked. "She's your mother, isn't she?"

Jacob shook his head and wiped the bottom of his nose with the back of his hand.

"She's not your mother?"

"She is," he replied. "But she doesn't like me. Michael, too. He sings so terribly that if I wanted to torture a person, I would tie them up and make them listen to him."

Thaddeus giggled.

And, for the first time, Jacob did, too. He looked at Thaddeus and, for the moment, they were two happy boys who had no fears or worries. Neither thought Thaddeus' mother would be searching for him, mad he'd snuck out of the house and was now outside, alone. Nor did they think about Jacob having to go back home to his mother—the very woman he did not like and who he claimed had no soft feelings for him either.

"Who's Michael?"

"The guy my mother is dating. He's terrible. They're both terrible. I guess it's why they fit each other so perfectly. All they do is do bad things together. *Wrong* things. I don't think the police would allow my mother to have me if they knew what kinds of things she does. They think she's a good person and my father is a bad person. I don't think they know that it's actually the opposite. My father would never think of doing the kinds of things my mother does. He would never even dream of it."

"Well…" Thaddeus scratched behind his ear and pressed both hands between his legs. He was slowly crossing the invisible threshold his mother had warned him against crossing—the border into other people's privacy. He stared ahead at the setting sun. It wasn't really trespassing when Jacob, his new friend, was more than willing to share this information. It wasn't like he was even asking. He might as well indulge the boy and keep him company until it was time to go home. Besides, he would probably never see him again, so there was nothing to be cautious of.

"Does your mother hurt you?" he asked, slowly turning his head to look at the other boy.

Jacob pulled a snack from his backpack and began munching on it as though he had not heard the question. Perhaps Thaddeus had misinterpreted the look on his face and the meaning of his words. Maybe he should not be asking this sort of question.

"She does whatever she likes." Jacob shrugged, then paused suddenly. He looked up at Thaddeus as though suddenly remembering something essential. "My mom should be waiting for me. If I don't go now, she'll think I ran away and call social services. Do you want to come home with me, Thaddeus? You're my friend now, aren't you?"

Thaddeus was taken by surprise. He didn't expect an invitation this early from someone he barely knew; not to mention his mother would be looking for him. Still, he found himself smiling at this strange kid and heard the word escape his mouth before he could stop himself.

"Yes."

"Well, let's get going, then." Jacob stood from the bench, put the rest of his snack into his bag and adjusted his glasses. Thaddeus rose shortly after him and took Jacob by his hand. They smiled at one another as though they had been friends for a long time and were about to go on a secret mission.

A secret mission that would change his life.

Chapter Two

It was as though Thaddeus were being hypnotized or placed under some sort of voodoo spell. However, he knew deep inside that there was nothing hypnotic about the way he was following the boy whom he'd only just met.

As Jacob led him down the winding lanes which led to his house, they passed through many dark, filthy alleyways. Thaddeus pinched his nose as he went through some of the worst ones, wondering why the people living there would allow such rot.

As they walked through, Thaddeus could see the scary-looking guys around, smoking and holding small bottles of alcohol in their hands. They were staring at both of them with a look in their eyes which implied they were wondering what young boys like them could be doing in such a neighborhood. Meanwhile, Thaddeus was wondering how

Jacob's mother could live in such a place. It was the worst place in the city. A place reserved for hoodlums and criminals. Not a place to live and certainly not a place to raise a child.

"Are we still far?" Thaddeus asked, glancing up at the ever-darkening clouds. There was no way he would make it home on time. He could almost see his mother's face burning with rage as she yelled at him, asking where he had been. When Momma got angry, it was never good. She would not hesitate to take out her rage on anyone she saw, even if they had nothing to do with it. Momma still had difficulty keeping her temper in check, but that was normal. Even his school teacher got mad and stayed that way when things were not done as he'd instructed, grunting and mumbling inaudible things for a long time.

"Are we close?" Thaddeus asked again, worried he had made the wrong decision by choosing to go on this adventure.

"Yeah. We're almost there."

If he'd known Jacob's house was going to be quite a distance, he would not have bothered to follow him in the first place. *It's fine*, he told himself as he almost tripped over a small block.

"Oh, I'm sorry. Did you hurt yourself?" Jacob asked, stopping to examine him.

Thaddeus had already sprung back to an upright position, as though the near fall had not rattled him.

"I'm sorry. The path around here is very rough. I trip sometimes, too. Adams says the trick is looking at the ground like you're shy or something."

"Yes, but you can't always look at the ground when you walk," Thaddeus informed him. "Who's Adams?"

"Adams is my elder brother. I don't like him either."

"You have an elder brother? I thought you were an only child."

"Why would you think that?"

Thaddeus wondered why, as well. He had barely been with the boy for an hour, yet he had come to that conclusion. Maybe because the boy had spent the time talking only of himself.

"I just thought so, I guess. Is he your only sibling?" Thaddeus asked.

"No. I have a sister, too. Tall. Talks too much and too often. Adams and her, they're twins."

"Oh, really? That must be cool. I have a sister, too. Her name is Tonya. She's really nice. I also have a baby sister. You have two siblings and I have two siblings. We already have a few things in common."

"I guess so. But my siblings aren't nice." Jacob stopped and took out a small package of peanuts from his backpack. Thaddeus wondered just how much was contained in that bag of his. If he kept all sorts of edible stuff in there and took some out to eat now and then, it was no wonder he was so fat. Tonya said people who overate were called gluttons and these people usually became obese and had lots of issues with their health. But Thaddeus wouldn't call his friend obese because, given the way Tonya always says the word, it didn't sound *kind*.

"Why do you say they aren't nice, Jacob?"

"They aren't!" The boy's voice rose dramatically. "Not one bit. They are not nice. They ask me to do all the work and run errands and take out the trash and clean the furniture, while they sit and play games with their stupid friends, make lots of noise, and talk about the celebrities they think are cool. They blast their speakers and the neighbors don't say anything because I think they are scared of Adams and his friends."

Thaddeus blinked, then sucked in a deep breath. "Why are they scared of your brother and his friends?"

"You will be too when you see them." Even as he chuckled, there was a note of finality to his voice. Jacob looked back at him and shrugged, as though attempting to nullify the fear he'd instilled in

21

Thaddeus. "Don't look so glum. *Pucker up.* I have a dog. His name is Buffy. You might like him. He's nice and fluffy and loves to make new friends. He doesn't bite, either. No, Buffy doesn't bite. He's a very good boy."

"I like dogs." Thaddeus smiled, allowing the fear of the previous moment to pass. He had never had a dog before, but they were adorable creatures. He would do anything to have one. He'd asked his mother countless times if they could own a dog, but she had always turned him down. She wasn't the only one who was against the proposal. Tonya was, too. Tonya was like a big baby scared of almost everything, so he didn't find her refusal surprising. What he couldn't understand was why his mother, of all people, who hardly feared anything, was against him owning one. He'd decided it had nothing to do with fear and more to do with an unnatural dislike for the animal. Either way, he thought her decision was unfair.

"What color is your dog?"

"He's white, with patches of black." Jacob chuckled. "Does that mean my dog is interracial?"

Thaddeus laughed, though he wasn't sure what the word "interracial" meant. Obviously, Jacob was smart. Only smart people wore glasses, for one; and Jacob's glasses, in particular, looked like the ones smart people wore. Thaddeus wondered what school he attended, what his grades were like, how many hours he spent studying. Then, he wondered how many hours he spent playing video games and watching television. His mother always told him he spent too much time watching television, and smart people—or people who intended to be smart people—did not waste as much time on video games entertaining themselves. She told him he would need to get more serious with his studies if he was ever going to become someone important like his father, who was a police officer fighting crime. But, he was still just a kid, and he believed kids should not be worried about things like that. Those worries were for teenagers, like Tonya, to fret on.

"The dog was a gift from my father on my last birthday. He said he saw all the drawings of dogs I made and thought it would be nice if I actually had one. My father is a very good man."

"That's really nice of your dad. My dad also gets me gifts, but I'm not sure he knows the things I like. It's kind of him, anyway, though."

"Well, what kind of things *do* you like?"

Thaddeus smiled and picked up a flower that lay on the path. "I like basketball. No, I *love* basketball."

Jacob broke into raucous laughter. "Basketball? You're too young to play real basketball!"

"I know." Thaddeus laughed and looked into the amused eyes of his friend. "But I play the junior games and, when I'm old enough, I'll learn how to play the real thing. Momma says she'll turn the old garage into a playhouse for me when I get older."

"Really? Can I learn to play with you too, Thaddy?"

No one had ever called him Thaddy. It felt new and somewhat soothing. He was getting a nickname. It was the kind of thing friends did. He had a friend.

"Of course, you can. Father says anyone can learn to play basketball. At school, they say you need to be tall—and you need to be this and you need to be that—but father says that with the right mindset, anyone can achieve anything. I choose to believe him."

"Looks like you're close to your father and you like him a lot."

"I do. He's cool."

"Mine, too. Dads are cool."

"I know, right?"

"Well, we're here," Jacob announced, stopping in front of a white fence.

Beyond a black gate, a small house sat. It looked moderate and inexpensive. There were small, colorful flowers out front, most of

23

which were dead already. Instead of beautifying the place, they did the opposite. Still, it wasn't too horrible. As a matter of fact, the place looked better than Thaddeus had thought it would. He didn't know what he'd expected (and he knew how wrong it was to degrade people), but the house *was* more than he'd expected. It looked even grander than the small apartment he and his family shared.

"You have a nice home," he said.

Jacob opened the gate carefully, as though he were afraid of waking or disturbing someone. "My dad pays for it," he said.

"Really? And he lets your mother live in it? I thought he didn't like her."

Jacob shook his head roughly and frowned. He removed a doughnut from his bag and began eating.

"I said *I* don't like her. I didn't say my dad doesn't. Daddy adores her. I don't know why. I think she did something to him—one of these voodoo spells they do on television—and that's why he still loves her despite all the bad things she does."

"What kind of bad things?"

"I can't exactly say, Thaddy. She's going to be mad at me if I do. And when she gets mad, she does all sorts of crazy things. She yells at me and then she calls Daddy and tells him I've been naughty. Or, she'll lock me up in the dungeon for days and never let me out."

"The dungeon?"

"Yes." Jacob reduced his voice to a whisper. "I'll show you. Before we leave, I'll show you."

"Alright, then," said Thaddeus.

He didn't know where all of this was leading, which excited him as much as it scared him. He wondered if he would be seeing Jacob after today. If they were now real friends, would they get to do cool stuff together every day? If this was the last time he would get to see him, that would be a pity. He was a rather interesting fellow. Strange, but intriguing. He seemed like someone who would be fun to spend time with.

Jacob climbed the front steps while Thaddeus followed behind at a slower pace. He was now highly aware he was either making a good choice or a big mistake. Who knew what his fate might be?

"Mom! I'm home!" Jacob yelled as soon as he opened the door. There was a small bark. A white dog flew out of the cat flap and jumped on Jacob, tugging at his leg. Jacob picked the dog up and, giggling, tickled his belly.

"This is Buffy. Buffy, say hello to my new friend, Thaddeus. You can call him Thaddy. I call him Thaddy and he seems cool with it. Right, Thaddy?"

Thaddeus wasn't listening to him. Rather, he was taking in his surroundings. Like the exterior of the building, the sitting room was modest in its décor. The paint on the wall was chipped and stained. Small pieces of art hung on the walls. Most were tiny portraits, hung crooked, fallen out of place like they had been knocked about. There were empty cans littering the floor—beer cans and half-burnt cigarettes dumped on the white tiles. Music played from a room upstairs, while noisy clatter came from another room.

There was no response, however, from whoever was in the house.

Thaddeus scrunched up his face as he took another glance around. Even the couches were out of place, bent out of position. Water was spilled on the centerpiece right next to an empty pizza box, filled with crumbs. The place was a terrible mess. It didn't look like someone sane lived there. He wondered what his mother would say if she ever saw this place. Momma made sure their home was always neat and respectable. "Spectacular" being her favorite word to use.

There was no way she could live in a place like this and no way she would not hit him upside his head to knock some sense into him if she knew where he was at the moment. *Such dirt*, he snorted silently. *Like a pigsty.*

Jacob didn't look like the place he lived in. On the contrary, he looked rather dashing and neat in his brown khaki shorts and grey Nike t-shirt. The feet peeking from his black sandals looked clean. Thaddeus guessed Jacob's father, whom he had lived with, must be a tidy guy. He had to be where Jacob learned his clean habits from, because he sure as hell hadn't learned from this place. This place stank so much Thaddeus almost felt like throwing up.

He moved and felt something against his foot. Looking down, he saw it was just the remote. He picked the controller up and dropped it onto the centerpiece. Jacob didn't seem to notice the place was a mess. It must've seemed pretty normal to him.

"Mom?" he called again. "Anyone home?"

Laughter sounded from upstairs—a female voice, loud and shrill.

"That's my sister," Jacob said. "I don't think my mother is here. What can I offer you?"

"I'm fine," Thaddeus replied. Those were the words he was told by his mother to say if anyone he didn't know well offered him something. In fact, he was instructed not to accept anything from anyone if she wasn't around or the person asking wasn't someone she knew closely. There was a look of relief on Jacob's face which Thaddeus didn't miss. Jacob was grateful he wouldn't have to share his food after all.

"Jacob?" a strange voice finally replied.

Thaddeus couldn't determine whether the voice belonged to a male or a female. He stood rooted to his spot while Jacob responded.

"Yes, Ma?" He turned to Thaddeus and whispered, "*My mom.*"

Thaddeus nodded and dug his hands into his pockets. He didn't know why he was a little frightened. What would Jacob's mother be like? What if all the things Jacob said about her were true?

Jacob slapped his shoulder, as if he had sensed his tension and was telling him not to be afraid.

"Where did you go?" Jacob's mother asked. Her words were soft but, even in a lazy slur, their intended meaning sunk deeply. Something told Thaddeus that his friend would be in trouble. The more he thought about it, the more he remembered that the same fate was probably awaiting him at home. "How many times did I tell you not to leave this fucking house? How many times did I tell you to be good?"

"Sorry, Ma. I just... I just went to the garden to watch the butterflies."

Jacob's mother emerged from the kitchen door dressed in a short chiffon gown. The scrap of fabric did little to conceal the angel tattoo covering her thigh. She was tall—tall enough Thaddeus had to angle his head upwards to see her face. Like Jacob, she was blonde and straggly, but he could make out the lines of grey that snuck in between the locks of her hair. She held a cigarette in her hand and her face was creased into a small frown.

Thaddeus was beginning to feel uneasy but tried (as much as he could) to fight his anxiety. He began singing an old song in his head—a song his mother had taught him back when he was much younger. Shanice had only just learned to walk. He used to have nightmares. The nightmares were scary enough and happened often enough that he could hardly sleep on his own. He would wake up and walk into his parents' room, shaking. His mother would usher him in, make space for him on the bed, and ask about the dream. After, she would assure him it was just a dream and he had nothing to worry about. Then, she would start singing the song 'The Red Fledglings Who Fell in Love' by The Stream, and he would fall asleep again. The song, funny and intriguing as it was, always had a calming effect on him.

Thaddeus was singing the lines in his head as he stood in the living room, watching as the frown intensified on Jacob's mother's face. He should never have come in the first place. What in the world was he thinking?

Her eyes were streaked with red, her lips black from too much tobacco. Looking at her, Thaddeus decided Jacob had not been wrong about her—she was a bad person. It was obvious just by looking at her. A terrible person. The only question now was if Jacob had been selective about the truth and if he, too, was a bad person. Either way, Thaddeus didn't like what was happening or where it might lead. It was too late to back out, though. He had decided to come on his own. He could only imagine what his mother was thinking or how scared she must be by now. He hadn't even told Tonya where he was off to because she wasn't home when he left. He thought she said something about going to the grocery store. Shanice would be worried, too. Everyone would be worried. His palms grew slick with sweat inside his pockets.

"Who's this?" A male voice echoed down the stairs.

Thaddeus looked up and saw a tall teenager with a blue mohawk. His eyes were dark and coated with makeup. His nails were painted black and there was a huge tattoo on his neck. From where he stood, Thaddeus didn't need anyone to tell him the boy was the one Jacob had called Adams, his elder brother.

"He's a friend," Jacob said.

Adams looked at Thaddeus for a long minute, then plugged in his headphones and walked back into his room, unconcerned.

"Leave," Jacob's mother said.

"W-what?" Thaddeus stuttered.

She moved closer and the stench of alcohol became stronger. Narrowing her gaze at him and, in a voice so strong it made him tremble, she said: "Go home."

Chapter
Three

The lone police vehicle lights flickered on and off as Nicholas Carter fiddled with them in the blazing afternoon heat. He had opened his shirt by a single button, allowing him to breathe a little easier. The squad car's air conditioning did little to keep him cool in the summer heat and his second option sat right in front of him. He was amused by the fact that it just so happened to be a doughnut shop. Regardless of his years of trying to fight the stereotype of being a doughnut-loving cop, Nicholas had loved doughnuts before he became an officer and always would.

The sugar rush from the snack would send anyone into overdrive. Perhaps not physically, but it would certainly put their minds to work. The sharp tingle—especially when taken with some coffee—could turn any downer into a productivity machine.

Nicholas knew he could be called in to respond to something soon. Crime rates rose as more people fled to the beaches to escape the heat. Risking it, Nicholas got out of the vehicle and hurried into the store. Checking the refrigerator, he pulled out three cans of *Monster* energy drink, ensuring that they were cold enough to reduce his body temperature.

At the register, the cashier stared at Nicholas as he pulled a five-dollar bill from his wallet. She was a black woman in her early thirties and looked incredibly discontent. He smiled at her, earning a snort from the woman as she turned back to the counter to bag his goods. Nicholas popped a can open before he reached the car, worried about the built-up heat which would be waiting for him inside the vehicle. He held the door open for a bit, allowed the hot air out, then rolled down the windows before climbing in.

He drank quickly, knowing he had only a couple of minutes before the heat would warm the beverage, making it undrinkable. Nicholas pulled onto the highway. He wasn't going anywhere, but he needed the wind in his face to help relieve the heat. The radio on his shoulder beeped, called for units on 10-33, the other side of town from where he was. Using the free time he had, Nicholas doubled back and drove by his children's school.

The red bricks of the school were pale from years of being beaten by an angry sun. He said a prayer that their air-conditioning would be working fine. He would give anything for it to be Bring Your Parents to School Day. He needed the A/C or even the portable fan at his office. Another call on the radio came in for a 10-48. He briefly considered responding, escorting the ambulance to the hospital, leaving a report for the doctor. Those few minutes would be precious time inside the hospital with its wonderful ventilation system.

He drove by a red vehicle parked behind a fire hydrant. Nicholas sighed and stopped the car. Parking behind a hydrant was avoidable and dangerous. He was especially irritated because of its proximity to his kids' school. Nicholas looked down at the fifteen-dollar ticket he was about to stash on the vehicle and noticed his pen hadn't written anything—the ink had gone dry.

Nicholas swore, shaking the pen vehemently and wondering why he hadn't gotten a Sharpie. The pen momentarily came back to life, allowing him to drop his ticket before getting back in the car. He knew there was a chance he would see the kids and didn't want to disrupt their day, so he drove off. As he rounded the corner, the dispatch radio crackled to life on his shoulder.

"Dispatch we got a possible S-21 on St. Vine Street. Units available?"

"Yeah, 10-4, this is Officer Carter, responding."

After receiving the address, Nicholas picked up his pace. While most break-ins happened at night while the owners slept or traveled, there were some which occurred during the day. There was a high chance the occupants were down by the beach—as were many people—or away for work, which presented the perfect opportunity for a burglary to take place. Apparently, the criminals hadn't considered the security system, which had been tripped when they went inside.

Nicholas parked his car in front of the house, to carry out reconnaissance first. The building appeared empty. He sat in his car for a while, watching the world around him. One thing that made Nicholas such a successful officer was his ability to put himself in the shoes of the people he was pursuing. His ability to think like them and to predict their moves before they made them.

Looking around the road, he concluded daytime burglars would not want to draw attention to themselves and would take only small items from the home. Small items meant a small number of criminals, maybe two or three men at most. The probability of them being armed was high. However, since they were burglarizing an empty house, they wouldn't expect much opposition, leaving him with a fifty-fifty chance of meeting an armed response.

As he analyzed their escape route, his instincts spiked when he spotted an unmarked blue van across the road. But then, Nicholas reconsidered. A van would be too much. Not only would it be too obvious, but it was also too big for a few men coming to steal jewelry and household items. They would want a smaller vehicle. A white Prius sat in front of him, looking very much in place in the fine neighborhood.

Nicholas quickly called dispatch and had the car traced to a rental company. The vehicle had been rented two days ago to be used for a fishing trip later that day. Seeing the vehicle so close to the house gave him the info he was looking for. Slowly, he inched his cruiser forward, blocking the car into the corner of the street before getting out of his vehicle with his gun in hand. He approached the house stealthily, moving in from the side and keeping low to hide his shadow.

He peeked in through the window and immediately saw two masked men. One of them stood directly in front of him, rummaging through a dresser. The burglar was so engrossed in the action he didn't notice the face centimeters from him. His partner behind him seemed to be working on a door that most likely led into the bedrooms. The man was crouched low in front of it, trying to pick the lock. Taking a few steps towards the back of the house, Nicholas spoked into his radio requesting for a backup unit.

As he spoke, a shadow grew behind him. At first, he was thankful for the cloud providing shade from the sun, but then he heard movement. He rolled out of the way just as the third burglar swung at him with a baseball bat.

The man froze at the sight of the gun in Nicholas' possession. As he raised his firearm, the burglar turned and ran, tossing the baseball bat behind him. Nicholas gave chase.

He entered the house from the back, narrowly avoiding a concrete kitchen table in the middle of the room. The criminal, who had clearly been inside before, vaulted over the table with no hesitation and called out to his colleagues. They dropped everything and ran for the front door. The few precious seconds Nicholas lost in evading the furniture was enough for the men to make it into their vehicle.

Nicholas burst onto the porch and called into his radio.

"Dispatch, suspects are in a white Prius. Plate number Seven-Charlie-Zulu-Tango-Four-One-Three. We're heading south on Henderson. Requesting backup."

Nicholas jumped in his car and kicked the engine to life in a two-step move. The car shot forward like a bullet.

His dash camera recorded the entire event as he drove, capturing the driver of the getaway vehicle as he veered between lanes, winding in and out of cars as he fought to get away. Nicholas turned on his sirens, signaling the other vehicles to get out of his way.

"Heading through San Jose now!" he said into his radio, swerving around a pickup truck. He kept his eyes on the Prius while trying to drive safely. The siren and bright lights cleared the roads as the chase continued. He'd lost the right-side mirror when the burglars scraped past him to get away. Nicholas knew it took only a moment to lose the subjects and a mistake in that small time frame could also result in a deadly injury for him.

A second squad car joined him in the chase, connecting through an adjacent road. Nicholas radioed the officer who had joined him, preparing for a game of tag. He fired up his engine, climbing up to seventy as he reached the vehicle they were chasing and gently knocked into the rear bumper. The Prius fishtailed, swerving left and right as the driver fought to gain control, then veered off the road. They crashed through the white picket fence of a small suburban home before coming to a stop by the patio.

The men jumped out of the car and ran into the house. One of them grabbed a young man who had come out to check what the commotion was about and stuck a gun to his neck.

Nicholas slammed on his brakes and took out his gun, aiming at the house. He watched as the suspects dragged the man inside and slammed the door behind them.

"They've got a hostage," Nicholas said to the other responding officer.

"I'm calling it in," he replied.

"I'll cover the rear exit. Keep your eyes on the front 'til we get more men. We don't know how many could be inside the building, but let's keep them locked in." Nicholas turned on the siren in his car, cranking its volume to the maximum level. Hopefully, the sound would be enough to make the criminals panic. As he went around the house, he tried to imagine what he would do if he were in their shoes. They were trapped with the police outside.

From the looks of things, there was only one armed man; the others probably only did the breaking in and stealing. Now that they had a hostage, they'd be looking to negotiate. Statistically, they had a meager chance of successfully escaping, but even so, Nicholas knew just how quickly things could take a turn for the worst. Since he wasn't looking to spend the night in the ICU, he simply kept watch. He heard through the radio the nearest officers were three minutes away.

A shot rang out inside the house. The sound of something shattering filled the air. Nicholas heard children sobbing, confirming there were more innocent bystanders in the house. He moved as close to the door as he could, then crouched low beside it, listening for another moment.

"Hey! Guys, listen to me."

A shot whizzed through the door, right where his head would have been if he were standing up. Nicholas recoiled, knowing the men would be waiting to hear the sound of his body drop to the floor. He pulled out the magazine of his Glock, used the butt of his gun to shatter the bottom half of the glass door, then tossed the magazine inside the house.

"That's the magazine of my gun. Check it out—still fully loaded. Listen, no one has to get hurt here today. In fact, I'm willing to make you guys a deal."

"I'm listening!" came a reply.

"I'm going to let you guys go. I'm unarmed. You walk out the back and my partner out front won't know. I won't chase after you. Just leave the family be. They don't have to get hurt."

It sounded like the men had huddled together and were having a hushed conversation. Nicholas fought the urge to say, *the government does not negotiate with terrorists.*

"You think we're stupid?" one of the men finally said. "Don't think we won't take our insurance policy!"

The suspects walked out—the armed man exited first, holding his gun against a child's head. Screaming and crying from the family inside erupted as all three men stepped outside. The hostage was a young boy, no older than Nicholas' son, Thaddeus. The boy stared at the officer as he was being dragged away, a gun to his temple. Nicholas knew he had to act fast. Only three feet separated the men from the vehicle of the homeowner—their new getaway car.

It took all of two seconds. Nicholas waited until the armed man broke eye contact with him, then lifted his gun. He had left one round in the chamber, hoping it would be the silver bullet he needed. He aimed and fired, right above the boy's head, hitting the criminal in the shoulder.

The man cried out, dropped his gun and released the boy to clutch the new hole in his arm. The boy took off, running back towards the house where his parents waited. Nicholas aimed the gun at the remaining two men, yelling orders at them to freeze. His empty gun was enough for them to comply before the other officer came running from inside the house, tackling one of the men to the ground and slapping cuffs around his wrists.

In the hours that followed, Nicholas was invited to the captain's office to give his statement, after which he was congratulated. But the warm handshake and pats on the back were nothing compared to the one thing he had gained from giving his statement. Right there, in the captain's office, was a perfectly functional air conditioning unit.

Chapter
Four

As a child, Tonya had everything. A father who absolutely adored her and a mother who brought up her princess in the best way possible. When her mother became pregnant with Thaddeus, Tonya was excited. The thought of a little sister fascinated her to no end. She wanted nothing more than someone to play with. While she wasn't disappointed when Thaddeus was born, she certainly was as he began to grow up.

As a baby, Thaddeus would sit and have tea parties with her, cooing and watching his sister with his bright eyes. But, as he grew older, he would ruin her setups by crawling all over them. He would stick her dolls in his mouth and cry when they were taken away. This always led to their mother whisking him away, as though Tonya had done some evil to the boy.

Once he learned to walk, Thaddeus couldn't get away from his sister fast enough. He was constantly on the move, zipping around the house like an animal on fire. Tonya watched the boy walk, run, and then fall face-first into the carpet, over and over. He would contort his face as though about to cry, but then the thrill of being able to walk would return and the child would be on his feet again. His face brimmed with glee as he continued his waddling, lips gleaming with saliva and the innocent smile of a child.

He wasn't what Tonya had wanted, but he was what she had gotten, and she loved her little brother regardless. Tonya drew closer to her father, the man who still cared for her as he always had, but she felt a change in her mother. A sort of switch in her demeanor, causing Tonya to wonder what it was about Thaddeus that made her go head over heels for the snot-nosed kid.

"Why does Mom prefer you over me?"

"Mom," her baby brother replied, holding onto his sister's legs for balance.

"Yes, *Mom.*"

Thaddeus stared up at her and repeated himself. "Mom."

Tonya scoffed and pulled her leg away, letting him fall. He dropped to the ground, landing softly on his diaper. She waited for the sound of crying, but none came. Instead, the boy scampered up her legs again, holding on and staring up at her with huge eyes.

When she did not do what he wanted, he said "Mom."

She pulled her leg away again.

Thaddeus dropped to the floor, this time, with a laugh. He rushed back and climbed her leg, his face stuck in a heartwarming smile which drained the jealousy out of Tonya and filled her with the child's shared happiness. She pulled her leg away and Thaddeus fell once more, bursting into contagious laughter.

At that moment, Tonya hadn't just found the love which her mother and father felt for the child. She had come to understand Thaddeus was a beautiful part of her life—one which was bound to stay and which she wouldn't fight. Thaddeus needed her to teach him all she knew, help him when he got into school, show him how to do his homework. Someone had to be there to protect him and she was going to fulfill that position with every breath in her body. She was only three years older than him, but Tonya Carter felt like she was a parent. Her solemn duty was to the baby.

***

"You're such a baby," Tonya remarked.

"I'm not!" Thaddeus replied, staring at a wild peacock who had joined the family on their camping trip.

The entire Carter family had gone camping at Fort Desoto State Camp. Their father had gotten two tents for the family—one for the boys and the other for the girls. They spent a night in the wild, with Thaddeus being the most uncomfortable. By morning, he seemed to be in better spirits, taking a walk around the area where they had set up camp.

As Thaddeus explored, he came upon a collection of what looked like fine chips of marble stones sitting in a small heap. Their shapes varied in size and form, with the biggest being only as large as a quarter. Some had pinkish hues to them, while others were plain white. A few rare ones were partly or entirely clear as glass, making them incredibly alluring to the young boy. He began to pick them up, stashing the loot in his khaki pockets.

"Is that a peacock?" Mrs. Carter asked her husband, who had pulled out the camera.

"It is," said Nicholas. "Aren't we a lucky bunch? Hopefully, he'll show us his feathers if we goad him enough."

"How'd you know it's a he, Dad?" Tonya asked.

"Well, the feathers on the males are a lot brighter than on the females. See the bright blue patterns?"

Tonya examined the bird's long tail. Walking majestically, only about ten feet away, the bird did not bother to cast a glance in their direction. It was almost as though the bird was aware it was being watched and enjoyed the attention. It walked around with purpose, occasionally stopping to peck at something on the ground before vibrating its body and rustling its tail feathers. The intricate blue and green designs which made up the feathers seemed to radiate in the sun, making them shine in an almost glassy manner. Tonya suddenly wanted a peacock feather she could keep.

"Here, here!" Tonya called out to the bird.

"Hey, leave it alone! You'll make it come over here," Thaddeus shot back.

"You're such a baby."

"I'm not!"

Tonya ignored her brother and continued goading the bird as her father took photos. The bird, however, seemed fine staying where it was—just far enough to be out of harm's way, but close enough to be adored by its captive audience. Tonya pulled out a cracker, only to be cautioned by her mother. The park had a rule against feeding the animals and, as much as Tonya hated the restriction, she obliged, not wanting to be in her mother's bad book.

Mrs. Carter seemed interested in doing nothing but relaxing in the hammock—which she had set up herself—and reading the novel she brought along, leaving the kids to Nicholas. Thaddeus was fine to wander around on his own, collecting rocks and being fascinated by the ants, which coordinated themselves up the bark of a tree. But Tonya was bored. She considered grabbing her dad's cell phone, but he had left it back at the cabin. She sighed, a sound which her father heard. He understood what the girl was going through. Tonya loved her father dearly. She had an unspoken bond with the man, which she questioned each time he refused to give her what she wanted. But in the end, he always did what was best for his little girl.

"Tonya, Thaddeus, let's get some firewood."

Tonya was glad to have something to do. She listened intently as their father showed her and Thaddeus the best type of wood to gather for a fire. He explained how hardwoods like oak, ash, maple, and fruit trees would burn hotter and longer. They collected more wood than they could ever need, but the kids didn't mind. It was their mission to secure the fires that would keep them safe throughout the night. As they gathered, Thaddeus suggested they make smores and even their mother lit up at the thought of marshmallows.

"Tonya, did you know that my mom and I used to go bird watching when I was younger?" her mother asked, catching Tonya off guard as she drew shapes in the dirt between the leaves.

"Like, on TV?"

"No, baby. We would come out to the great outdoors. She would bring her camera and we would spend evenings outside, trying to find the birds and take pictures. Listen."

The whistles and calls of birds somewhere far off in the trees reached them. Tonya took a moment to appreciate the scenery as she stared up at the trees, her gaze falling to the west where the sun was slowly setting, lending an orange hue to the clouds and the treetops. The shadows cast by the mammoth wooden creatures were long and tall, blending into each other as the sun's rays danced along with them. The gentle evening breeze rustled branches and sent leaves tumbling to the ground in slow motion. The tweeting of a nearby bird garnered their attention and her mother quickly responded, puckering her lips to replicate the sound.

Like a magic trick, the bird made the sound again, almost instantly.

Tonya watched her mom, who wasn't one to back down, make the sound again. They heard the flutter of wings as the bird came down from the treetops to perch on a lower branch before tweeting again. This time, its cries were drawn out, as though the bird were sending a message.

Her mother responded, keeping hers short and simple, quietly gesturing to Tonya, indicating she shouldn't move.

The bird switched trees, keeping a wary eye on the family, but looked left and right to find the source of the cry. It was an Eastern Wood-Pewee. Tonya was certain the bird could fit in her fist. Its feathers were dark grey, its underbelly a tainted white color. Tonya had learned the reason fish and some other animals had that type of coloring was because they had evolved to survive being hunted. It was harder for predators looking from below to spot the bird when flying because its white underbelly would match the sky. From above, the darker coat would blend with the ground below, making the animal near invisible and increasing its chances of survival.

Her mother pulled out her camera and caught a few photos before the bird flew off, leaving them with one final song before its ascent to the heavens. Tonya glanced over at Thaddeus, whom she thought was next to her the entire time. The boy had missed the entire bird show and was off with their father on the other side of the camp.

Thaddeus blew on the wood while their father rubbed a twig back and forth between his palms in a twisting motion. A bar of twix dangled from her brother's pocket. Tonya seized the opportunity and moved beside the men who were hard at work.

"What are you guys doing?" she asked.

"We're making a fire," Thaddeus replied with glee.

Tonya looked down at the wood they were working on. The back-and-forth motion of the longer twig had drilled a groove into the wood; Tonya had no idea how that groove would create a fire. She was certain she had seen her mom pack a lighter and a pair of matches just in case, but they didn't seem interested in any of that.

Their father's face was damp with perspiration. He groaned softly, evidence of his exhaustion in his shaking arms. Thaddeus' cheeks were flushed pink. Both men, more than anything, wanted to beat the elements and bring the oldest form of energy man had ever known into existence without external help.

The longer twig's top began to darken and, a few minutes later, smoke issued from the hollow groove. Father and son worked double time, eventually drawing Momma's attention, who smiled at the sight.

Soon, Tonya saw a faint red glow and a trail of smoke—enough to block her view of the twig temporarily. Thaddeus quickly handed his father a bit of tinder, which they had prepared while gathering wood. The tinder was smaller pieces of dried-up wood and leaves which their father told them would "catch a good flame." He packed a bit of the tinder into the hollow at the base wood and blew, even harder than Thaddeus had been, giving oxygen to the newborn as the tinder caught flame. A small fire crackled at first, then quickly burned through the leaves. Their father dumped more wood and branches on top, feeding the fire enough fuel to keep it burning for a long while.

Tonya watched her family as they donned sticks with marshmallows and slow roasted them over the fire. Her father laughed as he told stories of his time in the Boy Scouts and the wacky adventures he and his friends had. Thaddeus hung on his every word, listening as if his life depended on it.

Tonya loved her family. She had a good life. She knew she would do anything she could to make everyone happy.

As Thaddeus laughed, Tonya pulled open the Twix bar and started eating it in front of him with a knowing look on her face. In the dimness of the campfire, it took the boy a minute to realize the snack belonged to him. His face contorted into an angry frown. He looked like he would leap across the flames just to retrieve the candy bar from her.

"Those are mine!" Thaddeus yelled.

"Pipe down, Thad. We're all family here."

Chapter Five

T haddeus liked school. It was his go-to activity whenever he was down. Unlike most kids, when Thaddeus learned there was a place where people could go to obtain more knowledge than they could ever possibly use, he was beside himself. He enjoyed learning, basking in the increments of knowledge he gained, and his curiosity led him down a path to find more. He discovered physics long before he reached high school, finding Tonya's textbooks and indulging himself. Thaddeus would rip through pages to try the exercises out, trying and failing until he could do them perfectly.

Education was a challenge to him, but one which he was more than happy to take on. He struggled a bit with chemistry, which proved to be a little too much for him, regardless of how much time he dedicated to its study. Otherwise, Thaddeus was a marvel to behold. Which is why he was up before his sister, already in the bathroom and scrubbing his teeth.

It was another day of school, a Wednesday, which meant they'd have gym practice. Thaddeus wasn't overly athletic like some of the older boys in his class, but he was okay with that. Their better performance was something he couldn't achieve because he did not have the same build.

He turned on the shower and heard his sister waking up. She was playing Mark Ronson's 'Uptown Funk.' He bopped his head to the music as the warm water pelted his skin, washing away the grogginess which lingered after waking up. By the time he was done, his sister was at the door, knocking. She ruffled his still wet hair as he came out, neither saying a word to each other as they passed.

He danced down the corridor, into his bedroom, shaking the water out of his hair as he slid on a pair of briefs. Though he ran a comb through, his hair would set itself whichever way it pleased. Thaddeus knew his hair had a mind of its own and he was in no position to dictate what it should look like.

A set of Levi's hung on the closet doors, waiting for him. The boy pulled the pair of pants down and flipped them over, trying to remember if he had worn them this week already or if they had just come back from being dry cleaned. He shrugged and threw them on anyway. They were the most comfortable pair he had.

He pulled on the shirt his mom had bought for him at the fair—a deep-black tee with a stark-white omega symbol on the front. He collected his bag as he ran out of the room, then doubled back to grab a snapback, which he had gotten at a basketball game. Unlike most of his friends, Thaddeus loved basketball. They enjoyed watching the game and talking about the sport, but Thaddeus loved to play. He joined his school team and practiced for at least an hour every day after school.

Practice wasn't always fun. The boys who gave him a hard time during gym class were the same ones who made up most of the basketball team. Even though Thaddeus had made the team, they constantly bullied him, treating him as though he wasn't good enough. But Thaddeus never let negatives stand in the way of the things he loved. Those boys weren't his concern at the moment. What had crept into his mind was what his mother had made for breakfast.

"Hash browns and omelets!" his father exclaimed as Thaddeus arrived in the kitchen.

He looked at the clock first before mumbling a quick *good morning* to his father. The man would be late for work in ten minutes, but there he was, wearing an apron and a big smile on his face.

"Morning, Dad," Thaddeus repeated, taking a seat before he grabbed a fork and dug into his food.

"You like?"

"Mmm." Thaddeus nodded.

"Where's your sister?" His question came just as his daughter descended the stairs. She breezed over to the table with an iPod in her hand, fumbling with her headphones as she tried to untangle them.

"Morning, Dad." She glanced over at the clock. "Aren't you late? Where's Mom?"

"She had to take the car for some repairs. Apparently, I'll be dropping you two off today. I thought, what better way to start the day than with a badass dad who made breakfast?"

Tonya took a bite and realized he had gone incredibly heavy on the salt. He'd also used a spice she couldn't identify but which most definitely did not belong in an omelet. She looked up at her father, who had the same childish smile Thaddeus would often wear when seeking approval from her. She looked over at Thaddeus, who had been eating the entire time, before she took another bite and smiled at her father.

"Tastes amazing, Dad."

"I know," he said, grinning smugly. "You know, when I was still in college, I never dined out. Matter of fact, the first time I asked your mom out to dinner was at my place. I cooked. It was amazing."

"Definitely wasn't what made her stay," Tonya mumbled under her breath.

"What was that?"

"I said you definitely made her day!" Tonya smiled, flashing her teeth which had just been cleared of braces.

"Alright, then. Let me grab the keys and we should be good to go."

"Mom's with Shanice, yeah?" Thaddeus asked, realizing he hadn't seen his baby sister around since he woke.

"Yeah, they'll be together all day. Or, at least until you guys get home. So hurry back."

"I think we can only go as fast as the bus can drive us, Dad," Thaddeus said as they were getting into the car.

When Thaddeus was younger, he used to love riding in the car with his father, playing with the sirens and lights. Officer Dad would often take him for rides at night, just to see the glee in his son's eyes. Thaddeus was fascinated by the radios and asked how they worked. His father had been a bit lost for words since he didn't exactly know the answer. In the end, he took the boy to Ikea and purchased smaller radios for him and his sisters. Later, Thaddeus learned they operated on something called "microwave frequencies." Sometimes, he still wondered how they were connected to the microwave.

Tonya and Thaddeus slouched in the backseat as their dad drove them to Freedom Heights High. As they arrived, so too did the school bus, bringing its massive payload of students from around the city. A red vehicle behind the bus honked loudly before pulling to the side and driving off. The kids got out, said goodbye to their father and walked toward the building.

The school consisted of a simple set of three-story buildings spaced out with adequate greenery between them. It reminded Nicholas of his high school. He sighed as he drove off, remembering how his heart had been broken during senior prom.

The kids would have to face reality on their own.

Almost immediately, Tonya peeled off from her brother with a knowing look. It was a thing the two had developed from the time they'd both begun attending school together. Thaddeus wanted to be with his sister, but Tonya couldn't get away from him fast enough so she could play with her friends. Seeing her little brother look at her in that longing way hurt, so she stayed, leading him through for as long as she could before they had to be separated.

Before they parted, Tonya looked him in his eyes. A look which would later become one the siblings shared when they were being separated, a look which held a lot of unspoken words. It was a "take care and don't get in trouble" look they both understood.

Thaddeus hurried toward his locker through the crowded hallway. He received a few greetings from some of his friends on the junior chess team as he walked past to grab his books. First period was Biology—a subject he loved because he learned something new each day.

He arrived at class a minute before the bell rang and watched as the school technician screwed in the holder for the whiteboard eraser. Thaddeus wondered why they kept the holder on the lower end of the board if they knew it was a problem. Occasionally, a teacher's clothes would get caught by the holder, which jutted out like a sore thumb.

Then, the holder would be pulled free; or, if it were screwed in hard enough, the teacher's clothes would rip.

As the technician walked out, the teacher walked in. He was a cheerful, charismatic man, with one of the most entertaining classes in junior high. The kids loved Mr. Peters. His wit and sarcasm alone were enough to have the kids looking forward to class. He looked only a couple of years older than Thaddeus' father, with his sideburns showing the first hints of graying. He wore a friendly smile on his face as he entered, greeting the children.

"Alright, quiet down, kids. Today we'll be discussing evolution, carrying on from last class. Does anyone know...?" He'd paused, prompting the class to finish the question in their heads. Then, he proceeded to rip the carpet out from under them. "Who Goku is?"

The class erupted into chatter. Of course, the kids knew the character was a hero from a TV show called *Dragon Ball*.

Mr. Peters smiled, enjoying the little spur he had given the children. He enjoyed teaching, watching their faces come to life whenever he dropped knowledge. Mr. Peters considered teaching to be a privilege, something he was glad to be doing.

"You're probably wondering what Goku and evolution have in common. Well, you know how he keeps unlocking a new power level each time he fights an opponent who's stronger than him?"

Thaddeus nodded. He had seen Goku fight Jiren.

"That right there, kids, is evolution," Mr. Peters said. Everyone fell silent, hanging onto his every word. He'd baited them with something they loved and now he would exploit their minds and use the channel to give them the required data.

"Evolution—according to my latest Google search—is a process in which different kinds of living organisms are believed to have developed from earlier forms during the history of the Earth. The animals we see around today don't look the way they did millions of years ago. For example, the chicken evolved from dinosaurs."

"How?" someone asked.

"Good question, Djamila." Mr. Peters walked to the whiteboard and wrote down 'evolution;' then he wrote the word 'how' inside a circle with a question mark next to it. "How? How did the huge dinosaurs become chickens? Well, why does Goku become stronger when he's losing a fight?"

"So he can win the battle," Thaddeus answered.

"Very good. Living things evolve so they can win battles, too. Except they're not fighting an overpowered alien. They're fighting the battle of life. They're fighting to survive. Let's continue with the chicken, yeah? The dinosaurs died off billions of years ago, but the chickens managed to survive. Why? Because they evolved. They were able to withstand the harsh conditions that killed the other dinosaurs and survive."

Like the rest of the kids, Thaddeus listened with great interest, enthralled by how he weaved a tale into his lecture. As he spoke, the classroom door opened and a student walked in, followed by another teacher. Thaddeus squinted to make sure he was seeing properly because he instantly recognized the new student.

The visiting teacher whispered to Mr. Peters before leaving.

"Students, this is Jacob," Mr. Peters announced. "He transferred from Hillsborough High and will be joining us. Jacob, please find a seat."

Jacob walked down the row of chairs, making eye contact with Thaddeus briefly before taking a seat behind him. Thaddeus fought the urge to turn around and greet his friend. He held himself back, quietly revealing that he knows there would be one person in the school he could understand and trust. Someone he genuinely wanted to be friends with. As the lecture continued, Thaddeus allowed his mind drift slightly, waiting for the class to end. He would show Jacob the ropes, take him around school and introduce him to everything needed to survive Freedom Heights.

With a smile, Thaddeus shook his head free of thoughts and focused his attention back on Mr. Peters.

Chapter Six

*N*o one is above sin. Everyone sins. Even I find myself enthralled by the simple pleasures of the flesh. I find myself wanting to go back to another cigarette, a bottle of beer, a woman's thighs.

The problem is not with life or man—but with the mind. The mind needs to be corrected. The mind needs to be cleansed of the illness that is sin. Men are too far gone. Too hard to be corrected. It is easier to correct man when he is innocent, devoid of the evil machinations of the world which corrupts.

I will correct it. I can correct it. This gives my life purpose. The good Lord will bless me for the work of my hands. They will be cleansed. All of man will be cleansed.

Chapter Seven

As far back as his memory went, Thaddeus had never really heard his parents argue. That did not mean they didn't argue or have the usual fights customary in every relationship. Thaddeus could have bet they did, but he was too young to be bothered, looking out for the days when his parents were at each other's throats. He learned to watch out for this because of a neighbor they'd once had when he was six, named Flora.

Flora was a beautiful, brown-skinned lady with sleek black hair. Her skin shimmered, as though coated with honey. Her eyes were a startling shade of brown and she was always smiling.

Once, Tonya had been walking him and Shanice to the front of the street where they usually caught the school bus when they saw Flora on the opposite side of the road, struggling to hold some files as she hurried along. They assumed she was late for work or an appointment and, when they called her name, Flora Bay glanced up to find the three of them with their hands linked. The loveliest smile Thaddeus had ever seen spread across her face. And when Flora Bay smiled at you, you just had to smile back.

Another time, Momma was driving them to church and almost ran into her on the subway. Momma jumped down from the car, calling on the name of Jesus. But there was Flora, barely perturbed, laughing, assuring the shaken older woman nothing had happened to her.

Once, she was with her husband, Andrew Bay, who seemed to be angry about something. They were in front of their house when he lost his temper and began to yell. He grabbed a bottle that had been close by and folded his fists in rage. Nobody knew what upset him but, whatever it was, it had to be really bad.

Thaddeus had never seen anyone so angry before, least of all a neighbor. What surprised him most was Flora—who had been beside Mr. Bay at the time—had the warmest smile on.

Thaddeus had wondered how the man could manage to be angry even with Flora smiling at him, so he'd asked his mother. She had looked at him with a glare that, even to the present day, still burned in his memory and told him it was rude to be curious about the affairs of another family. It was none of his concern.

Afterward, things went on pretty normally, as though that day had never happened. It did not seem important, anyway. Everyone got angry once in a while. Tonya got mad when she found out that Shanice was experimenting with her makeup, wasting the products on her dolls. Shanice got mad when she found out that her dolls were not where she left them. Momma got mad when someone ate her fruits without her permission and their father got mad when someone was wasting his time. It was nothing new.

However, there were rumors that Mr. Bay had lost his job.

Thaddeus had awoken from a bad dream and gone to spend the rest of the night in his parents' room. Soon, after they thought he'd fallen asleep, they began talking. He heard them bring up the neighbor's name.

"Such a pity for the young couple," Momma said, in a tone she reserved for bad news.

"I know," said his father. "They were only just starting to make a good living for themselves. I wonder what he did."

"Oh, honey, isn't it wrong to conclude he was the one who did something wrong? Some of these employers are just crazy. He might have done nothing. In fact, maybe there was a bribe to replace him with someone even less competent. Maybe it just wasn't, you know... designed."

"I don't believe anything is *designed*, but maybe—by some chance—you're right."

"You don't believe much, Nicholas. You're pretty much out of the question."

They both laughed. Thaddeus faked a light snore to convince them he was still asleep.

The other time, he was climbing up the stairs to their flat when he saw the old man who lived on the ground floor with his granddaughter standing in front of his door, leaning on his cane. Thaddeus looked closer and saw he was not alone. Flora was beside him and appeared to be leaning towards him. The old man, whom everyone called Pops, including his granddaughter, was saying something to Flora, only his voice was deep enough Thaddeus heard his words as a low rumble.

He heard the old man clearly when he said, "Andrew will find a better job. It's only a matter of time, dearie."

Pops called everyone "dearie." One of the reasons people loved him was how kind and affectionate he was. A good father figure. Flora had then said something to him and leaned closer to his chest. There were small whimpering noises as Pops drew her into an embrace and kissed her hair, his eyes closed, his lips moving in gentle prayers. Thaddeus didn't need to look at her face to know that Flora wasn't smiling. No one could smile in such a condition. And it wasn't just then. After that night, Flora Bay didn't smile as often as she used to.

***

Usually, Thaddeus loved going to visit Flora, and not just on Sundays, which Momma thought should be the official day for family and friends' visitation. He would go when he got back from school or when Shanice was too busy with her dolls to notice his existence. Tonya didn't have much time for him that particular year; she was preparing for an important exam. Most of his time, when Momma was not around, and Tonya was busy, he spent his afternoons with Flora or Pops, who were both a joy to be around.

The old man told him stories from when he was younger, about the war and his time in the army. Pops had many interesting stories and his granddaughter, Pearl, was always there to entertain him even more. She baked the best cookies and sang many beautiful songs. Pops had said she got her beautiful voice from her mother, whom she had never met. Thaddeus thought that was rather sad. He could not imagine what it would've been like to have grown up without his mother. Scary, no doubt. Momma was everything to him. To Tonya and Shanice, too. Even to their father.

The times he didn't go to Pops for leisure, he went to Flora. She cooked as wonderfully as she smiled and served her food with an accompanying grin that was impossible to resist. Whenever she cooked, the aroma traveled for blocks. Sometimes, she had unwanted visitors, but she didn't mind. Most people who regularly paid Flora visits were children and she never had the heart to drive them away. So, whenever Thaddeus visited, she would prepare such a lovely meal and serve him. Despite how shy he felt about eating outside his home, he always enjoyed Flora's meals.

Momma had always warned him against eating other people's food. People were bad. You never knew who was rubbing you on your shoulder but, beneath the façade, meant you harm. However, the first time he'd had a meal of chicken soup and salad in Flora's house and told Momma, she didn't yell or say a single word. And Thaddeus knew it was fine to eat in her house. That Flora was not part of the bad people who rubbed your shoulders but meant you harm.

However, after her husband lost his job, Momma's feelings seemed to tilt. For one, she told Thaddeus, Shanice, and Tonya they needed her permission before they paid Flora a visit. Thaddeus thought this was weird. Her husband had lost his job, which was a tragedy, and people who suffered tragedies needed all the comfort they could get. Why would Momma restrict the way they visited her? Little Thaddeus, however, was more clueless than he could have ever known.

One day, after school, Thaddeus returned home while Momma was out at the office. Their father was working overtime to catch a criminal who seemed pretty important. Tonya was busy with an assignment and did not seem to care much about him, even though she was his designated nanny. Shanice was somewhere doing God knows what with her dolls.

It was the perfect chance to go out without being noticed by anyone. Not like Tonya would tell on him anyway. Tonya only told him when they were fighting. Otherwise, she kept quiet, even though she knew they could both end up in trouble. Blackmailing was a powerful tool and she used it to her advantage well.

He was going to tell Flora about the recent happenings in school and all around. He was going to tell her Father was working hard to catch a criminal and, when Father succeeded, he would get a promotion. That meant his pay would become bigger and they could even afford to get out of this "shitty town." Then, a thought struck him. If his father received a promotion and his salary was raised, he might even be able to help Flora's husband secure a new job. Father said all the time that people in important positions could do just about anything. A smile split his face. He couldn't wait to tell her about his great idea, nor could he wait to ask his father if he could help. Flora was such a good person and good people deserve good things.

The door opened. There she stood in a red gown and a blue denim jacket. Her hair was woven into cornrows, but that wasn't the only thing different about her. Her usually smiling eyes weren't smiling this time. Her left eye was red and puffy; her face was darker than usual. When she looked at Thaddeus, she appeared scared. *Frightened.*

This was not the Flora he knew at all.

She peeped outside like she was checking if there was another person with him. He found this weird, too, because Flora loved company. She never had a problem with him coming along with friends or many people visiting her. She always welcomed them.

"Hey, Thaddeus," she said, a slight tremor to her voice.

Thaddeus noticed, but didn't say anything. Tonya's voice did the same thing plenty of times when she was scared of something, or even just before her exams when she was extremely on edge. It would quiver and thin out as though she was about to burst into tears, only she never did.

It was the same thing Flora's voice was doing at the moment. Did she have a big exam that she was nervous about? Or an interview that adults always went to? Mother always hugged Tonya, braided her hair, or made her favorite lunch when she was having one of those moments. Thaddeus could not braid Flora's hair, which was already braided. Neither could he cook for her. Once, he had almost set the house on fire while trying to heat something and his mother had been furious when she returned. She warned him never to set foot in the kitchen again unless there was an adult around. So, cooking surely was out of the question. Thaddeus wondered, if he gave her a huge hug, would it help her stop worrying?

"Hey, Miss Flora."

She smiled a weak smile. She stood by the door still, not drawing back to allow him in; merely glancing from him to the open corridor and back.

"How are you, Thaddeus? Did you want to get something?"

He shook his head, his forehead creasing into a small frown. "I just wanted to see you. May I come in?"

"Oh, yes, of course." She slapped her head and held the door open for him. "Come in, love. Make yourself at home, as always."

Her place was like his home, after all. Though it did not seem much like one today.

There were empty bottles on the floor, shattered in pieces, as though there had been a fight. Like those scenes in the adult movies where someone stepped on someone else's toes in a bar, and they got into a big quarrel. They'd bump tables, exchange words, and bottles would end up as tiny splinters on the ground. It was exactly the scene he saw.

On the table, there was an empty pack of cigarettes atop a brown leather jacket he knew belonged to her husband. He had seen him wear it a couple of times and fantasized about growing older so he could own fancy clothes like that.

The place smelled rotten, as though it had not been cleaned for days. Thaddeus looked around the small apartment. It was graced with expensive glass figurines. Momma had once said, Andrew was a man of taste—unlike his wife, who really couldn't care much about such things.

The wedding photograph on the wall was broken, almost fallen from its hold. Thaddeus did his best to hold in a small gasp. Tonya always said it was a bad sign when family photographs broke. She said bad things would happen to that family most of the time and, although she did not believe in such bad luck theories, she seemed particularly adamant on that one.

He couldn't even sit on the couch because there was something sticky on it, like a patch of vomit or forgotten food. His belly began to fill with nausea. He should have listened to Momma and not come here in the first place. She would be mad if she found out he went without asking her first. Did Momma know about whatever was going on? Did Momma know that Flora now had a black eye and a swollen face and smiled a lot less than she used to? And if she did, how come she never said anything about it? Not like she would disclose anything to either him or any of his siblings, but he might have overheard something if she discussed it with his father.

"Sorry about the mess," said Flora, sensing his panic and calming him with a smile. "Andrew had a couple of friends over yesterday. They had a few drinks and *uh*... This." She ended with a nervous chuckle, which Thaddeus couldn't return.

Just as she mentioned him, her husband appeared from behind a curtain, swaying to his left and pointing absentmindedly into thin air. "Who's that?"

His voice sounded different then Thaddeus remembered. More akin to a drunken slur.

The fear in Flora's eyes returned. "No one. It's just Thaddeus. The next-door kid. You know Thaddeus, right, honey?"

"I thought I told you not to let anyone in? Of... of all the people you c-could decide to disobey this rule, it had to be the cop's kid?"

"Come on, honey. He's just a kid." She was moving backwards, her eyes growing larger.

Andrew, who was dressed in nothing but checkered shorts, pounced on her so quickly neither of them had seen it coming. Flora started screaming as his fists landed on her. Thaddeus stood there, shocked to the point he couldn't move. When he finally regained his wits, he turned on his heels and sprang out of the apartment.

He never told Momma about the incident, but he wondered if he'd told his father if he would've been able to help somehow. His father was a police officer and police officers were known for catching bad guys. From what he had seen that day, Andrew was an unbelievably bad guy. The kind of person his father caught and put in prison. Who else would do such a thing to Flora? She was the gentlest and kindest person he knew. He told Tonya, but his sister, older and much wiser, did not believe him. She thought he was spinning a tale or something. He had shown Tonya that he had no reason to lie—that he was too young to think of a lie filled with so much violence, especially against dear Flora.

He had told Tonya because, on his own, he did not know what to do. If he told Father, Momma would hear, and he would be in so much trouble. On the flip side, if he didn't tell anyone, Flora would keep on suffering.

Why could she not report that her husband was a bad man and that he beat her up when they were alone? His father had told him it was easy to contact the police department if anyone had a person they wanted to report or a case to settle. So, why couldn't Flora just pick up the phone so the police could arrest him and give him the punishment he deserved?

Tonya finally believed him two days later.

They were returning from school when they saw Flora walking fast in the opposite lane on her way home. Her head was bowed, hidden in a hoodie, staring at her feet as she moved. Thaddeus wanted to run to her, but Tonya stopped him. So, instead, he called her name. She looked up and saw them both. Without answering or even smiling, she quickly turned away, as though trying to prevent herself from being seen.

But Tonya had seen everything her younger brother had told her about—the dark eyes, swollen face, split lips.

Tonya held her breath until they arrived home, her face ashen. She had agreed they shouldn't tell Momma because that would mean they were sticking their nose in another family's affairs and she must have already seen for herself. Whether or not they were making a mistake, they had no way of knowing.

Two weeks later, when Momma was cleaning the house, the family portrait which hung by the corridor shook from its place. The portrait fell and broke into pieces.

Chapter Eight

March 28th, 1980

"You know I always wanted to be a singer. Out there on Broadway, using my voice to melt hearts and bring tears to the eyes of all who heard my voice."

"Well, table three needs extra dip. You won't mind now, would you?" Sarah asked her coworker and best friend.

The red-haired woman scowled at her through a pair of small grey eyes. Sarah was a bit jealous of them. They were beautiful and, even with their size, they allowed Candice to hold the attention of everyone she spoke to, especially customers. Candice did not always have an enthusiastic personality. She was often blunt, though with no ill intent. Even so, her eyes captured the hearts of whoever she spoke to and they didn't seem to mind.

Candice was from Texas but growing up in coastal cities had faded her accent. She had traveled to thirty states and was hoping to continue her journey someday. Sarah had suggested she join a travel agency, but all her applications came to naught.

Sarah met Candice during her finals in college. The young woman landed in Tampa during her stint to cover the coastline. Bubbly and full of energy, she had desperately needed a place to stay while she awaited the next check which would allow her to continue her travels. Sarah, who had just gotten into a fight with her previous roommate over her drinking problem, needed someone to join her for a drink. Candice didn't seem to mind. In fact, she indulged Sarah, both of them getting wasted often.

Candice had a simple rule to life: *Live it*. Sarah was fine with that. She had fallen into the habit of drinking since the passing of her father a year ago. Against her mother's wishes, Sarah felt the need to hide her sorrows in the misty clouds of intoxication and find solace in the throbbing head that had become her morning calling. Sarah would wash down an aspirin with a sip of Budweiser before passing out on the bed. Her grades fell. She'd watched idly as her life slipped through her fingers.

At first, Candice thought Sarah just really loved to party. But a few weeks in, she understood that the girl she had become close to wasn't a big shot Friday night person. She was a sad and broken woman who needed her heart mended as soon as possible. One night, she came up with a plan. Candice seized every single credit card her friend owned, sold all the booze Sarah had bought, and used the money to buy her friend a few new dresses. At first, Sarah had withdrawal. She slept in late, ate little, and refused to do anything else. Candice dragged her out of bed constantly, trying to get her to go to class and meet people.

"How old are you?" Candice asked.

"Twenty-five."

"And you don't have a boyfriend. Not even someone looking in your direction?"

"Maybe they see the drunken state I'm constantly in and decide I'm not worth it?" Sarah shot back with a wry smile.

"Then I guess it's time we got you back in the saddle, eh? Who did your makeup?"

"Rebecca."

"Oh, well, since your old roommate is gone, you're stuck with me. I have no idea how makeup works, so you'd best be fine with a dose of mascara and lipstick."

The country girl's attempt to get Sarah back on her feet didn't seem to be working. Sarah simply had no interest in any of the activities they did. Spas, massage parlors, even a strip joint didn't seem to make any impression on her. She only smiled when she was offered alcohol.

Sarah graduated with a low GPA, which sent her into a deep depression. Her mother didn't help. The woman didn't mince words, nor did she care about hurting her daughter. They fought often and Candice could only watch as the girl told her mother she never wanted to see her again. Her mother seemed unperturbed as she shut the door in her daughter's face. Both women were grieving the loss of a father and husband, allowing the worst of each other to be shown.

Candice quit her travels to live with Sarah, both women becoming closer than ever. Candice became the sister she never had and didn't know she wanted. They both got jobs at a nearby diner where they waited tables. Candice was the preferred waitress there and, while she knew as much, she never flaunted the fact. They worked eight hours a day and spent nearly a third of that time gossiping about the regulars who came in. One, in particular, had captured their interest.

"He's with a different girl today. It's Friday." Candice pulled out her notebook and flipped to the back page, where she had scrawled all sorts of ramblings. Among them was a detailed graph, recording the patterns and movements of this particular customer. "He should have a blonde, take his seat at table... *nine*. Order the lobster and white wine—which he's certain we don't have—then settle for either a cocktail of pineapple or lime."

"You really got him figured out, huh? Funny how he keeps getting your name wrong. I feel like he's doing it on purpose, just to get on your nerves... Oh, here he comes," said Sarah.

The man walked in, savvy as ever. He appeared to be in his forties with dirty blond hair and a constant five o'clock shadow. His baby blue eyes cut through the diner before he took a seat at table nine, as Candice had predicted. She wrote down the color of his suit and the style, certain he was a creature of habit.

Sarah noticed the man seemed on edge. Each time he came, he would check his watch constantly, like he was rushing to get back to something more important than the date he had. He would arrive a full thirty minutes before his date, order a cup of coffee and a bagel while he waited. Candice had already gone inside, readying the order before the man even asked. His date walked in soon after. Sarah recognized her not just because she was blonde and walked in with a smile—looking to dazzle the date she hoped was looking at the door—but because the man with the dirty blond hair rose to greet her.

"Hey, Charlie, right?" the man asked, his smile exuding confidence.

The woman's face lit up at his voice, her lips curling in recognition. "Nice to finally meet you in the flesh, Jon. How are you doing?"

"A lot better now that you're here." Jon leaned in and, as always, kissed the lady on the cheek before pulling out her seat for her.

With a wave of his hand, he flagged a waiter. Sarah responded, walking over to the table to take their requests. She had already written down what he wanted on a sheet—his lobster and drink—with just enough space for what the lady would take. Like clockwork, Jon made his order in the most flamboyant way possible, while the lady ordered a plate of spaghetti and a smoothie. By the time Sarah returned to the kitchen, the lobster was already steamed, ready for its impeccable customer. Sarah wondered how Jon was able to keep so fit with an appetite like that.

"You ever think a man like that would come for you?" asked Larry, one of the boys who operated the stoves, in the midst of making fries.

Sarah scoffed. "If your mom doesn't come to pick you up later tonight, I probably will."

"Burn." Candice laughed.

"The fries?" Larry asked.

"No, your love life. Now mind your business, boy."

Sarah watched the two at the table enjoy their food, exchanging shy glances at each other with the occasional giggle. From where they sat, she could only pick up bits and pieces of their conversation about online chats and their pets. The wine was served, which seemed to loosen the lady's tongue even more. She relaxed, rattling off at Jon, who listened with the attention of a cat with a ball of yarn dangled in front of him. He interjected a sentence or two at the appropriate times when she paused to take a sip of her drink.

Sarah hadn't been in a serious relationship since her first year in college. The guy had moved on with his life, only occasionally calling to check up on her. She had figured out how to bury the loneliness deep down, reveling in the companionship Candice brought her. But even Candice went on dates. Men looked at her longingly and she was able to curve them, control them like nobody's business. Sarah had told herself she didn't care for all of that, but she was beginning to desire more for some reason.

Charlie cocked her head back and laughed heartily. If she had driven over, there'd be no way she would be able to drive herself back. Jon beamed at her, his words striking like a well-placed blow that put her at ease, filling the woman with a sense of calm and joy. With his comical nature, he exuded pure wit and humor. She was spellbound, just like every other woman Jon had brought into the diner. The man repulsed Sarah and she hoped someday, someone would see through his bullshit. But today, just like every other day, was not that day. He asked for his check with a wave. While he paid with cash, Sarah sat the woman down, hoping she would somehow connect with her telepathically.

Charlie was clueless.

***

Later, Candice walked up to her roommate from behind and whispered into her ear. "You know, if you put in a good bit of effort, we could find you someone to go home with tonight,"

Maybe one night she would put herself out on the line. Sarah could feel her old compulsions coming back. The music, the alcohol, a chance to indulge again. She couldn't say no, regardless of how much she knew it wouldn't end well.

As their shift ended, they took a taxi home for a little nap before their night out. The women dressed in the best clothes they had (or in the most street-savvy dresses they could find). Sarah donned a crop top with a leather jacket and tight-fitting jeans, while Candice wore a short skirt that left little to the imagination and a sleeveless top with an evening jacket.

The guy in front of the nightclub didn't need to check them before allowing them inside, as two beautiful women were always welcome in any club. The odor hit Sarah hard as they walked in—tobacco and nicotine and beer and liquor mixed to create some groggy stench. For a moment, she wondered how she had ever allowed herself to enjoy alcohol. She felt the weight of her irresponsibility begin to weigh on her, her mother's words ripping at her mood again.

But Candice was what Sarah often called a "pocket-sized miracle." After she retrieved shot glasses from the bar, the night flew by. They took shot after shot, venturing onto the dance floor and laughing and dancing off-beat without a single care in the world. Nothing mattered to Sarah then. Not her father, who had passed away, shattering her relationship with her mother. Not her job, not her education, and certainly not her relationship status. Sarah felt her body fill with the euphoria of the moment and, after four more shots, Candice decided they were done.

"No. No more. We have to go."

"But we don't have to work tomorrow." Sarah giggled as the first signs of drunkenness hit.

"Maybe, but I don't want to be cleaning up puke at four in the morning, so we have to go, Sarah. Come on." She held her friend by the hips, struggling to keep her upright as she flagged down a taxi.

Outside, as a vehicle went around the center divider, Sarah heard footsteps behind her—moving quickly, as though numerous people were running. Candice heard it, too. She turned around to see a man with a gun, running as fast as his feet could carry him.

The armed man saw the two women standing in front of him and raised his weapon, firing at Candice. The bullet hit, causing both women to fall to the ground. Sarah felt the man reach for her, lifting her with one hand and putting the warm barrel of his pistol to her head. She tried to scream but the adrenaline-alcohol mixture in her system prevented her from doing so.

A second gunshot echoed through the night air.

Chapter Nine

Present Day

"Wait, I don't understand. How did you get transferred? I thought you were on the other side?" Thaddeus asked.

They stood in line at the cafeteria, waiting to get lunch. Jacob had a lollipop in his mouth. His mouth watered as he waited for his food to be served. The aroma wafted into his nostrils, alerting him of the wonders which awaited his tongue in a matter of moments.

"Mom moved out here so she can get to work faster and stuff. So..." Jacob trailed off.

"Well, that's a surprise. Welcome to my little corner of hell. Basketball tryouts are today, after school. You should come."

"I don't know. I just got here," Jacob replied, moving up the line. His tray was handed back to him and he took the food with a smile. Sliced peaches laid in the bottom corner next to a milk box, with oven-baked potatoes, a sandwich with lettuce and tomato, and a few chicken fingers. "I should be worried about my grades and stuff."

"Jacob!" Thaddeus called his friend, who was holding up the line while staring at his tray. "Let's go."

As they walked to a table on the left side of the crowded cafeteria, Jacob and Thaddeus glided between the bodies and elbows, protecting their trays while trying to squeeze through to their table. When they finally did, Jacob wasted no time digging in.

Thaddeus watched him for a while, not realizing how much he had wanted Jacob at his school until it actually happened. Thaddeus had more acquaintances than actual friends, but he enjoyed the nature of those relationships. He would simply provide a service for them—like helping out with homework in exchange for joining their chess club and learning the game.

With Jacob, it was simpler. They had only known each other for a little while, but he already felt a connection. It was shaky and fresh, like dipping into a pool without knowing its temperature. Somehow, though, Thaddeus knew they were going to be close. Returning to his food, he grabbed the sandwich, satisfied with having someone he could talk to next to him. As he chewed, someone walked up to their table. When he looked up and noticed who it was, he stopped chewing.

Toby Ryan was a grade ahead of him and hated having Thaddeus on the basketball team. Being the team captain, he wanted his best friend to take a position the coach had reserved especially for Thaddeus. Toby was nimble, quick on his feet, able to outrun and dribble past opponents. Thaddeus could only make free shots; and, with any pressure, he would miss, which was why his job was to get the ball from the back to the shooting guard. Toby wanted nothing more than Thaddeus off the team and, from time to time, he would attempt to scare him away.

He was tall for his age and walked around with a toothpick between his lips. Toby fought hard to cover his country accent but was unsuccessful. His arms were toned from his time working at a ranch. There was a reason he played defense—Toby knew how to draw blood.

And that was exactly what he was coming to get from Thaddeus.

The other three people at the table picked up their trays and left, leaving Thaddeus alone to face the threat. Toby reached the table and placed his shoe down right next to Thaddeus' tray. He stared at his target, narrowing his eyes as he swirled the toothpick in his mouth. For a moment, Thaddeus wondered how many toothpicks he carried since he always had one. Did he bring them from home or did he have a deal with the cook? Shaking the thoughts from his head, Thaddeus held the stare of the boy in front of him.

"Carter. You know tryouts for today are a closed event. Only members of the team can watch."

"I am a member of the team," Thaddeus replied, dropping the peach back on his tray.

Toby leaned over and picked up the slice of peach, sucked the juices off of the fruit, then tossed the husk at Thaddeus' face. Thaddeus shut his eyes, fighting the urge to push Toby's leg off the table. He knew any form of violence he attempted would result in him getting a beating once he left the school premises. He had seen it happen to other students, the ones who thought putting up a fight would earn them their freedom. But with seniors, even when operating alone, had a pack mentality.

Cooper Lee had once gone up against Edward Bim, a senior two classes ahead of him. The seniors had constantly picked on Cooper because of his difficulty with speaking English correctly. He had spent most of his life in China and was still adjusting, but the seniors kept making racist jokes and shoving him around, daring him to do something. One day, in the hall, Cooper walked up to Edward, grabbed him by his hair and smacked his face into two lockers before knocking him down with a kick.

The fight had taken all of five seconds and Cooper was already gone before Edward could even see who hit him. Cooper believed he was in the clear and the seniors would know not to come after him considering what he'd done to Edward. But, three days later, they tracked him down to an alley as Cooper was riding his bicycle home. Cooper put up a fight but was left with a fractured arm and bruised ribs.

Toby threw another piece of the peach at Thaddeus with a laugh before he picked up the last piece on his plate. A small crowd had begun to gather, knowing a fight was going to happen sooner or later. Either Thaddeus would be used as a table rag now or he would stand up for himself and be sent to the ICU later. The students knew the drill and they were ready for their show. Toby sucked on the last peach before throwing the piece at Thaddeus' face again.

Jacob shot out a hand. Catching the piece right before it hit his friend's face, he flicked the fruit back at Toby. It hit the senior in the eye, causing him to blink and take a big step back, stumbling as he tried to find his footing. Gasps came from everyone watching, then a disturbing silence fell over the cafeteria. Toby rubbed at his eye before looking at Jacob. The blond-haired boy had not left the table as he approached, but Toby hadn't even noticed he was there. He had never seen Jacob before, nor did he have the slightest clue who he was. Jacob seemed intent on finishing his sandwich before he spoke, downing some of his milk before addressing Toby.

"Do you have a problem with Thad?" Jacob asked.

"Thad? Oh, no. What I have with *Thaddeus* is private and not any of your business," Toby fired back, glancing from Jacob to Thaddeus and back.

"He's my friend and I'm sure he doesn't mind if his business is spoken about with me here."

Toby scoffed, realizing he was being bodied by an unknown junior. He cast his gaze around at the gathered crowd—they assumed he was on the defensive now. Truthfully, Toby wouldn't fight someone he didn't know, therefore, he relented.

Glaring at Thaddeus, he pointed with his finger as he spoke. "I'll see you on the court, Thad."
With that, he turned and left.

Like clockwork, the entire cafeteria fervent discussion as Toby walked away. Everyone was talking about what just happened, looking over at their table and pointing fingers. Even those who had sat there previously refused to return, leaving Thaddeus and Jacob to themselves. Jacob returned to his food, as though nothing had happened, picking at a piece of lettuce that had fallen from his sandwich.

"Jacob, why did you do that?" Thaddeus asked.

"Because he was picking on you and you weren't doing anything about it."

"You don't understand. He's the captain of the basketball team. He has been trying to get me off the team for a long time now and you just gave him a reason to."

"I thought you already made the team?"

"I have, which is why I'm trying to stay on it." Thaddeus ran a hand over his face and sighed.

"Toby wants me out so his friend, Eric, can be on the team. Eric will be at tryouts today, trying to make the sub spot for my position. If he succeeds and I'm injured or something, Toby will get what he wants. I'll be booted from the team. I've been trying to exist without actually having to deal with him, but now? It just had to be today. The day of the tryouts itself."

Jacob squeezed the last of his milk into his mouth before crumpling the carton in his palm. "Well, I guess I'll have to attend tryouts…"

Thaddeus went through the rest of the day with a nervous expression. Every senior he made eye contact with gave him the same look of rage. At the end of the school day, Jacob followed Thaddeus to the locker rooms, where he was given a spare jersey. Since there were no sneakers available, Jacob went onto the court with his regular shoes.

The court was huge, with rows of seats covering three walls of the room. The court serves multiple purposes as both a gym and an assembly hall. The bleachers rose five feet from the ground, with a small bench for the subs. A single scoreboard loomed over the main entrance to the court, with its huge double doors. Fluorescent lights hung from the roof, illuminating the veneered wooden floors which squeaked wildly as the boys ran over their tennis shoes.

Coach Hutchinson stood at the center of the court, one foot on a cooler, as it always was. To Thaddeus, the man looked as though he were only moments away from devolving into a full-on mental breakdown and screaming at everything. He was the most impatient person Thaddeus knew. Students had often reported seeing Coach Hutchinson talking to himself alone in his office—a long, erratic discussion which involved lots of theatrics.

"Alright, everyone. Three laps around the court. Get that heart pumping. Hopefully, we can pick out the weaklings among us before we even get to the main event."

Jacob stayed close to Thaddeus as long as he could during the laps. The three-lap run turned into four before Coach called in the main team for a small game of two on two. As they organized, Coach instructed the newbies to run two extra laps before they could sit and watch. Toby was paired with Thaddeus, leaving them to face off with two other members of the squad. It was a simple game—the first to score two points wins.

The other team started with the ball, dribbling towards Toby and Thaddeus. They passed the ball between themselves, searching for a way past their opponents. Toby didn't want Thaddeus to have a piece of the action, so he jumped in front of him to catch both opposing players at the same time. They evaded him with a simple feign-and-pass before coming to Thaddeus. With a behind-the-back pass, the other opponent caught the ball and dunked.

An ear-splitting shrill from the coach's whistle—which Thaddeus and a few others were already too familiar with—filled the air. "See? That right there is what I'm looking for. Players who will capitalize on their opposition. Players who can work together like a well-oiled machine imported from China. That's who I want on this team and that's what I'm going to force out of every one of you who makes the cut."

The whistle blew again, signaling the start of the second round. Jacob watched with keen interest while secretly chewing a piece of gum.

Toby looked at his teammate with eyes which spelled discontent and rage. Thaddeus knew a repeat of what had happened in the first round would happen again.

The coach threw the ball into the air and, after the second bounce, Thaddeus stole the ball right from under Toby's arms.

He bolted straight for the defender at the back, knowing Toby would be hot on his tail, looking to get the ball away from him. Thaddeus tried the under-leg dribble, but the defender had more experience than the average Joe. Pulling back, he listened for the sounds of boots coming up from behind him. Thaddeus knew he wasn't good with the dribble, but all he needed was a good spot to take a shot. With a single step to the side, Toby passed Thaddeus, who had stopped running forward and changed directions to his left.

Momentum carried him and the defender forward, not giving either a chance to react. With the only person who could stop him sliding away, Thaddeus jumped and made a three-pointer, catching the net cleanly.

Chapter Ten

J acob wanted ice cream to celebrate their win. He'd learned from his father it was always good to celebrate a victory, no matter how small a victory was. Both he and Thaddeus making the basketball team was no small win. Jacob was glad. He had just met Thaddeus, but he felt like theirs was a friendship which would span a lifetime.

He was too young to be thinking about lifetimes, Anna always said. She had a boyfriend—some flimsy sleazeball of a man she would be on the phone with for hours—and, just as she was about to hang up, she would tell him she really loved him and he was the kind of person she wanted to build her life with. So, as far as Jacob was concerned, she wasn't one to talk.

She didn't know he'd overheard her most times. Actually, he overheard a lot of things. For example, he knew Anna had been pregnant once and aborted the baby. She'd spoken in hushed tones over the phone, kind of like whisper-screaming. Jacob had been walking to his room at the end of the hallway when he heard little noises coming from inside her room, He'd stopped to listen. From the sound of things, her boyfriend didn't seem like the child's father. Then again, it didn't seem like *she* knew who the father was. He never mentioned what he heard to her or anyone else; just as he never mentioned the things he had heard about his brother who, in more ways than one, was worse than Anna.

Recently, Jacob had overheard the team leader, Toby, was angry and planning a round on both of them after school. He didn't tell Thaddeus. Truthfully, he forgot about the information until this moment. Still, he wasn't bothered. He had received too many beatings in his life to be afraid of a fight from a bunch of punks. A small part of him thought he should inform Thaddeus he might be walking back home with his nose bleeding and a black eye. And, okay, maybe he wouldn't exactly be *walking*.

But, in his defense, if he hadn't stood up to Toby, Thaddeus would have been attacked right then. Milder, because they were on the school premises and Toby wasn't crazy enough to pull a stunt that would get him in trouble. But Jacob couldn't just stand there and watch something like that happen to his friend. He had to do something, which was why he'd done what he did.

Thaddeus wouldn't understand, but he had spent a lifetime watching people suffer because they refused to stand up for themselves. It turned his face an unhealthy shade of grey to think, too many times, he had been one of those people. He still was. Jacob felt a cold feeling in his chest and sucked in his breath. After taking a pack of cheese balls from his bag and stuffing a couple in his mouth, he started to feel a lot better.

"Are you okay?" Thaddeus asked him.

He nodded, stuffed in another mouthful. The cheese balls these days tasted amazing. Not like the shitty ones his mother bought from the corner store or wherever she got them from. Nothing his mother ever did was right.

"How long have you known Toby?" Jacob asked, sitting down on a bench in front of the school gate. He was exhausted. It was probably the sun beaming down on him; or, like his father used to say, his high intake of sugar. Jacob didn't understand what his intake of sugar had to do with anything. He knew his father was just trying to get him to stop overeating because he ate like a diabetic, avoiding sugar like the plague. Jacob had often tried to convince his father that he was nothing like him and the sugar actually gave him a boost. In some ways, though, he knew he was a lot like his father. Especially when he thought about the relationship between him and his mother.

"Toby has always been the man," Thaddeus said, startling him out of his thoughts. His friend sat beside him on the bench and took a large gulp from a water bottle, wiping sweat from his forehead. The sun was way too hot; one could easily pass out. "I think his father is a member of an important committee and that's why he has such an upper hand. There are rumors his father is even close friends with the principal. You see, Toby's always known he's untouchable." Thaddeus frowned. "That's why he'll do anything—he thinks he can get away with it. One day, someone even stronger than you, stronger than both of us, will stand up to him. Put that stupid bully where he belongs."

"His body gives him an advantage," Jacob said thoughtfully, sipping his orange juice.

Toby had a muscular body that should not belong to a boy of his age. It infuriated Thaddeus. Maybe, if he started going to the gym, he could have a body like that. The idea was ridiculous—Momma would never let him go to the gym at this age. Thaddeus had a problem on his hands. He had made it onto the basketball team and Toby's friend had only gotten in as a sub, as had Jacob. The thought made him smile. He hadn't thought Jacob would make it onto the basketball team. He hadn't even thought Jacob knew the slightest thing about basketball. But he had, and now Thaddeus knew he had so much to teach him. It would be a lot of fun.

There was a traffic jam building up on the road. It was the hour parents were rushing to pick up their kids from school. Next to the school gate, where they sat, a commotion grew.

Everyone seemed impatient, honking at each other as though the car in front of them would fly its way out of traffic. A red sedan pulled out of the line and stopped by the sidewalk, the car behind it taking its place.

"We can't sit here forever," said Thad. "Let's go."

He was probably right, but Jacob felt so lazy at the moment. He groaned, wishing he had a million servants, half providing him with whatever food he wanted and the rest meeting his every demand. Just the thought filled him with glee. He had told his father about this wish once and he'd told Jacob if he wanted such dreams to come true, he would have to work extra hard to make them happen. Jacob did not like the sound of that. He could not imagine a life filled with too much work.

"What about your sister, Thaddy?"

"Oh." Thaddeus had forgotten all about Tonya because she usually stayed after school to prepare for an exam. Recently, it seemed like she was always preparing for an exam. Thaddeus hoped he wouldn't have to be like that when he was her age. It was a terrible life to live in constant fear and anxiety. He shook his head at Jacob. "She's not coming now. It's Wednesday. She stays back for lessons with her math teacher."

"Oh."

"What school do your elder siblings attend?" Thaddeus realized he knew so little of them. Perhaps, he could have learned a lot more if he had not been sent off the way he had. Remembering the scene again made his stomach churn. He had been trying his best not to think about that day ever since.

"They're done with high school. Anna thinks she wants to go to a catering institute and learn how to cook. Last time she tried making a bagel, she almost set the house on fire. My mom said men like ladies who can cook and, if she doesn't learn how to cook, she might end up as a lonely old lady with two cats and a dog constantly trying to kill each other and her constantly trying to break them apart."

"Your mother said that?" Thaddeus asked, laughing.

"*Uh-huh.* She also said if Adams went into music like he's planning on doing, he would go broke faster than it takes to pronounce the word 'circus,' then come crawling back to her house. And she would kick his ass out because she warned him in the first place."

Thaddeus was still laughing. "Well, what does she say about you?"

"Oh, nothing." Jacob lowered his head to stare at the ground. "She doesn't know if I'll become useful to her or not yet. She says I'm still young and there's still time for me to not end up like my siblings. Or my father."

"What about your father?"

"I think he's an awesome fellow. My mother is just mad because he once had sex with a girl from Albany—which is not such a bad thing if you ask me. I mean, it would be a blessing to be with someone else besides my mother, if I was my father. All she does is overdose and yell at me. If I didn't know better, I'd say I wasn't her original son."

"But you are," said Thaddeus.

Jacob shrugged. "I am, I guess. It's just... *hard.* I wish she would be a better person. She says she wishes I were a better person, too. I don't think my mother likes anyone other than herself."

Thaddeus could not imagine what he would have done if his mother was like that. For sure, he knew his mother loved her children very much, even though she lost her temper often. He knew it was because she wanted them to do the right thing. Suddenly, he felt a wave of sadness on his friend's behalf. He had seen Jacob's mother before. He may be young, but he was not sure she was capable of the kind of love Momma showed him. Perhaps it was wrong to compare her to his mother. No one would ever compare to Momma, anyway.

He didn't think Jacob was all that bothered about it, though, watching his friend. What he lacked in terms of parental love and care, he made up for in the unfading comfort food provided.

"These chips taste amazing, Thaddy. You want some?"

Thaddeus nodded and Jacob placed three thin slices into his hands. They continued their trek, Jacob walking under the canopy of trees to avoid the harsh sun rays.

"Do you miss your father?"

"I do. I know he misses me, too. He didn't want me to leave, as I said before. My father is brilliant, so I'm sure he'll find a way to bring me back, though."

Thaddeus nodded, but he was thinking of something else. "How come Anna and Adams weren't living with you and your dad? And how come he didn't fight for their custody like he fought for yours?"

Jacob thought about the question for a while. Right from his birth, there had always been an invisible line separating him from his siblings, but he had not bothered himself about it.

"They don't want to be with my father," Jacob said, realizing the truth wasn't as simple as he'd made it sound.

They were too busy in their conversation to notice what was coming. Toby and his squad were making their way towards them with sticks in their hands.

Jacob saw them first. "*Uh oh.*" This was not going to be good.

The bag of chips fell from his hand. He stared angrily at the ground, hating his chips had to pay the price. He would pick them back up, but half the contents had already spilled onto the pavement and there was no retrieving those.

"What do we do?" Thaddeus asked.

"We run," Jacob answered absentmindedly, staring at where his chips were being kissed by sand.

"We *run.*"

He looked up at Thaddeus and grabbed him by the hand. He knew exactly where they were going.

They ran a long way from the school, with Toby and his clique chasing after them tirelessly. Jacob was exhausted by the time he got there, but at least he knew they would be safe.

It was an old garage, the walls covered entirely in graffiti, with faint light barely penetrating the space. Thaddeus didn't understand why they had come there or why they were stopping. Jacob collapsed near the garage's entrance, his breath heavier than lead. It took Thaddeus a while to realize they weren't alone.

"What's going on, Jacob?"

Thaddeus, startled more by the cool manner of the voice than by the fact the person knew his friend's name, looked at the person. He had seen that face before. And, of course, the hair—a flaming blue mohawk. It was Jacob's brother. Adams.

Toby and his friends finally arrived. Jacob pointed at them and said, breathlessly, "These guys... They are trying to beat us up."

Toby's expression was one of confusion. He didn't know if he should be scared of Adams, who didn't have much of a well-built frame. While he had his six friends, a quick count revealed Adams had only three. Toby smiled. This was a fight he could win. Thaddeus Carter and his friend had to pay the price for their foolishness and they were crazy to think these three guys could stop him.

Adams looked at the exhausted boys and asked them to go behind a door in the garage to some sort of storage room.

Jacob and Thaddeus sat in the dark, dank space—which smelled of crude and cigarettes—wondering if Adams was talking to Toby or sending him away. Neither said anything, but they each knew what the other was thinking. They felt the tremulous fear on each other's breath.

When Adams told them they were free to come out, Toby and his guys were gone. There was blood on the wall.

Neither Toby nor his six disciples were in school the next day. Later, the principal received a call that Toby had been involved in an accident and was hospitalized.

Chapter Eleven

Nothing changed immediately. In fact, nothing changed for quite some time after Momma accidentally broke the family portrait. She was really sorry when it happened and even tried her best to fix the frame with adhesive glue, but it was shattered. The glass came off in shards. The old picture beneath still held the charm and love the family had for each other, but the frame was ruined.

Thaddeus was about four in the photo. Momma held Shanice in her arms and the small babe looked up into her eyes. Tonya was smiling wide enough one could see the sun reflecting in her smile. She had pressed her head against their father's cheeks and was wearing a southern Native pearl necklace which had belonged to their grandmother. Thaddeus couldn't understand why anyone would ever wear the necklace. It looked like it was choking Tonya. She hadn't minded, though, and seemed happy wearing it. Now, the necklace was lost to the bottom layer of her trinket box. She never wore it because it made her look old. Instead, she would borrow Momma's jewelry whenever she had a party to attend; or ask Emily, her best friend.

Father stood at the left end of the photo in a white open-neck shirt, a boat pendant dangling down his open chest. His lips were smiling, but his eyes were not. It was the kind of smile Thaddeus was used to seeing on adults.

When Tonya found out the portrait broke, she burst into a frantic sweat, her face growing slightly pale. As far as she was concerned, the incident with Flora had confirmed her theory.

"You saw what happened with Ms. Flora, didn't you, Thad?"

Thaddeus sat on his brightly colored carpet, trying to assemble playing cards into a pyramid or any kind of shape. His goal was to build the structure without anything distracting him or destroying his efforts. The wind was attempting to thwart him but was not strong enough. Shanice was outside, playing a game of her own invention with Momma's plant. Therefore, most of his problems were solved. There would be no one to run around, no prospective threat to be scared of. *God*, Shanice was such a bother. He wondered if he had been this irritable to Tonya when he was Shanice's age and, if he had, how she had survived the persistent torment.

He hadn't considered Tonya would get in his way. Normally, she entertained herself by reading a book or talking on the phone with Emily for hours about God knows what. But, now she was here, interrupting his game, trying to bring up a matter he thought was settled.

"You saw what happened, didn't you?" she pressed. Her hands dug into her coffee brown hair, pushing the wayward locks from her face. "You saw what happened when Ms. Flora's photo with her husband got broken."

"It didn't get broken. He broke it."

"And how would you know that? You said you went in and found a mess."

Thaddeus placed an ace on top of a red heart and picked up the next card from the pile beside him. "I know he's a bad man and Ms. Flora could never have done such a thing. She could never break her family photo. Didn't you say they were important?" He paused, a distant look on his face. The scene had begun to replay in his mind. His mouth was agape, but he didn't notice. "When I got there, he came out and started yelling, throwing things around. He smelled like alcohol. He was... It just had to be him," he said with finality, bending to resume his invention.

"Still, all of those bad things started to happen because the picture got broken," Tonya insisted.

"Momma says he became a bad person because he lost his job. Momma says something like that could do a lot of damage to a person."

"When did she tell you that?"

"She didn't tell me. I heard her discussing it with Dad when they both thought I was asleep."

"Why, you little..." Tonya smiled.

He giggled and paused to admire what he was creating. He had built three layers already and the structure was beautiful. He only hoped he could make it to at least the seventh layer before the cards were exhausted. He would have to beg Momma to get him another deck of cards the next time she went out. For that, he had to be on his best behavior now. There were many things besides the cards he hoped Momma would get for him.

"What else did you hear?" Tonya asked.

His sister loved gossip. He had learned this about her and used it to his advantage many times. By holding back a piece of information he knew she desperately wanted to hear, he could get her to do almost anything.

That was how badly she loved gossip. It was why she would spend hours with Emily on the phone even though she had assignments to do. And, why they found it hard to leave each other whenever Tonya went visiting or Emily came over. They talked like the world was coming to an end and they had one day to tell each other every last thing.

"I didn't hear anything else."

"You're lying," she said.

"No, I'm not. Why would I lie?"

Tonya shrugged. "Is that really all you heard?"

"Maybe."

"So, you are lying."

"I can't remember."

She gave an exasperated sigh and picked up one of Shanice's teddy bears. She stroked the toy gently, like a child. It was a large pink teddy called June—one of Shanice's favorites. Thaddeus thought it was insane anyone would name a toy in the first place; but then, if that person were his younger sister, the craziness was not too far-fetched.

Just then, Shanice sauntered in wearing a purple, wool gown dotted with little butterflies of different colors. Her hair was held back beneath a tight polka dot band and her feet were bare, which earned her a scowl from Tonya.

"How many times have I told you never to go out with your feet bare? Don't you know you could get pierced by a nail or something even sharper?"

"Daddy says there are no sharp objects outside," Shanice said in her defense, smiling.

The next hour, their father returned from work, tired and sweaty. Tonya heated his bath water to just the temperature he liked and took his shoes outside to let the sunshine get rid of the stench. Momma was not home yet, and as long as that was the case, Tonya was the woman of the house.

She heated some food for her father and served him while he sat on the couch to watch *Sanford and Son.*

She was going to ask him about the portrait and how he planned to fix it but was too scared. Well, not scared per sé. N*ervous*. It was an easy thing to do, she told herself. She took a deep breath and made her shot.

"What are you planning to do about the frame, Dad?"

He didn't hear her. His eyes were fixed on the television screen, as was his attention.

She took another deep breath. "Dad?"

His eyes shot up.

"What are you going to do about the frame?"

"What frame?"

"The one that got broken. That *accidentally* got broken," she corrected hesitantly.

"Why, replace it, of course. I'll just get a new one," he said, returning his attention to the television. His eyes dilated in view of the current scene.

Tonya wasn't watching. She did not like how casual he was being about the picture. Replace it, of course, but that wasn't the problem.

What exactly was the problem? Her subconscious probed her, but she had no response. She could not place her fingers on what, but she knew things would go wrong. Just as things had gone wrong with Flora. God, she hurt just to think about the woman. Good ol' Flora, who was everything anyone could ever ask for. The one all the kids loved to be around.

Tonya looked at her father, whose eyes were still glued to the television and whose beard shimmered in blue light, and felt a painful constriction in her chest. It would tear her apart if her father turned out to be, well, a different person than he was today.

That night she went to bed and had a dream. A terrible dream. Or, more precisely put, a *strange* one. It was Thaddeus who usually had these sorts of dreams. She would often dream about riding a unicorn or an alien invasion. Instead, she dreamt they were in a dark room. The whole family was there. For some reason, the lights were out, but they could still make each other out using the light breaking in from the window.

Tonya was alone in the corner. She tried to speak, but her voice was gone. It was like there was something over her mouth, drowning out her voice, except nothing was there. Her mouth formed words, only—there was no sound.

Tonya tried to walk to where the rest of her family were, but couldn't move, either. She heard a voice behind her, though the words were unintelligible. It sounded like someone was laughing; then, the next moment, like an angry rumbling. She could not turn her head to see where the voice was coming from. She was stuck.

Her father sensed she was in distress and began moving toward her, but as he came closer she realized he wasn't her father. A beam of moonlight fell across his face. It was, in fact, Thaddeus as a full-grown man.

Tonya could understand why she'd mistaken him for their father—he was wearing their father's police uniform. It was stained with blood. He stood in front of her, tears filling up his eyes as he watched her on the floor. She was trying to ask for help and, from the look on his face, she knew he understood. But he didn't do anything to help. Or, maybe, he *couldn't* do anything.

Tonya woke up in a frantic sweat, breath rushing into her lungs.

She explained the dream to her parents, but they said it was only a dream. Thaddeus, who she thought was much too young to decide whether it had been just a dream or if it was some sort of premonition, agreed. He said it was called a nightmare and he had them all the time. Tonya rolled her eyes at him. Later, she still wanted to talk about the dream with her dad, but he had this overly flippant way of discarding topics he was not interested in that hurt her. She was terrified but, over the next few days, her fear alleviated.

***

One Sunday afternoon, after church at the Gilbreth Parish, what Tonya had been waiting for happened.

Their father came home from a meeting and didn't seem pleased at all. He didn't say anything, but Tonya knew something was eating away at him. She knew her father well; she knew when he was happy and when he was worried, despite how he tried to conceal his feelings and "be a man." She knew one-word replies meant he was irritated and needed to be left alone.

That day, he had hung out with his friends for a few drinks. Their father did not usually drink. He said one bottle often led to ten too quickly and the kind of friends he hung out with weren't ones to place a safe bet on. He hadn't said the last part, but she had deduced as much from the grimace on Momma's face when he mentioned the name of the friends he was going out with.

There was something different about him when he returned that night. He said something about bad news from work. Then, he picked at his food and paid no attention to the news. He always enjoyed watching the news. He didn't even stir when Thaddeus told him he had gotten an A on his last assignment. It was obvious he was there, but his mind was not. He was in a bad mood and she really wanted to know what had happened to upset him like that. As it seemed, so did Momma, who asked for details in as polite a manner as she could, careful not to step on his toes. But he had only mumbled a few lines and retracted into silence.

A few hours later, he donned his jacket and said he was going to the office to check out a few things. Momma had gotten mad because it was Thanksgiving and a few people from church were coming over. In return, their father had lost his temper, and said Momma was too demanding and insensitive. Then, for thirty minutes, Tonya had watched her parents exchange words with each other, voices raised. The argument ended with their father storming out of the house.

Afterward, Tonya had cried in her room while Thaddeus played with Shanice.

Tonya knew the broken photograph had something to do with this.

Chapter Twelve

March 29th, 1980

Sarah felt a throbbing sensation in her head and her vision was blurry. There was a bright white light coming from above as she lay on her back. She wondered what it was. At first, she thought it was the sun. Why was she on her back and staring at the sun? She had just come out with Candice and was heading home. Her mind raced as the memories came flooding back. Candice had been shot. They had both fallen. She remembered hitting her head before everything went black.

Sarah shut her eyes tight, not wanting to see her surroundings. The pain radiated from the back of her head, hitting her in waves like a migraine. Shutting her eyes wasn't enough. Her mind wouldn't allow her to escape what she had seen. The man in the mask running up from behind, the sound of the gun *cracking*, the flash of the reddish-white light. The sound had stunned her ears. Candice, who was right behind her, had taken the impact. The bullet was meant for Sarah, though, and would've hit her if she'd been walking on her own.

Tears ran from the corners of her eyes through closed lids. Tampa, Florida was rampant with crime. Robberies and homicides occurred every day. They never imagined they would become the subject of another tragic story, which would top the news tagline for a day before being swallowed by sports and politics. As Sarah struggled to come to terms with her reality, she heard a name. Then voices all around her.

She slowly opened her eyes. The lights weren't from the star in the solar system but from a light above her. She squinted, pulling away from the light and triggering a sharp pain in her forehead. The pain jerked Sarah awake and she reached for her head, only to be stopped by the doctor who hovered over her, a weak smile on his face. He looked middle-aged, with wrinkled skin at the corners of his eyes. His mouth parted as he spoke softly to Sarah, but she couldn't hear a single word. Slowly, the muffled sounds cleared as she regained her hearing.

"Is it any better?" the doctor asked.

"Yes." Her voice came out in a croak, like she had been asleep for a long time. She didn't know what he was asking, but hoped he was referring to her hearing. She cleared her throat, rattling the ache in her skull to a new degree, causing her to grimace. "Where is... Where is Candice? My friend. She was shot."

"Your friend is in the next room with excellent doctors. We've been patching her up. She will be fine. In the meantime, I need to stitch you up. You have quite the gash on your head. I need you to lie as still as you can, alright?"

She had to playback most of what the doctor had said in her head for her to understand. Sarah nodded and the movement caused the skin just above her left eyebrow to tug. That was where the doctor began stitching. She winced as he worked, wondering what the injury would look like. He stated his name and reassured her any scarring would be minimal.

"When can I see her?" Sarah asked, the words tumbling out of her slack lips.

"Someone will give you an update when she's out of surgery. In the meantime, you need to rest. You've suffered a concussion. I will take a look at your results when the remaining scans are done processing, but right now, all you have to do is rest. I'll check on your friend." The man exited through and Sarah heard him whisper to someone standing in the hall. He argued she needed rest and wouldn't be able to take questions, then sighed. The doctor stepped back into the room. "Sarah, this is Officer Carter with the Florida Police Department. He would like to have a word with you." The doctor turned to the officer. "Two minutes, then you let her rest."

The officer entered the room. He had jet black hair and brown eyes burning with the passion of someone new to the job. He looked young, with his strapping uniform and look of unbridled ambition. Officer Carter was proud to be a police officer, Sarah could tell with a glance. Although, it might've just been the painkillers.

"Ms. Jones, I'm Officer Nicholas Carter. Sorry for the inconvenience, but I'm going to need you to recount everything you saw last night."

"Last night?" Sarah looked out the window beside her, seeing nothing but darkness. "What time is it?"

"Five forty-four in the morning," Nicholas replied without missing a beat.

"Okay. I didn't see his face. He was wearing a mask and I... I was intoxicated at the time, so I don't think my word could hold up for anything." Sarah felt the tears well in her eyes as she realized the one who had held her up was undergoing surgery to have a bullet removed from her body.

"I'm sorry. Look, I can come back later," Nicholas said, glancing behind him to see if the doctor was watching. The other man had hurried away, heading to another patient who needed his attention.

"I'm fine," Sarah replied, stifling a sniffle.

"Maybe you *could* help us. I was chasing down a lead in the area with my partner. We're in search of a suspect but have nearly nothing on him. My partner saw the man in the mask trying to break into a store. When he called him out, the guy took off running." Nicholas adjusted his belt along his waist. "That was when we bumped into you. We were chasing after him and heard the shot go off. My partner shot the man right after he shot your friend. Once the doctors clear him, we'll take him into custody. He's going to pay for what he did to you two."

"We didn't find the man we were looking for," Nicholas continued. "But, we believe he's connected to a few missing persons' cases. All we have is this single photograph of him. This was the last place he was reportedly seen. Recognize him?"

Nicholas held out the photo for Sarah to see. It was a colored image, distorted, as though taken with a low-resolution camera. Sarah peered at the picture but couldn't place him. The man had a bland look, a square jaw, dark blond hair—a face which might blend in anywhere in Tampa. Sarah took a deep breath and drew her face away, turning back to the officer.

"I'm sorry, but I don't think so. I'm still a bit hungover from the drugs or alcohol, I guess."

"Or maybe both?" Nicholas added with a smirk.

Sarah laughed, then groaned. The officer took his cue but left his card in case she remembered anything of importance. Once she was alone, Sarah fell into a deep and troubled sleep as memories of the evening flashed constantly in her head. When she awoke, she climbed out of the bed and hurried down the corridor as quickly as her legs would allow without toppling over.

She approached a nurse seated at a desk and saw the woman peering down at her desktop, making notes on what looked like a chart. From a distance, the woman seemed too cheerful for someone who had to be at work by six in the morning. Sarah peeked at the doors as she passed by—they had no names. As she reached the desk, the woman looked up at her with a wide ear-to-ear smile. Sarah began speaking and the nurse cut her off no sooner than the first syllable had left her mouth.

"Ms. Jones, you should be resting. Here, let me take you back to your room—"

"No, I want to see Candice. My friend. We were brought in together. She was shot. Redhead." Sarah spoke erratically, her voice strained as much as her body. She was exhausted and her heart was beating like it would explode out of her chest. She couldn't lose Candice. The woman had been a rock to her. Losing her was unimaginable. The tears came, unbidden and hot, flowing down her cheeks as she weakly wrestled with the nurse for information.

"I don't have any details about her, I'm sorry. We need you to rest."

"I'm not going to! I need to make sure she's okay. I can't go without knowing."

"Then I'll tell you," another voice said.

Sarah and the nurse turned to see a middle-aged doctor, quite younger than the one who had stitched her up. She had eyes that spelled years of tiredness, regret, and loss, but also a bit of hope. She smiled at Sarah and adjusted her glasses before speaking.

"Are you family?"

"Yes," Sarah replied instantly. "Not exactly. She has no one left. Her family is nomadic. They travel the world."

"Alright, Ms. Jones. Your friend has been stabilized. Ms. Farrelly suffered some internal bleeding, which we were able to clear. We are waiting for her results from the test lab to know more. But, the combination of a concussion and a gunshot wound has temporarily placed her in a coma. The bullet did some damage and we're hoping to straighten everything out soon. All of that can only be done, however, after the scan."

Sarah looked around the corridors of the hospital. For the first time, the dreaded stench of antiseptic and death reached her nostrils. She had hated hospitals ever since her father had died, even if the place was built to save lives. Sarah felt like it was a prison for those whose souls were absolutely loved. Her father and now her only friend. She saw a few nurses and patients staring at her and turned back to the doctor.

"Can I see her?"

"Not now. Your body needs time to heal and so does hers. She just got out of surgery. You'll see her soon. I know you're in pain, but for both of your sake, Ms. Jones, please return to bed. I promise I will update you personally once her results are in. Alright?"

Sarah nodded gravely and allowed her gaze to drift to the left, where she saw a male nurse. His dirty blond hair reminded him of someone she had seen not too long ago. She remembered the man from the diner and the connection was made instantly. Her mind was trying to connect the man she had seen in the photograph shown to her by the officer with the man who had come into the shop. She shut her eyes and compared both images in her head side-by-side. There was no mistaking. They were the same person.

"I need my phone. I need to make a call."

"Ms. Jones, I think if it's something that can wait—"

"It's regarding the man whom the police are looking for. I remember seeing him."

The officers hadn't left the building. Both Carter and his partner rushed back to the room where Sarah had reluctantly resigned herself to. She could get a better look at them as the drugs had started to wear off. Her left side ached from her fall and she was certain she'd have some sort of bruise underneath the hospital gown.

"You're saying you know him?" Carter asked.

"No, not exactly. He comes to the diner where my friend and I work once a week. He's very predictable, never misses a week. Candice even documents it. She knows what he'll wear, what he'll order, and things like that. He always comes with a different woman. You're saying he's kidnapping them?"

"We're saying some of these women have been missing for months on end and the last anyone heard from them, they were driving or flying across the country to meet with some guy in Tampa. They were never heard from again. This guy is our suspect and we can't find him."

"I know where he'll be next week," said Sarah. "I know when he'll be arriving and everything. I just need to see Candice's notes. *Jon*, that's his name. That's what the last woman he was with called him."

Chapter
Thirteen

*Present Day

Nicholas loved being an officer. Several years ago, his mother's house was destroyed by a dreadful fire and Carter had watched the police solve the case. They had said it wasn't just any fire—it was arson. It had taken a week, with the officers constantly returning to their house to update them, but eventually, they found who was responsible for starting the fire. Not only was the arsonist responsible for burning his mother's family home to the ground, he was also wanted in connection to three murders and three separate acts of arson. The young Nicholas had seen justice play out quickly and swiftly. He had seen the system work and the bad guy be caught. After that, nothing else mattered to Nicholas Carter except becoming a part of the police force and protecting the people. Catching the bad guys. Upholding the law.

It had taken some work, but Nicholas succeeded in joining the force. He worked his way up until he could finally become an officer. He'd considered applying to be a detective, but knew he would need to boost his intuition first. Until then, he was stuck as a regular cop.

Truthfully, he loved walking the beat and going on patrol. He felt a deep sense of connection and confidence whenever he did. He was giving back to the country in which he'd been born, keeping its people safe. There was no greater honor to Nicholas. He was proud to be an officer.

Driving his vehicle back to the precinct, Nicholas caught a glimpse of himself in the mirror.

He looked left to see the other cars parked around the precinct and was surprised to find more than eight cars docked at once during the morning. It was a rarity, as most would be out on patrol, as he had been before he was radioed back to the precinct. He received a beep from the captain of the department on his pager, requesting his immediate presence. Nicholas tried to guess why he was being summoned—hoped for good news—but he knew Captain Cosmo. The man was naturally unpleasant. He liked little and despised a lot, using the anger and frustration of the men who worked for him to get things done.

The fact someone else was being transferred to be his replacement soon put him even more on edge, causing him to bark orders at everyone. The man was rarely in a good mood.

Nicholas strode into the precinct. The building was buzzing, busy as ever with officers taking and making calls, following leads, filing paperwork—the makings of any precinct around the world.

Nicholas nodded to a few of his coworkers and made a beeline for the captain's office. Through the glass door, he saw the man on the other side. Cosmo's muted voice angrily grilled whoever was on the receiving end of the phone in his hand. His hair had grown to counteract its unequivocal retreat from the top of his head, while the rest was fashioned with a slick gel and hung limply down his back. Blooms of acne spotted his vampire-white skin, making his cheeks—which tended to flush with anger—look like the perfect source of blood for said creature. He looked up before Nicholas could knock and waved him in.

"Yeah. Look, I'll call you back. You better have him ready within the next two hours or I'm coming there myself." Whatever was said in response caused Captain Cosmo to stare at the receiver as though the device itself had insulted him. "Alright, listen here, *you*. I'm going to give you two hours. After that, I'm coming for you. And nothing on the face of this goddamn earth will keep me away from you, got that?"

The line clicked dead. Nicholas thought the man would throw the phone across the room and erupt into a fit of rage. Instead, he sighed, dropped the phone casually on his desk and picked up a cigar. He gestured at Nicholas, silently asking if he wanted one. Nicholas declined, not because he didn't smoke, but because he wondered how it would look if anyone saw him smoking with his captain before ten in the morning. He sat quiet as Cosmo stalked towards the south window in his office, overlooking the city below. The man pulled long drags of smoke into his lungs, held until he was certain all the damage a single puff could do had been done and his brain begged for oxygen, then let the smoke through the window. After a minute, he turned around and put out the cigar in an ashtray hidden behind a potted plant before taking a seat.

"The boys down at Ybor have a suspect of ours. They're trying to use red tape to keep the arrest from our hands. Honestly, I don't even want to go over there with the mood I'm in. Someone would end up hurt."

"Sorry about that." Nicholas cleared his throat. "I could be there in an hour, talk to the captain, get our suspect back. What's the case? The only one I'm aware of from Ybor is that unsub McCaughey and his partner—"

"No, no. I'll get the suspect myself. You're here for another reason." Captain Cosmo squinted at Nicholas, a look which men and women at the precinct had dubbed the death glare. "The breaking and entry case with the Millers."

"I've given my statement everything has been checked and recorded. What's the problem?"

The captain scoffed. "The problem is your damn scrawny ass broke protocol."

"Sir," Nicholas began. "I made a judgment call. If I hadn't done something, matters could have sp—"

"What you did was fire a weapon at a criminal holding a kid. You barely missed his head, and that was *after* you negotiated with criminals, told them you'd let them leave the house and handed them your weapon. You know it's punishable to let go of your weapon like that? Willfully giving ammunition to criminals is something you should very well know not to do and you did it anyway!"

"Sir, I didn't give away my weapon. I gave away the magazine."

"Does it look like I give half a rat's ass, Carter? Protocol is protocol and you went straight in there and broke it. Didn't wait for backup, didn't listen to dispatch, tried to let them go *and* handed your weapon over. You know what the higher-ups are saying to me? You could be kicked off the force for this, Carter. For this little stunt of yours—"

"What's with the sudden change? I saved their lives!" Nicholas shot back, restraining himself to his seat.

"Great job! Now the commissioner has to lobby with the Millers and pay them into silence. They wanted to sue the department for putting them in danger. I can't deal with this kind of backlash right now, so you're going to have to do things by the book or—"

"If I may, sir," Nicholas cut in, trying and failing to hide the anger in his voice. "Our job is to protect and serve the good people of this nation. At that point, a child was being taken—held at gunpoint as collateral to ensure those criminals could escape. A human shield, of sorts. If I had not acted, if I had waited for things to be done by the book, a child would have been taken away from their family that day. I understand why we have protocol, sir, but sometimes it's not enough and we need to act—"

"Shut your goddamn mouth. Twenty-five years on the force and I've never seen a more self-righteous prick. You saved a life? Big whoop. Here's a cookie. You broke protocol. If you can't follow the rules which govern us, what makes you different from the very criminals you were trying to apprehend?"

"Sir—"

"No. Shut up. Let me finish. You think you're a wise-ass, so here's how it's going to go down. Out of the respect I do have for you, I'm going to take the brunt of this whole thing because that's what a captain is supposed to do. But, if I see you breaking protocol again, for *any* reason, well… You better start reading up on your traffic laws and be ready to sign in your weapon. Keep your calculated risks to yourself and allow the system to do its job. Do you understand, Officer Carter?"

"Yes, sir." The response sounded like rocks passing through a blender, mixed with iron filling then shaken together in tin cups. Nicholas ignored his inner voice telling him to leap across the table, grab Cosmo by his neck and smack his bald head into the hardwood table until he passed out.

As Nicholas left the captain's office, he noticed rows of eyes glaring at him. Apparently, the conversation had been loud enough for some of his coworkers to catch what was said. He evaded their eyes and headed straight for the door, quickly reaching his car.

Nicholas sat still for a moment, allowing what had been said to wash over him. He swore. Smacked his steering wheel in a fit of rage. He had done the right thing, he knew he had, but somehow rules made it as though he hadn't. If the laws which existed to protect people were insufficient to protect the very people they were made for, then the only sense which could be made would be to go outside the law and to do what was required.

He put the car in reverse, stepped on the gas and hit something hard. Nicholas looked into the rear view to see he had run into another police vehicle parked behind him. Nicholas bit his tongue, strangling the anger flooding through his chest.

Chapter
Fourteen

N icholas spent the entire day stewing. He had to take money from his personal account to fix the other officer's car, as he didn't want the captain to know. After, one piece of bad news arrived after the other. First, he got a flat tire as he was handing out a speeding ticket. Then, the jack which he had used to lift the car off the ground fell loose, causing the inner mudguard of the vehicle to slam into his forearm. Nicholas put ice on the injury and drove the rest of the day with only one arm.

After that, he made a routine stop of a man who had parked wrongly, only to be verbally abused by the man. Nicholas knew with his temperament at the time, he would have said something which would have landed him in big trouble. The man was African-American and the police had been accused of several incidents involving police brutality within the community. Protests had broken out earlier in the year and tensions were still high from the event. Nicholas allowed the man to go with a stern warning.

Dispatch called out an S-13 in his vicinity for a suspicious vehicle. As much as Nicholas was not in the mood for work, he knew he had to do his duty. He immediately took the call and turned onto an intersection which led to the highway, radioing the police vehicle closest to him to check the opposite end.

He waited in the middle of the Leroy Selman Cross Expressway and, three minutes later, spotted the Toyota driving down a one-way street to get on to the expressway. Nicholas turned on his sirens, signaling for the man driving to stop. But the man continued, driving the vehicle onto the expressway.

He zoomed after the Toyota, using his siren to clear a path in front of him while the Toyota made sudden turns, darting left and right through traffic. Nicholas radioed the situation in, calling out the license plate numbers and the road they were currently on. His arm ached from where it had been struck by the car, but he held onto the steering wheel and plowed forward.

His police cruiser managed to catch up to the fleeing vehicle. Nicholas turned on his speaker and directed the driver to pull over repeatedly. The man disobeyed the order and continued to drive recklessly. The Toyota drove on the left side of the road, barreling straight through as other drivers had either pulled over or given way to the police chase.

Nicholas knew he could stop the driver. All he would have to do was match his speed and use his rail guard to tip the Toyota's tail. The vehicle would spin out and, if the driver kept his foot on the gas, the car would flip and crash. But, if he were not a complete madman and hit the brakes, the car would come to a halt in the middle of the road.

Nicholas looked ahead and realized they were approaching the city district, congested by people and small businesses.

He had to stop the driver before someone got seriously hurt or killed. The police cruiser picked up speed quickly as he pressed down the gas pedal, maxing out the horsepower to match the Toyota.

Nicholas looked over at the driver for a split second before focusing back on the road. It would take him only a moment to perform the move and he needed to time it perfectly.

As he approached the suspect's vehicle, additional units provided updates of a potential roadblock at the next intersection. Nicholas considered simply going forward with his plan, but he had been given orders. The new plan was to force the suspect's vehicle to continue in the same direction towards the roadblock. As he pulled back, he was joined by two additional vehicles. All three squad cars squeezed in around the escaping vehicle.

As they came to the roadblock, he and the others slowed down, allowing the suspect to reduce his speed. Only, he didn't. He drove right through the stop sticks, causing him to crash into another police car and sending his vehicle into a coffee shop.

Nicholas watched as officers rushed to the scene, dragging the man from the vehicle. He had survived the crash, albeit in terrible shape, but injured an innocent bystander. A young woman who had worked at the coffee shop died instantly from the impact.

Nicholas felt responsible for the woman's death.

His former partner had died because he had been a stickler for the law. Since then, Nicholas worked alone. He understood the importance of having a partner cover his six—and the pair system worked—but he couldn't shake the conviction if he had his way, a lot of crimes could be prevented.

By the end of the day, Nicholas had bought himself a small bottle of scotch, poured the liquor into his coffee mug and drove down the street which led to his home.

The officer stayed on the street a long time, slowly sipping his drink. He had memorized each of the houses, the features, the people who lived inside them. He wasn't really friends with any of them, but they were still a community. He admired his neighborhood's serenity and was grateful for how the craziness of the city never found its way this far. A red Sedan drove by, obscuring his view for a moment. He dumped the rest of the alcohol and drove home. Pulling the cruiser to a stop in the driveway before manually lifting the garage door, he drove in.

"Hey, hon." Sarah stood by the door. She planted a kiss on his cheek. "Did you get the eggs?"

Nicholas raised a confused eyebrow, then remembered the text he had received right before the alcohol. Sarah had asked him to buy eggs and he had completely forgotten.

His wife frowned, her face twisting with disappointment. He felt the urge to apologize, but he didn't. He was too mentally drained. Looking around the living room for his kids, he sighed when he didn't see them.

"I need the eggs to make dinner. If I had the car fixed, I would have gotten them myself, but you know it's not back from the shop yet."

Maybe it was the way she said it or the alcohol, but Nicholas had been pushed to his wits' end.

"I cannot deal with your shit right now," he said. "If you want eggs, get them. If you can't, that's not my problem. Either way, get the hell out of my face."

He shut the door behind him and made his way to the shower, allowing the cold water to wash the day's stress off him. It took him less than ten minutes to go from the shower to the bed.

Tonya listened from the thin walls of her bedroom, her eyes brimming with tears.

Chapter
Fifteen

*T*he problem is not with life or man—it is with the mind. The mind needs to be corrected. It needs to be cleansed of the illness that is sin. But men are too far gone. Too hard to be corrected. It is easier to correct man when he is innocent, devoid of the evil machinations of the world which corrupts.

I will correct it. I can correct it. This gives my life purpose. The good Lord will bless me for the works of my hands. They will be cleansed. All of man will be cleansed.

I have found the perfect man to cleanse. Young and smart, so full of life and energy. It is a true sorrow to see that all men are born into sin. Regardless of who they are, there is sin. From birth, they have already seen too much, felt too much. Thirsted for the milk from their mother's bosom. How do they not know what they want is nothing but a manifestation of the sin itself?

I will protect man. I have to. For the sake of the future.

The man wasn't Stanley Barr. Right now, he was the reformer. A man who existed only to cleanse the world of its sins.

The man parked his car in front of the mall and watched his target walk in. The shopping center was full of people. Consumers. *Sinners.* Men who bought multiple cans of beers. Women who stared longingly at expensive makeup.

The pleasures of the flesh—a sin greater than any.

Barr's face was one which easily blended into the crowd, allowing him to be wherever he wanted to be at any time. No one ever suspected anything. He had never committed a crime and no one was looking for him. His high-necked coat covered the sides of his cheeks. He kept his head down but maintained a visual on his target with his peripheral vision. He watched as his target found an air hockey table, bought a few tickets and proceeded to play against the man who operated the machine.

Watching from a safe distance, Barr saw the smile which erupted across the target's face. Positive emotions were something he despised—a waste of time and energy for a simple rush of chemicals in the brain. They were like addicts, hoping for a spurt of dopamine, a burst of adrenaline. Chemicals which were to be reserved for special moments were being misused. As he watched, he felt rage build within him. He couldn't watch the target any longer.

I will protect.

He walked up to the table where the game was being played. The man who operated the table capitalized on the distraction of his opponent and sunk the puck. The target looked up at Barr and fear spread across the boy's freckled face. He took to his heels instantly, running away as fast as he could.

Barr chased after the boy, leaving the confused table operator.

The boy pushed past people, attempting to make his way through the crowded mall. He kept looking over his shoulder to see the man coming after him. When he turned his head forward again, his vision was filled with a pyramid of stacked scented candles. He ran right into the display.

A nearby security guard turned toward the commotion and began making his way over. Not wanting the boy to be taken away, Barr distracted the guard by calling out the name of his target.
    "Jared! Jared, wait!"

The boy looked back at the man in the jacket. Gaining new inspiration, he took off running again. Barr slowed down to offer an apology to the guard.
    "He's my son and I found out he's been skipping school. Please don't let him leave the building."

The guard obliged, using the short-range walkie on his shoulder to warn his colleagues at the door, asking them to be on the lookout for the boy.

Barr hurried towards the door and found Jared struggling with two guards. When he reached them, he explained the situation and apologized.

Exhausted, the boy readily gave up his struggle and allowed himself to be walked toward the car, the man holding his arm in a vice-like grip. He climbed into the front passenger side seat while the man retrieved a handkerchief from the glove compartment. Before Jared could resist, the fabric was over his nose, knocking him unconscious.

No one noticed the man lift the boy out of the car and place his limp body in the trunk. There were no cameras around to catch the action and no onlookers. He had succeeded in retrieving his target. Now, the cleansing could begin.

He drove back to work and completed his duties for the day, occasionally returning to his car to make sure his target was still unconscious. The moment he was done for the day, he started his car and drove home.

Home was a single suburban-style house. Just like him, his house blended in with the neighborhood. Nothing about his house stood out. He reveled in going unnoticed, in *not* being the center of attention. He regretted the whole debacle at the mall. Three people had seen his face, even if barely for a moment. They would not be able to recall his features and, even if they did, the description they gave would be wrong. Once inside, Barr washed the makeup from his face, revealing the features only a select few people knew about.

The wrinkles on the side of his eyes, the scar which ran across the left side of his face, his darker skin which he had made light with makeup. He had become a different person, one which no one could recognize.

The sun was beginning to set, and the suburban mothers were calling their kids inside. He had watched those families with their children for many nights on end, fighting the urge to *cleanse.*

The last family disappeared into their home, allowing him to retrieve Jared from his trunk. The boy was gagged and bound, only slightly conscious with all the chloroform still running through his system. He was as limp as a doll. But, for what he would do to Jared, Barr needed the boy to be conscious.

When Jared finally came to, he found himself surrounded by three incredibly bright lights. He narrowed his eyes, squinting as he tried to make out the room he was in through the blinding light. He screamed but heard nothing in response. His hands were tied behind his back. He was strapped to a chair. Jared screamed again. When he looked down at himself, he could see only a white cloth draped over his body. Everywhere he looked, all he could see was the white light.

White is not just a color—it is godliness. It is purity. It is all that is good about the world. The white light will take away all sin, leaving the boy a pure blank slate without a single bit of sin left in him.

Barr approached Jared, his rubber-soled boots making almost no sound as he walked across the room. The boots weren't so much for the noise. He had made the room soundproof, so none of his captives' cries would reach the outside world.

Barr waited until the boy cocked his head to just the right angle, then strapped noise-canceling headphones over his ears and ran duct tape underneath his chin to lock them on.

Jared screamed again, but the boy couldn't even hear his own cries, regardless of how loud he tried to be. The bonds on his hands didn't allow him to move them at all. Jared couldn't see or hear. He could only feel the intense heat bouncing off of the lights. Even when he shut his eyes, he could still see the white. The white had become his body. It had become the floor beneath his feet and the sky above his head.

Once a day, Jared would feel a straw touch his lips. He would suck down water before being fed five spoonful's of a sponge-like food— most likely unseasoned rice. At first, he rejected the food, screaming at

119

his captor, swearing the police would catch up with him. But, as time went by, Jared lost all sense of time. He had no idea how long he had been there or where he was. He knew the face of the man who had abducted him, but even that face had not been real.

He'd been skipping school and thought the man had come to report him. He'd had no idea the man had come to take him to his personal hell.

On October 1st, Jared Evans was found in the same mall parking lot where he was abducted three months prior. He was curled up in a ball, malnourished, wearing the same clothes he had worn the day he went missing. Doctors treated him with antipsychotics, as he was plagued by constant hallucinations and an inability to remember people. His parents, siblings, and teachers were all unfamiliar to him. Jared couldn't speak for fear of his voice and other sounds. Most days, he stayed alone in his room, staring into a white bulb and whispering to himself.

Jared no longer knows who he or who anyone else is. He has been wiped clean. Devoid of all sin—all imperfections of the flesh. It had been a productive three months. The reformer set his gaze on a new target. He will cleanse little Carter. He has been watching for a while and he will do his duty. He will ensure a world without sin.

Chapter
Sixteen

June 4th, 1996

Adams Norman lit up a cigarette in his room and blew the smoke out through the window. The sky was bluer than usual. Most of the time, the sky was an impure bluish-grey. Something to do with all the pollution released by the town—all of that dirty material no one was willing to do anything about. Not the so-called environmental scientists or the city politicians or the engineers.

He was listening to an old Tupac record and hoping someday he would be like him—making music from all the madness and dirty shit he'd grown accustomed to.

Adams didn't like the wildlife. He didn't appreciate drugs, alcohol, guns, or anything associated with criminals. But, growing up and receiving all the blame for the things everyone else had done wrong made him realize no one was ever going to be fair, even in his own home. Life was not a game of fairness. It was survival of the fittest.

When Jacob was still a little boy, he'd played around in his father's room one day, throwing his files around. Their father had told Jacob to stay away from his things, but Jacob wouldn't listen because he was stubborn and always needed to have his way. Adams hated babysitting Jacob. It was the most annoying job anyone could ever be asked to do, and he was always the one asked to do it.

Jacob was too rough. Anything he found either ended up smashed on the ground or in his mouth. He pooped a lot, too. He was always yelling, making a ton of noise whenever Adams was trying to concentrate on his music. And, on that particular day, when Jacob was making a mess of their father's room, Adams stayed in his room, listening to music, tired of watching over his little brother.

Jacob would make the house into a mess and Adams planned to clean the mess up when he was done, instead of cleaning while he was still in the process of destruction.

Then their father came home early to find his reading glasses and Hermes watch broken. He'd exploded into a rage. Adams tried to explain to him there was only one person responsible for the damage, but he had been the one to take the blame as usual.

"Weren't you supposed to be watching him?" his father asked, his eyes full of a deadly sort of fire.

Adams explained, but his father wasn't listening. He didn't listen when the left pair of his brown shoes went missing—God knows what Jacob did with that—or when his car receipt was used in building a paper plane, or when the glass piece on the center table broke. He blamed Adams for *every single thing*. Even when Anna got drunk at her first party and returned home late. Their father blamed him for not watching over his sister and letting her drink too much, even though they had not seen each other until the party ended. When she received an F in mathematics, he said it was Adams' fault for setting a bad example; now none of his children were going to be serious about their academics.

In his words, Adams was "a bad egg." One which needed to be flushed before any more damage could be sustained.

Adams didn't understand what he had ever done to make his father hate him so much. It was obvious from the way he looked at him and the way he spoke to him, he regarded him as different from the rest. Often, Adams thought he was not his father's actual son and he knew as much, which made him mistreat him. Deep down, though, he knew this was only wishful thinking and his father simply didn't like him. Jacob was his perfect child, who he needed to be taken as far away from Adams as possible.

When his father came up with the idea for Adams to move to his grandfather's place in Michigan, he wasn't the least bit surprised. He wasn't hurt, either. The suggestion wasn't too far outside the wheelhouse of things he expected from his father.

Adams had packed up his things the next morning and was ready to move. His grandfather was a good man. He taught him how to change a car tire and how to drive. He taught him a few things to do with carpentry and how to milk a cow, too. Adams enjoyed the times he'd spent with his grandfather, however short-lived they were. He was mostly able to visit him during the holidays, but each time was spectacular. He was more than happy to go live with him.

He quit his job at the mall, where he'd worked night shifts to make some extra cash. Just as he'd been about to leave, his mother found out and stopped him. Apparently, she'd been unaware of her husband's arrangement to send him away and was outraged when told. He had hardly ever seen her that furious. The last time had been last New Year's Day when she lost her cool with the filling station's attendant.

She'd looked Luke Norman in his eyes and told him if her son left, she sure as hell was leaving with him. His father couldn't bear to let that happen—she was his weakness. Each time she threatened to leave and file for divorce, he would beg, promise to do anything to change her mind. At the end of the day, she would take him back and forgive him for whatever he'd done. He knew she loved him, just as she knew he loved her, but their love was suffering. Every single day was suffering. She wasn't happy and they knew it.

Maybe, she was not as in love with him as she had been once. Maybe, she was in love with the idea of being in love with him; or, a memory of being in love with him. Maybe, she loved the power, having the upper hand.

One morning, she woke up and decided she wanted a divorce and he knew that was that. There was nothing to be done to change her mind. Not his father promising to treat him better—treat him like his actual son—nor deciding to buy a house for her parents (which he eventually did). They knew it was time. There was nothing which could change her mind.

She told Adams he wouldn't have to worry about his father's cruel treatment towards him anymore, or his indifference, because they were going someplace far away where they would never have to see him again. Adams believed her. As far as he knew, she was going to make what she'd said happen. He had that much faith in her.

At first, Luke refused to sign the divorce papers. He wasn't willing to let her go for anything in the world. But she was insistent and he knew if she was adamant on leaving, she would leave one way or another.

There was nothing he could do to stop it. Her tenacity was one of the reasons he loved her.

That night, she made love to him better than he had ever experienced, Adams knew because he could hear his father's voice from the next room. He could hear his moans, his shrills of delight. The following day, he noticed a glow he had not seen in an exceedingly long time— since the time Jacob first called him "Dada." He saw a smile which faded the wrinkles on his face. Adams had no idea what his mother had planned, but in that moment, he couldn't help but feel sorry for him, regardless of how much he hated to feel anything other than hatred for those who'd made his life a living hell. He knew what was about to happen would tear him apart.

Who knows how she got a gun? All they knew was she had one and she was going to use it to get what she wanted.

Adams heard his father scream. He had rushed to his parent's door. He was used to peeping through the crack, watching even when they had no idea he was there. His mother sat on a chair, stark naked, her hair pouring down the sides of her face, a gun poised between her legs. His father sat on the bed opposite her. The gun wasn't pointed at him and that was the one thing Adams didn't understand. She'd pointed the gun at herself. She was smiling and had widened her legs so her husband could have a better view. Even though she was holding a gun, Adams watched as the bastard grew an erection.

He expected her to shoot him, at least his leg or something. He thought she would do something terrible to him—something which would come close to all the maltreatment Adams received from him over the years— but she didn't. He couldn't understand why. She had pointed the gun at herself and was talking and laughing, as though this were the kind of conversation one might have over coffee or dinner with a close friend.

125

The following morning, his father signed the divorce papers. She packed her things and told Adams to do the same. They were moving to Tampa. From the pictures he had seen on the internet, he already loved Tampa. Jacob stayed behind. Adams didn't understand why their mother wasn't bringing him with the arrangement. Jacob was his perfect son; best he stayed with him. Besides, the more he saw the boy, the more he was reminded of the terrible life he'd had to endure.

Anna had always been nothing more than a middle child. She was troubled, but she was also a girl, so his father, being the absolute prick he was, had not seen a reason to give her the same kind of attention he paid his sons.

"She can't take over the company or handle my estate when I'm gone. Hell, I'd be damned if she even knew how to change a tire!" he'd once said.

Anna, in the truest sense, was good for nothing. She was spoiled rotten at birth, having been left to live the kind of life she wanted without any form of supervision as she grew. Not even their mother paid her much attention. As the years went by, Adams could see her growing more rotten. He knew in his heart she would end up as total waste material if she didn't die of STDs first. Even now, as he walked past her room, he could hear her tangled with someone else.

"Oh, *yes*. That's right, baby. Oh, my. Hit me harder, baby. Yes, go slow..."

"I'm doing it for you, girl. Anything you want."

Adams slammed the front door shut as he walked out. He had business to deal with now.

He was on his way to Jacob's school.

Chapter Seventeen

"I'm kinda tired," Thaddeus said to Jacob as he placed his books back into his locker.

After school, the hallway gradually became empty. Lately, he'd enjoyed staying late. Shanice was always pissing him off at home, touching things which weren't hers and going places he didn't want her to go. It was becoming harder for her to mind her own business. Tonya, whom he found more enjoyable to talk to, was hardly around. If she wasn't staying at school for an extra lesson, she was at home doing all the motherly duties their mother would do if she were around. Momma had her job and she was very dedicated to it. Sometimes, he thought she loved the job because it took her away from them and the headaches she said they gave her, but he knew that was crazy thinking.

"What do you think happened to Toby?" Thaddeus asked abruptly.

Jacob was placing one of his books into Thaddeus's locker because his locker was too far and he didn't want to walk all that way.

"I don't know. Whatever happens to bad people, I suppose. Adams said he's dealt with many bad people before and gives them what they deserve. In a way, you could think of him as a cop." Jacob chuckled. "Or the Green Arrow." He shook his head then. He loved the Green Arrow too much to think of him as his despicable elder brother.

"Why does he deal with so many bad people when he's not a cop?"

"I don't know. Can we go out and get some peanuts now? School's over."

"Jacob." Thaddeus hated he was concerned, even when he knew he shouldn't be. He should be happy because the problem with Toby was finally over, but he wanted to know. To quell his curiosity, perhaps, he needed to know.

"Do you have any idea what happened to Toby?"

"Do you know what I love most about peanuts, Thaddy? It's how crunchy they are, but also how easily they melt in your mouth. Oh my God! I could bust a nut just by thinking about them, pun intended."

And then Jacob was racing down the hallway, out of the school building.

Thaddeus caught up to him outside, where he had just bought ice cream from a vendor parked by the school gate.

"You're going to get a runny stomach," Thaddeus warned.

"They say if you're going to suffer, make sure it's the good type of suffering."

"No one says that."

"Yeah, you're right. I made it up. Still, have a taste. It's really good, I promise."

"Everything tastes really good to you."

"Not everything. Anna's cooking is horrible. Makes me puke every time. It's why Mama wants to send her to that cooking school, you know? Waste of money, if you ask me. The girl has no brains!"

"She's your sister," Thaddeus said.

"Doesn't change the fact she has no brains. If I have homework I don't understand, I *never* go to her. The one time I went to her for my algebra assignment, I got a ten over ten, *until* I looked closer and realized there was no one. Just a zero."

Thaddeus was laughing. "Well then, who do you go to when you need help with homework you don't understand?"

"Adams. He's smart."

"Why don't you like him?"

Jacob pulled off his glasses and cleaned them on his shirt, then returned them to his face. "*He* doesn't like *me*."

Though he wanted to, Thaddeus didn't ask again.

"Tonya's really helpful. She helps with any homework I don't understand, and she explains well enough for me to understand. Must be all those extra lessons and stuff, but she's really good with whatever she does."

"Guess we're both lucky. To firstborns," Jacob said, raising his cup of ice cream.

Thaddeus raised an empty hand into the sky.

"Do you want to be a cop like your father when you grow up?"

Thaddeus didn't know where the question had come from. He stared at Jacob as he scooped another spoonful into his mouth.

"I don't know. Never really thought about it." Truthfully, he had thought about the prospect a few times, though never seriously. "I mean, being a cop is good. You get to save lots of people and capture criminals." But, he saw what the job did to his father—the stress and anxiety it gave him—and knew he didn't want to be like that. "I guess I could." He didn't think he would.

"Yeah, that's cool. I want to be a police officer, too."

"You? I thought you said you wanted to be a doctor."

"I changed my mind. Being a doctor is too scary."

"You said that about being a pilot."

"Yeah, I did."

"Can't be sure you won't change your mind again."

"Maybe."

"Hey, what's up? You guys are leaving without me?" Tonya had approached them from behind.

"Don't you have your lessons today?" Thaddeus asked.

"If I had lessons every single day, my brain would go up in flames," she joked. "Hey, Jacob." She'd met Jacob two days ago. "Can I have some of that?"

Jacob hid a frown as he handed the cup over to Tonya. He was only letting her have a little because he liked her. She was pretty and smart. He was, however, going to be upset if she took more than just "a little." He didn't show it because he knew it would make him look selfish and, despite what most people said about him, he wasn't selfish.

He was about to take the cup back when a blue Mercedes truck pulled up in front of them. It was his mother's car. Jacob looked behind the wheel and saw Adams, who honked the horn at them.

A confused Tonya looked at the boys. "Why is he honking at us? Do you know him?" she asked.

"He's my brother," said Jacob.

If he hadn't said that, Thaddeus wouldn't have recognized him. His blue Mohawk was gone and in its place was a charming, low cut; the tips of his hair golden brown. He was wearing blue sweatpants and a white T-shirt. He looked like any regular, teenage boy. Thaddeus was surprised to see him that way; and, as it would appear, so was Jacob. Apparently, he hadn't seen his brother's new haircut.

Adams was charming. Even a few girls were turning to stare.
"Hey, boys," he said, smiling at Tonya.

Thaddeus couldn't tell if he was stuck up or shy, but he didn't look at Tonya long. Tonya, on the other hand, stared at him longer than was required. There was something about him she found undeniably striking.
"I was hoping to have a word with you two," said Adams. "Alone."

He would've preferred to speak only to Thaddeus, but that was impossible, as Jacob was his brother. Thaddeus would probably tell him what they discussed, anyway.

The boys looked at each other, then Tonya.
"What about her?" Jacob asked.

Adams glanced at her again. This time his smile was tight. "Is she—"
"She's my sister," said Thaddeus.

The word he'd been about to say was "important."

It was bad business. Regardless of who she was, Adams knew he couldn't have her knowing anything about this. If Thaddeus agreed to his offer, he would know why secrecy was crucial.
"I won't take much of your time," Adams insisted, delicately.
Tonya went to wait for them both in a coffee shop nearby while they hopped into the backseat of the truck.
"I can't," was the first thing Thaddeus said in reply to Adams' request. "I could never do something like that. My father trusts me. What would he do if he found out? What would he say?"

"He's not going to find out. I am doing you a favor, you know, Thaddeus Carter. This is fucking *Tampa*. You don't think you're going to get in some deep shit again and need my help?"

Thaddeus was growing hot. Beside him, Jacob sat quietly.

"I'm really happy you saved us last week, but... I can't—"

"I'm not asking you to hold a gun or sell drugs. I'm only asking you to be my mole. You get into your father's head. Tell us what the police know about the shit we're involved with. That's all. Look, you owe me, man." Adams' eyes were piercing.

Perspiration dotted Thaddeus' neck. "We?"

"Yeah. Me and my homies. The ones who saved your ass the other day. We work together. Ain't nothing to be scared of, boy. It's just small hits and you'll get a cut if that's what you're thinking. We'll save your ass every other day, come after anyone who even touches a hair on your head. I know what you're thinking. Your father's a cop and he can save you, too, right? But he can't. Was he there when Toby was after you? We're in the streets." Adams looked around before continuing, his brows coming together in a bow. "We just need to keep the police off our backs. You're the perfect guy for this. No one would suspect a high school kid, even though his father's a cop."

"How did you know about my dad?"

Adams sighed. "I had my man run a few checks on you after that day. Besides, it's a small world. Everyone knows everyone's shit." He looked out the window, toward the coffee shop where Tonya was waiting for them. "So, are you in or not?"

Thaddeus was not *in*.

"See? I told you he's a bad guy," Jacob said later as they made their way to the coffee shop.

Tonya thought to catch a glimpse of the curious stranger again, but he was gone.

***

Two days later, Thaddeus saw a girl named Rosa in a bookstore close to his house. Rosa attended his school and was in the same class as him. She was a pretty, brunette girl with a Scottish accent and deep green eyes. In second grade, he'd had a huge crush on her. Now, he still liked her, but not as much as he had back then.

He was walking her home when two guys jumped out of the blue, stole her bag and beat them both when he tried to stop them. Rosa hadn't suffered any major injury, but his entire face was swollen. He had even lost a tooth.

He crept out of his house the next day once his mother, who'd taken care of him, fell asleep on the couch. He went to Jacob's place. Jacob wasn't around, of course. He was at school. But Thaddeus found the person he was looking for.

Adams answered the door in sweatpants, an expectant tilt to his thin mouth.

"I'm in," said Thaddeus.

Chapter Eighteen

Jacob visited him the next day. He didn't know how he had heard about the beating, but it wasn't too hard to guess. His brother must have told him or word must've been going around the streets.

Thankfully, Thaddeus did not feel as terrible as he felt the previous day. He was able to bear the pain when he ate now and walk around without the agony he had suffered for the past day and a half. Also, his face was not as swollen and much less of an eyesore. He almost looked handsome again.

When he had first been brought home and Shanice had seen him, she'd screamed, refused to come close to him. God only knows what she must have been thinking. He'd been in insufferable pain. Their father was at work and would most likely have been unreachable at that time of the day, therefore their mother was the best option.

Tonya had dialed the number, her heart beating fast and hard in her chest as she waited for her mother to pick up the phone. The call connected after the third ring.

There was a frightening silence on the other end of the line after Tonya finished narrating what had happened. She could almost see Momma's face, drained of color, her hands shaking. She could almost see her eyes dilating in panic, lips parted with no words forthcoming. Tonya knew how easily Momma went into a panic and could only imagine the terror she was going through now.

God, she would not have been able to live with herself had anything happened to Thaddeus. She would not have been able to endure the torment. She had seen him covered in blood and knew then she would give anything to find the bastards who had done this to her brother; to find them and make them pay, no matter what she had to do. Deep inside, she hoped this had nothing to do with the boy who'd shown up at their school a few days ago. The one who had asked to have a chat with Thaddeus privately—Jacob's brother.

Momma arrived exactly ten minutes later, her hair flying around her face madly. She called the family doctor, a short bald man who wore large spectacles and a long mustache. His name was Dr. Gregory and he was skilled at what he did. Even though Momma was confident he'd treat him and Thaddeus would be back to his normal state in no time, she was beside herself with worry.

As was Tonya.

She sat by his bedside all night, even though the doctor had told her it was best to leave him alone to rest. She'd read a few chapters of Moby Dick to him while his eyes were closed and even after he fell asleep.

By eleven p.m., he'd regained consciousness and she was able to ask him if he remembered trying to climb an orange tree when he was six. Momma had told them to stay away from the tree because it belonged to their neighbor. And, even though the neighbor was not around because he lived in Miami, Momma still said it was wrong to climb his tree. Thaddeus had stubbornly shimmied up the tree when Momma was away, while Tonya had conspired with him to get the oranges. While trying to climb back down, Thaddeus had sprained his right foot. Tonya helped him treat his foot, but he had to walk in a certain way, taking extra care to disguise his limp when Momma was around.

"I thought I'd never walk well again," said Thaddeus, laughing.

Tonya laughed, too, and sudden tears fell from her eyes. She didn't know where they came from or how to stop them.

"I'll be fine," he said weakly.

She held his hand under the faint moonlight and pressed the skin of his palm against her lips. Like her father, she was not one to wear her heart on her sleeve, but she would not be able to bear if anything happened to Thaddeus. He was the only brother she had.

"You'll be fine," she echoed.

He had to be.

Tonya stayed with him until morning, but Momma simply wouldn't allow her to stay a minute longer because she needed to go to school.

"The babysitter will look after him. You prepare for school, Tonya. Get Shanice ready, too."

Momma kissed Thaddeus' head before she left for work, assuring him he would be fine. Their father gritted his teeth and swore he would find whoever was behind hurting his son.

Now, as Jacob sat beside him on the couch, the morning felt like a lifetime ago.

"School is boring without you, you know?"

"Oh, yeah?"

"Yeah. There's nobody to talk to. I just walk by myself and it's lonely. I miss you, Thaddy. When are you coming back?"

"As soon as the doctor gives the okay."

"*Hmm.*" Jacob took something out from his bag and smiled. "I brought peanuts. Want some?"

He forgot Thaddeus' gums ached. Bad timing.

"Sorry. Ice cream then?"

Thaddeus smiled.

Jacob was trying to help and hated there was nothing he could do to make his friend feel better. He had a strawberry smoothie in his bag, too, but he couldn't risk giving that away. He bought them from the new mall that had just opened downtown, and they made them so beautifully Jacob found he was becoming an addict. But, if it was going to make his friend feel better, then… He guessed he could share.

"Smoothie?" he asked glumly.

Thaddeus agreed.

They talked for a whole hour and Jacob told him everything which had happened in school that day. Thaddeus realized he actually had missed him.

He didn't tell his friend he had accepted Adams' proposal.

Chapter Nineteen

April 1st, 1980

Sarah spent the second day out of the hospital in the precinct with Nicholas. Both poured over Candice's notes, trying to make something coherent out of what she had scribbled down. The notes had started as something lazy—a thing Candice had begun doing in her spare time while watching customers—then become more erratic, written in between shifts and in a hurry. Some pages were soup-stained, others were written in shorthand and impossible to read. Sarah felt a bit embarrassed, but Nicholas laughed her off, writing "the quick brown fox" on a sheet to show just how bad his handwriting was.

"We had no idea he was some sort of kidnapper," said Sarah, looking at the measly two pages which made up all the information they knew about the man. "Wait, he has how many women locked up at his place?"

"Can't say. We just want to find them. That's what's important right now."

Sarah watched as Nicholas typed into a computer. In the end, they managed to partially decipher Candice's notes. The man known as Jon was halfway through his two-month cycle, after which he would start the entire thing again. This gave them a time frame for when he would be arriving. They could tell his next target would be a blond, but they couldn't determine what time he would be arriving.

Jon always visited the diner on Fridays during two windows—late afternoons or evenings. They knew his target would be someone who was coming from out of town, so there would be no way for them to know who they were or where they were from beforehand. They would have to wait for the targeted woman to show up, then take him. Sarah was instructed not to tell anyone about the plan.

***

Like any other normal day, Sarah went to work. Except Candice wasn't there with her and she was on edge. Maybe because she had been a little jealous of the women who had been with Jon and now she was scared for their lives; or, maybe, because a kidnapper was going to walk into her place of work at any moment.

Sarah found herself staring at everyone who entered the diner, even when she knew they weren't the man she was looking for. Just to be sure, she would double-check. The jittery feeling was one she couldn't shake and exuded itself externally, resulting in her serving with a shaky hand and a bit of a pitch to her voice.

Nicholas pulled her over to the side as she went to his table to deliver his order.

"Sarah, I know this seems like a lot, but I'm going to need you to take a deep breath. I need you to relax so you can confirm Jon for us." He referred to the four other men who had come along with him. Nicholas sat at the table in front of the one which Jon would use while his other two colleagues sat at the table by the door. Another stood outside, watching and being bitten badly by the frigid air. "Everything is going to be fine. Once he comes inside, take his order and step away. We'll take care of the rest."

Like clockwork, Jon walked into the diner wearing a burgundy suit and a plain-white undershirt. If Sarah didn't know who he was, she would not have minded going out with the square-jawed man. He looked around sheepishly, like always, before taking his table. He waved a hand at Sarah; as she approached him, she tried to keep her wits in check.

Jon smiled up at her, a look which instantly made her reject the oatmeal she'd eaten that morning.

"I'd like a slice of pie while we wait," he said. "Preferably the chocolate. Is it available?"

Sarah's eyes darted to the notebook in her hands. She scribbled down his order, as if it mattered. From Candice's notes, they already knew he would ask for a piece of marble chocolate cake. She smiled at him briefly before briskly walking away. Usually, the cake took a few minutes to heat, but Sarah had already heated it and found herself pacing. She double-checked her watch. Time was running *slow*. Peeping over the counter, she saw he was still there and his date had not yet arrived.

The cake was ready in another four minutes. Sarah walked straight for him, holding the warm plate. She placed the cake onto the table.

"Anything else?" she asked, following procedure.

"Please, sit," Jon said, a friendly smile on his handsome face. "Sit down with me. Have a slice of cake."

"I'm afraid that's against our policy, sir." Sarah swallowed hard, looking into the man's eyes as she spoke. "Employees aren't allowed to sit with customers."

"Well, you're not an employee right now, Sarah. You're my date. Now, please sit. I don't want to use this." Jon casually placed a handgun on his lap.

Sarah fought the impulse to run. The muzzle of the weapon was aimed directly at her stomach. She wondered if Officer Nicholas could hear their exchange. Jon had spoken in hushed tones and even she had to pay extra attention to hear him properly. The officers were only a few feet away. Why hadn't they done anything? Then, it hit her—they were waiting for her to step away. She heard the hammer of the gun click, giving her all the motivation she needed to become one with the chair.

"I heard about your friend, Candice. I'm so sorry." His tone was almost genuine, making Sarah's brain falter for a moment. "What did the doctor say?"

"She'll be fine."

"Good. Maybe I'll visit her when I'm free or send a card. One of those "Get Well Soon" cards with a pop-up song inside. Maybe a few balloons. That'd be nice, wouldn't it?" Jon's tone became icy. "Officer Carter, a word?"

Nicholas quickly rose from his table. He spun, drawing his gun and pointing it at the man five feet away. "Hands where I can see them!"

"Oh, but you *can* see them, Officer. If I were you, I'd be more worried about what you don't see." Jon opened the side of his burgundy jacket to slowly reveal what was underneath. Small red sticks strapped to what looked like a police vest, with wires running in and out, held together by duct tape. There was a smaller device with a green light resting just above his heart.

It took Nicholas a second, but—when he realized that he was staring at a bomber vest—he took a step back.

"Here's the thing, Officer. This, in my hand, is a dead man's switch." He produced his left hand from his pocket. In it was a small device resembling a lighter. His thumb pressed down on the top. "If I let go of this, for any reason, the bomb goes off. If my heart stops beating, the bomb goes off. If my main course isn't served, the bomb goes off. It's safe to say you want to cooperate with me if you don't want this bomb going off."

Sarah felt faint. How the man was able to keep such a cool demeanor while threatening the lives of nearly three dozen people, she couldn't understand. The other officers had begun ushering people out of the diner, including the cooks and other employees. Jon kept the gun on the table and picked up his fork, digging into the slice of chocolate cake in front of him. He was completely unbothered by the police and more interested in his "date."

"What do you want?" Nicholas asked.

"Oh, you know what I want. Consult your little notes and see what I am supposed to order today. Your friend Candice has a keen eye. See, when she started building a profile on me, I started building one on her, too." He took another bite of his cake. "Officer, when this is over, you have to try their chocolate cake. Blows me away every time—*pardon the pun*. So, get me the meal I want, some wine for my date here, and a bit of privacy to finish our food. Then, we can discuss."

Nicholas backed away. More police vehicles were arriving at the scene. A few men from the bomb squad were waiting for the go-ahead to enter. They'd tried to look under Jon's suit, but the man had a hankie covering the front portion of his shirt as he chiseled away at the rotisserie chicken he had been presented with. He smiled at Sarah as he ate, occasionally swallowing his food with some wine. Sarah didn't touch her plate.

142

Instead, she kept looking over frantically at Nicholas, who stayed in view the entire time.

"Aren't you hungry, love? You haven't touched your food," said Jon.

"Are you insane?" Sarah shot back, fueled by fear and shock. "These men are looking for a way to kill you and the only thing stopping them from doing that is *me*. The minute they can drag me away, you're dead."

"I'm aware."

"Why are you doing this?"

"Why not? I'm having dinner with a beautiful woman and, hopefully, I'll be able to invite her home with me. Maybe we can talk a bit more intimately."

"What did you do to them?" Sarah asked.

"Who?"

"You know who. The women you've brought here for the last couple of months. Where are they?"

"*Where?*" Jon asked with a chuckle. He cast a questioning glance at Nicholas before taking a sip of his wine. "I think your officer friend kept something from you. See, the women have already been found. *Where* they were found isn't as important as *how*, I'd say."

Sarah felt her heartbeat triple and threatened to explode in her chest. She was seated two feet away from a man who she had thought was just a kidnapper, but he'd murdered them, too. He was a *serial killer* and her place of work was where he picked up his targets. "You are a monster," she seethed.

"Nice to officially meet you." Jon cleared his throat. "I've had my fill. You? Oh, never mind. Officer Nicholas, a word, please?"

Nicholas approached their table, his gun back in its holster. "Alright, Jon. Enough games. Let her go. She's got nothing to do with this."

"She was the one who identified me to you, no? Then, she definitely is involved."

"You've had your meal. Let her go. If you comply, I'll talk to the prosecutor for you. We can still salvage this thing."

"No." Jon used the sharp end of his fork to pick at his teeth before dropping it on the table and wiping his hands on a napkin. "If you want Ms. Jones here to stay alive, then your only chance is to let me go. I want a car and, when I'm sure no one is following, I'll let her go."

"Can't do it."

"Look, Nicholas. You've seen my face. I can't keep working. Let me go and I promise not to do it again... In *this* town."

"Is this some sort of joke to you?" Sarah demanded, rattling the table a little too hard.

"It has to be. If not, my heart rate will increase, which could trigger ol' boy down there. And we don't want that to happen, now do we?"

"I can't have you leave here with her," said Nicholas.

"Oh, Nikky, my boy. I'm leaving here one way or another. What you can influence is how many people I take with me when I go." Jon smiled cheekily at the officer, who was staring at the trigger in his hand. "One push of the button and boom. So, just let me go and everything will be fine. You'll never have to see me again. Talk to your boss. Come on."

After copious arguing, they came to a decision. They couldn't determine what kind of explosives they were or what the blast radius would be if it detonated. They were in the middle of the city, with possible casualties all around, even though they removed every civilian from the scene and cordoned the onlookers as far back as possible. It was the life of one for the life of many and it was not an easy decision to make. Nicholas was uncomfortable with the choice, but it was one he'd been forced to agree with.

Jon had walked out of the diner with the gun to Sarah's hip, getting her to walk in front of him; his slow pace methodical, as though he were enjoying the show. They walked towards a Volvo parked on the side of the road. Everyone watched as he broke the glass of the back seat with the butt of his gun and popped the lock of the front seat. After unlocking the car, he followed Sarah around to the front passenger side and held the door open for her.

Shutting the door, he walked back around the car with a smile at the officers.

A loud *bang* permeated the evening air. The burgundy on the right side of Jon's body exploded as two bullets struck him in rapid succession. The bomb squad leapt into action, catching the man's hand just as his body hit the ground and pressing his thumb against the trigger as another placed a makeshift beat machine right next to the device to mimic the sound of a beating heart.

Nicholas rushed over to the side of the car and pulled Sarah from the vehicle. Her face was strewn with tears as the emotions of the moment overwhelmed her.

Jon had survived the shot. The vest he had worn turned out to be a very well-made bluff. The wires were randomly collected and taped together; the sticks of explosives were painted pieces of a mop handle. Even the green light was a single LED from a Christmas light.

"But how did you know it wasn't an explosive?" Sarah asked, once her teeth stopped chattering.

"I watched his thumb," Nicholas replied. "Noticed a slip when he opened the door for you. That, and he said everything would be over with the single push of a button. A dead man's switch has a two-way button. No way he could have clicked it."

"And you fired on him, just like that?"

"Just like that," Nicholas replied, smiling.

Chapter
Twenty

*June 10*th*, 1996*

"This is a bad idea, Adams. What the fuck were you thinking, bringing a little kid into our business like this, huh?" Jogo said. "What, you think this gon' be one of those brilliant plans of yours? Ain't no way you're fucking serious. That kid's gonna' get our asses busted. They're gonna' send us to prison and I'll never get to see my son. Did you even know Stacey is pregnant?"

Adams bore a look of genuine surprise. He'd noticed a recent change in Jogo, a newfound sense of responsibility, but he hadn't because he was expecting a child with his girlfriend.

"Yeah, that's right. We expecting' a son soon—"

"How do you know it's gonna be a son?" Leo cut him off, blowing on a pipe.

Jogo ignored him. "She's due in three months, man. Three *fucking* months. And you know what? I wanna be there when he takes his first breath. Hold his hands, watch him grow, all that shit. I ain't finna do all of those if I'm locked up in the pen, bro. My son ain't gon' grow up without a father."

"Nobody's going to prison," Adams said coolly. He sat on a bench in the garage where they usually had their meetings. Leo sat on the other end. Jogo was pacing, running his hands through his gold dreadlocks. His ripped jeans sagged low on his buttocks; the band of his Calvin Klein briefs on full display. Jogo didn't give a fuck about how he appeared to people or what they thought of him. He did whatever he wanted.

"Oh, someone's going to prison, alright. I see only one way this could end and it ain't good." He paused. "For any of us. Y'all ain't gon' tell me you don't see it. His father is a fucking cop! What the hell are you thinkin', man? You think this some kind of—"

"Why don't you just shut the fuck up!" Leo yelled, tossing his pipe onto the couch. His eyes were red from smoking and listening to Jogo whine like a child for hours. It was sickening.

Adams couldn't stand the incessant complaining, either, but he understood Jogo had fears. He was the shaky one of the trio and, with a baby on the way, it was to be expected.

"Now you ain't gonna tell me to shut the fuck up," said Jogo, his greyed fists curling. "You don't get to tell me to do shit because, last I checked, there ain't no boss around here."

"The fuck could you possibly know about having a boy?" Leo taunted. "He's gonna call *you* 'Pops'? You don't even have the guts to come out here and talk to *me* like a man?"

Leo was spoiling for a fight. Adams noticed the two had been at odds with each other lately. He had no idea what in the world was going on, he only knew he had to put an end to it.

"You watch your tongue, boy," Leo continued.

"No, you watch your fucking tongue!" Jogo yelled.

At that moment, Leo jumped on him, landing a heavy punch to his face. Jogo bounced back, hurling Leo into the nearest wall and jabbing his elbow into his stomach. He gave him a punch to his jaw area strong enough to knock him out; but because Leo was a well-trained ex-marine, he was merely dazed. Blood had begun to trickle from his mouth.

Adams jumped in the middle of the scene and broke them apart. Jogo was tearing at his shirt, itching to be let back at Leo.

Leo was cleaning the blood from his lips, scoffing, trying to contain his own anger. If he really wanted to fight, Jogo would be a dead man in minutes. To him, Jogo still thought like a little child. How was that same person going to be a father?

"What the hell is wrong with you both?" Adams yelled, anger blazing in his eyes.

It took Jogo a few minutes to calm down. And, when he had, he still fumed like a lion whose tail had been pulled, still cursed and called Leo names.

Leo, who was leaning back on the couch, used his shirt to clean his face. His chest was covered in ten beautiful tattoos. One was the face of a goat that represented his zodiac sign, Capricorn. Now, he looked at the goat tattoo on the upper side of his chest and muttered something under his breath, staring at Jogo. He was saying something repeatedly, like a prayer.

Jogo was still yelling. Adams held the man back. He was going to hit him in the stomach with his knee when Jogo ceased fuming and crashed to the floor, spitting angrily and raking his hands through his hair.

"Will you cut it out, you two? What the fuck is going on with you lately?"

Leo shook his head. "Jogos' is the one trippin', that's what."

"Shut your mouth, you cocksucker," Jogo spat.

"You both shut the fuck up. What the fuck you think this is?" He directed his question at Jogo.

"You think I'm dumb or something?"

"You tell me."

Adams picked Jogo up and punched him in his face, sending him back to the ground. Jogo looked Adams in his eyes and asked for mercy. Adams wasn't planning on hurting him anymore. Hell, he hated fighting with his guys; but, in this case, it was necessary. Jogo was in his head, thinking and acting like a damn fool. He needed to stop before he made a huge mistake and, knowing him for as long as he had, Adams could see he wasn't far from it.

"I ain't playing, man. I know what the fuck I'm doing. All I'm asking is for you to trust me. Damn it, just trust me for once. Trust someone besides your cynical self. That little kid has a name and his name is Thaddeus," Adams said. "We're not bringing him because this is some kinda after school program or shit. We're bringing him in because I see how valuable he's gonna be to us in the long run. He's gonna be our inside man, get all the information we need from his pops, steal his files, get onto his computer. *Fuck*—whatever we need, whenever we need it."

Jogo was silent. There was a long awkward silence, disturbed only by Leo's coughing. Then, Jogo staggered to his feet and leaned against a nearby fence.

Adams went to sit on the bench next to Leo, who was still rubbing bloodstains from his face. He was breathing harder than usual. Everyone was, in truth, just tense.

He knew Leo thought Jogo would become dead weight soon—more of a problem than a solution. They could find someone else to take his place, but Adams wasn't buying into Leo's train of thought just yet. He knew Jogo. Letting him go was not a good option. Sure, they were at each other's throats lately, but they patched things up quickly enough there were no scars left.

Later, when Adams climbed into the backseat of his mother's truck, he sat there for a while, thinking about his next step. There was no way he could discuss anything with Jogo at the moment, not with the way he was acting. He couldn't discuss anything with Leo without inflaming any conspiracy theories Jogo might have rattling around in his head. He would have to wait until the idiot cooled off.

He did not regret hitting Jogo hard, nor did he regret anything he had ever done to keep Jogo in check. He had known the guy for a long time now and knew, despite his hotheadedness and his stubbornness, he never really meant any harm. If Adams had done anything more than a few punches—if he had done something truly terrible to their friend— he would not be able to live with himself.

***

He was coming back from the mall one evening. It was cold and drizzling. His mother had asked him to pick up some groceries. Adams struggled to carry the things home in two gigantic, white plastic bags. He couldn't get a cab to drop him off. By some weird universal twist of fate, there were none in sight.

He would stop every few steps to muster up the energy to continue. He was opposite a dark alleyway when he noticed a woman taking out a knife from her waistband and flashing it at her two assailants. Her other hand clutched hard on her cell phone. They already had her purse. She tried dialing a number on the phone and the device was quickly taken.

Adams guessed she was calling the police. The woman stood, one foot before the other, knees crooked, daring them to make another move.

They did not see him because he was hidden in the dark. He could have jumped in to help her but didn't. He hesitated. Adams had hardly been able to forgive himself for that day. On recollecting the event, he realized there was probably nothing he could have done. Still didn't stop him from blaming himself every single time he looked at Jogo.

One of the assailants raised a gun and the girl's stance instantly weakened.

Next thing Adams saw, a car stopped right in front of the scene and a boy jumped out. He wasn't wearing a shirt and looked like he had flown a million miles. From the look of relief which washed over the girl's face, he seemed to be the person she had called. Which Adams thought was *outrageous*. Why hadn't she called the police? What was one boy going to do against two guys, one of whom had a gun?

The boy tried knocking one of the guys down. Adams heard a shot fire.

Then the girl was on the ground, bleeding from her stomach. The guys flee before sirens could come wailing and the boy who had come to her rescue went into a mad rage.

Suddenly, free from the invisible shackles which had held him captive, Adams ran forward and helped carry her to the boy's car. They sped to the hospital. All the while, Jogo kept saying, "If anything happens to my sister, I swear to God, I'll find those bastards if it means burning the whole fucking city down."

His sister did die and the guys who killed her were never found. Adams spent the next few weeks with the boy, getting to know him and helping him mourn the loss of the only family he had left—perhaps because the guilt of witnessing the incident and not doing anything to help ate him up inside.

***

The first excursion they brought Thaddeus along on was at a small supermarket. All Thaddeus had to do was sit in the car and dial a number if he noticed any suspicious movement.

Thaddeus did not know what Jacob's brother and the two other scary-looking guys were going to do inside the store, but he had a few ideas. He only hoped no one would be hurt.

A few minutes later, the boys jumped back into the car, shouting victoriously and fist-pounding each other.

Before Thaddeus went back home, Adams gave him a generous share of one-thousand dollars. He had never had a sum of money that large before and had no idea what he would do with it.

Leo watched Thaddeus as he walked away and said to Adams, "He really bought that little stunt we pulled. Wonder what happened to the girl, though. I told Grizzly not to hit her so hard."

Adams chuckled and popped open a can of beer. "Fuck what happens to her. The plan worked. Thaddeus Carter might just destroy his father without even knowing it."

"What a fool."

Chapter Twenty One

Nicholas might have loved working as a police officer, but one thing he wasn't a fan of was paperwork. It seemed as though he had been getting more than his fair share recently. He had done everything he could to avoid the rage of the captain, but the human irritant still found a way to work himself under Nicholas' skin.

He had reached out to Sarah the previous morning to apologize for his demeanor the night before. She left the house in a hurry, apparently not in the mood for him either.

He spent the day with a scowl spread across his face, angry at everything. Tonya had reminded him of the family portrait, which he kept forgetting about. She left a sticky note in the car to remind him to purchase a new frame, but he'd accidentally left the window down and the night's rain had washed most of the words off the yellow paper. It was only after he had seen Tonya, with her extremely disappointed eyes, he realized what the note was for. The following day, Nicholas made his way to the store with the photo in the glove compartment of his car. When he arrived, however, they didn't have the exact dimensions. They promised to have it ready by evening.

Everyone at the office regarded him as some sort of pariah now. Nicholas did not have a partner. His only one, Lewis, had been diagnosed with a progressive heart condition and was unable to continue operating in the field. Nicholas hadn't bothered with a new partner; neither had the captain offered to give him one. He would occasionally work with random people—men and women he knew well—but Nicholas was alone in the end. He didn't mind initially, but now it seemed as though no one was willing to associate with him.

Nicholas found a huge stack of documents waiting for him on his desk when he arrived at work. Cosmo requested he update all the files and log them into the database. Nicholas knew the captain was on a power trip.

He was quite aware of who the boss was and wasn't looking to disrespect the man. He had seen people go against Cosmo before and wasn't willing to be at the end of that smoking gun. Nicholas worked on the documents, typing and filing, arranging by date and in alphanumeric order. It wasn't only cases he investigated; also included were cases where he assisted his colleagues. Over the past nine years, he had investigated over seventy-seven cases. A lot of them brought back memories.

He stumbled upon the case which had led him to his wife and wondered just how lucky he was to have met her. Since then, he had done everything he could to ensure that Sarah was never put in harm's way. Overall, he'd been successful. His wife lived a pretty normal life. He loved her dearly and still did, even though work was taking a toll on their relationship. He picked up his phone and flipped open the screen.

The radio on his shoulder cracked to life just before he could press six, the number to her speed dial.

"10-4. We've got a possible robbery in progress off Wilbert and 5th."

The store on that corner was the same one he inquired about the picture frame. He frequented the business, as it was only a few blocks from where he lived. From the station, it was only about ten minutes away.

"Don't even think about it, Carter. I need those documents back in storage. You can forget about patrol for today," Cosmo said from the fountain behind his desk. He hadn't even noticed the man had walked up behind him.

"Sir, I have to follow up on a few special cases. If you don't mind, I would appreciate it if I could leave early."

"I do mind. Get to work," Cosmo responded with a grunt, not even bothering to drink the water in his cup.

Nicholas forced a smile and continued with his duties. It was a battle suppressing his rage. Just as he was about to calm down, he received a message from his wife. Sarah had sent a long text, highlighting how badly he treated her and the family. Nicholas felt his composure snap.

He knew he had been busy working overtime lately. He wanted to save enough money to take his family on vacation. The increase in Shanice's daycare fees had set back his plan by a few months. If Sarah did not see how hard he was trying, then she did not deserve an apology. Nicholas threw his phone into a drawer and shut it.

By the time he looked up from the computer again, it was past eight. He had worked through the day and only completed half the files. He sighed and placed the ones he'd finished back in storage, keeping the rest at his desk.

As he left, he saw Cosmo in his office. The man held A cigar between his lips and nursed a small glass of rum. Nicholas pictured himself in his shoes and fancied a drink for himself, too. As he grabbed his keys, a photo of Tonya and Thaddeus on his desk reminded him of what he had to do.

He drove in the direction of the store he'd visited earlier that morning. It was an ongoing crime scene and, when he got inside, the storekeeper was gone, most likely giving his statement. There was a single camera in the store, showing who entered and who left. If the camera was operational, it would aid the investigators greatly.

Nicholas couldn't find a frame for the picture and was too exhausted to search for another store.

A drink before he got home would loosen him up a little bit. As Nicholas drove towards a small pub close to his house, a vehicle blew a red light, missing the passing cars by inches. Nicholas quickly turned on his lights and drove off after them. He caught up with the Nissan, flashing his lights and using his intercom to alert the driver to pull over. After ten seconds, the man pulled onto the side of the road and killed the engine. Nicholas exited his car and walked up to the man slowly.

"Sir, would you mind putting your hands on the wheel?" Nicholas asked, once at the window.

"I didn't do anything wrong," the man said, his speech slurred. "What do you want, Officer?"

"You blew a red light is what you did. Care to explain yourself?"

"I don't gotta explain nothin'. I was driving just fine and the light was green when I passed."

The stench of alcohol burned. The man had been drinking. Sweat glistened on his skin and his speech came in quick bursts which made little sense if the listener hadn't lent a considerable ear. Nicholas had a breathalyzer in his car, but he didn't need to get it to know the man was drunk.

"Have you been drinking, sir?"

"No," the man responded with the straightest face he could muster.

156

"Then you won't mind taking a breathalyzer, Mister...?"

"Penn. Devon Penn. Officer, might I suggest you let me go? Could cause a lot of trouble for you."

"Is that a threat, Mr. Penn? Are you threatening an officer?"

"Just making a promise, that's all."

"Dispatch, we got a DUI on Morrison Ave. Heading in now. Over." Nicholas spoke into his radio before turning back to the man. "Sir, I'm going to need you to step out of the car, please. Do you have some identification on you?"

"Do you have any identification on you?" the man parroted, before stepping out of the car.

Nicholas escorted him to his squad car, then secured the man's vehicle and called a towing service. A few minutes later, the tow arrived to take the car and Nicholas drove the man down to the precinct. It took all of ten minutes before the man was processed and secured in a holding cell.

At his desk, waiting for him, was Cosmo.

"Carter!" his captain yelled.

"Sir?"

"I thought I said something about you *not* going on patrol today?"

"Sir, I observed a crime and apprehended the suspect. I believe it is our job to—"

"Spare me the bullshit, Carter. I tell you not to do something and you go right ahead and disobey a direct order. Not the first time. Are you trying to prove something?"

"Sir, I—"

"Let me finish." Cosmo seemed to enjoy the display he was making in front of those who were left behind at the precinct. "You know that's the lawyer who lobbied against those twerps at the senate trying to take away our funding? The reason you're able to have that car to even pick him up in the first place is because he's been fighting tooth and nail to keep this city in the hands of the most capable officers."

"Captain, regardless of his contributions to the state, no one is above the law. Not even Mr. Penn. He committed a crime and he will have his day in court."

Cosmo scoffed. "Carter, your keys." He held out his hand, palm up.

"Sir?"

"Consider it a favor, it's only the car I'm taking. I want you to listen to me very carefully, Carter. I don't care *who* or *what* you think you are, the next time you go against a direct order from me, don't bother about coming into work the next day. You can mail in your gun and badge for all I care. Now get the hell out of my sight."

The cold outside paled in comparison to the iciness he felt inside. Nicholas felt disconnected from the world around him. Nothing was going his way. He called a cab and rattled off his home address to the driver. His phone vibrated in his pocket as he received another text from Sarah. He didn't want to look at it. The thought of going home to face an irritable wife haunted him. Then he remembered he had left the family portrait in the squad car. Nicholas still hadn't been able to get it reframed.

He tapped the driver, giving him new directions to a motel. They stopped at a liquor store and he bought himself a bottle of brandy and a pack of cigarettes before continuing to the establishment. Nicholas wasn't in the mood to deal with his family. More than anything, he wanted to be at peace; somehow, it was constantly being ripped away from him. He fell asleep in the motel room, his phone silently ringing on the nightstand, an angry wife and worried children waiting for their father to return home.

For once, he didn't care.

Chapter
Twenty Two

It was time for a break—Jacob's favorite time of the day. As he and Thaddeus strolled through the cafeteria, he spoke more than usual. Perhaps he was only excited to have a few minutes out of the learning environment. Once back inside, he would be as mute as a child with speech impairment.

A few minutes ago, his math teacher had asked the class a question. Mr. Darby was feared for his habit of writing complicated questions on the board and randomly calling on students to answer them. He had called on Jacob this time. The boy had simply stared back at his teacher through his round glasses until Mr. Darby angrily asked him to retake his seat. A few snickers had circled the room. At least he hadn't received detention. *God*—anything was better than detention.

The one—and he prayed it would be the only—time he had received detention was when he was caught passing letters during history class. The letters weren't even his. He had felt a tap on his shoulder and been given a scrap of paper. On top of the paper had been two words: *For Jenny*.

Jenny was the tall Briton who sat at the front of the classroom. She was only ever interested in what the teacher was teaching and taking care of her smooth, curly blonde hair. Jenny had grey-blue eyes and a taut chin. All the boys thought she was extremely pretty, but Jacob hardly noticed. Thaddeus said it was because the only thing he was interested in was food, but Jacob had noticed pretty girls in the past. There was Grace, who had taught him how to make pancakes. She had been wonderful. There was Bella, who always brought fun-shaped cookies to class and gave him a taste. They were delicious.

But everyone thought Jenny, who never had time for anyone else and was much too stuck-up for his liking, was beautiful. *Yuck.*

The letters kept coming and, though they grated on Jacob's nerves, there was nothing he could do to stop them. Not unless he was looking to make new enemies. And, on the fourth letter, the teacher had caught him. He had spent the next hour after school, bottled up in a classroom with Jenny, staring at her big ugly toes peeking out from her leather sandals. It was a horrible day. One he would make sure to never repeat.

"Do you think Toby will be back soon?" Jacob asked. It was after school and they were both on their way back home. Tonya had her lessons.

Thaddeus' eyes shot up in alarm. "Why do you care if he's back soon or not?"

He didn't know why the question irked him the way it had, especially when he knew Toby was not a problem anymore. Still, a chill had run through Thaddeus when his name was mentioned.

"I don't," Jacob replied. "I asked Adams what happened to him, but he wouldn't answer me. He never lets me know his business, but you? He likes you. He must have told you something."

"I haven't seen him since that day when he showed up at school."

Jacob didn't believe him but, since he had no real reason to doubt his friend, he shrugged. "Who cares anyway?"

"Does Adams talk about me at home?" Thaddeus looked off toward the road, carefully avoiding Jacob's gaze.

"No. Why would he talk about you?"

"No reason. Just, you said you thought he liked me. I was wondering what he might've said to make you think that…"

"Hey, do you want to go get some parfait?" Jacob came to an abrupt halt. "Roma Time's over on Wilmette Drive makes them so perfect it's like an art they've mastered for years."

Thaddeus loved how easily Jacob was distracted. Loved how easy it was for him to forget things.

"Yeah, sure. Let's go."

The café was on the west end of Sing Sing Avenue, between an antique shop and a large boutique. The lights were fancy lanterns, hung lowly and spinning slowly. A beautiful tune played from the store's speakers and the afternoon air was scented with the aroma of freshly cut fruit.

Once Thaddeus had a taste, he realized Jacob had not been lying when he said the parfait tasted wonderful—especially the vanilla flavor with strawberries on top. Thaddeus asked for another cup, but Jacob said he didn't have enough money. That was okay. Thaddeus paid for two more and Jacob looked at him with teary eyes of gratitude.

161

He was glad he had been the one to introduce this beautiful place to Thaddeus. He was also glad his friend appreciated the parfait just as much as he did. They visited Roma Time's almost every day after that, especially when Tonya had to stay after school. They didn't want her to know about this place. It was their little secret. They also tried the pizza and apple pie *a la mode* and found they both tasted just as wonderful. Everything Roma Time's sold tasted divine and Thaddeus was more than happy to foot the bill.

"How come you have so much money now?" Jacob had asked once.

"Tonya pays me to do her chores."

Again—Jacob didn't really believe him. His answer was as good an answer as any, but he had a hunch Thaddeus was lying. And Jacob's hunches were never wrong.

***

Days later, they all drove to Yola's Bar—Adams, Leo, Jogo, and Thaddeus. Thanks to Thaddeus, the boys knew the cops were shorthanded and would not be patrolling that area.

Thaddeus sat in the back seat, wondering what they were about to do and if he would be allowed to go inside this time. As always, he hoped no one would be hurt. He also wondered if he would make it home before Momma returned from work or Tonya started questioning his whereabouts.

He was perspiring. His body felt hot, though he knew he did not have a fever. He was breathing faster than usual, too. There was nothing wrong with him. His "symptoms" were the result of adrenaline and would vanish the minute he was back home.

Thaddeus was not scared of Adams. Adams was nice to him and spoke as though Thaddeus were his own brother. Sometimes, Thaddeus wished the relationship between Adams and Jacob wasn't as complicated. No, complicated was not the word. The two brothers did not like each other and it was as simple as that. He wished things were not as strained between them and they had the kind of relationship he and Tonya had. But, as the saying went: if wishes were horses, beggars would ride. He had no business making wishes on another man's behalf when there were still wishes of his own he hoped would be granted.

For example, he wished to go back home in one piece.

Thaddeus rebuked the thought as soon as it flashed through his mind. He was thinking too far ahead, too soon. Of course, he was going to be fine. It would be just like the last time he had stayed in the car and waited for them to come out. There was nothing for him to fear (except maybe Jogo and Leo).

Leo was not all that bad and Thaddeus liked his tattoos. They were neat and different from the kind he was used to seeing around. Artistic. There was writing on his neck in Italian. Thaddeus had worked up the courage to ask what the words meant and Leo had told him they translated to: "You only live once." Leo also told him stories about his time in the Marines and about visiting Africa and about his little sister, who had died in a car accident. For a man of his demeanor, Leo had a soft side.

Then, there was Jogo. Thaddeus wasn't quite sure Jogo was entirely sold on the idea of him being there. Jogo never spoke to him. He hardly ever spoke to anyone. Thaddeus had a feeling he didn't like him much.
"You stay in the car," Adams directed, glancing back at him.

Through the windshield, Thaddeus could see three men carrying suitcases entering into the bar. He guessed they were the men they had been waiting for when Adams looked at his friends and gave a slight nod.

As Jogo and Leo exited the car, Adams stood by his window, holding a suitcase. He said, "If we are not out in ten minutes, call this number." Then he pressed a small piece of paper into his hand. Adams' face was hard, his eyes intense as he stared into Thaddeus'. "Then and only then should you dial this number."

"You hear him, boy?" Jogo said, a cynical smile on his face.

Thaddeus nodded slowly. Then they were gone. He didn't know why he had to come with them to this bar in the first place. Wasn't it enough he told them what he had managed to find out from his father? But, apparently, Adams had other plans for him.

For the next five minutes, Thaddeus sat in the car, praying. He had no idea what he was praying for, but his lips were moving in what could only be called a prayer.

He wanted to play a game on the cellphone Adams had given him, but, as he reached down to retrieve the phone, he heard a gunshot.

Boom.

He looked up and saw people running out of the bar, pandemonium breaking loose. Adams and his friends were nowhere to be found. Thaddeus panicked. Goosebumps prickled all over his body. Now was not the time for hesitation. He picked up the phone and, staring at the paper, dialed a number.

Instantly, a female voice came alive on the other end of the line.

"911, what's your emergency?"

Thaddeus swallowed the lump in his throat. "A shot was fired at Yola's Bar." He wanted to say something more but couldn't. The lady on the phone must have been saying something, but he couldn't hear her.

Before the call ended, two additional shots were fired. Another five minutes passed and the bar was surrounded by police vehicles.

Adams and his friends were still inside.

Chapter Twenty Three

The problem is not with life or man—it is with the mind. The mind needs to be corrected. The mind needs to be cleansed of the illness that is sin. Men are too far gone. Too hard to be corrected. It is easier to correct man when he is innocent, devoid of the evil machinations of the world which corrupts.

It had been a long time since Barr had corrected someone. He'd gone a little over two months without putting his good work to practice. He knew he had to be careful. Acting frequently and sporadically would be bad in the long run. If anyone were to find out about the work he did, there would be consequences. He needed to continue his work. He needed to go on for as long as he lived. Otherwise, the world would be in ruin and the only man who could save it would be gone.

Barr knew what he had to do. He had kept a close eye on Jared and all the others he had cured. A few had moved out of the state to medical facilities where they believed they would be cared for until they were back to "normal." Only there was no going back after being cleansed. Once you'd seen the light, returning to the darkness was impossible. He planned on using them—his seedlings—and sending them out to carry his mission to the rest of the world.

He had kept meticulous files, arranging his seedlings by date, age, and area. He would cultivate at least twenty before he could do no more and would need to continue on his way. So far, he had corrected seven children and was looking to cleanse the eighth.

I have to. They must be cleansed. I cannot postpone the mission. It is the will of He who is greater than I. This fire burns inside of me. I am like a hammer which cleaves stone into pieces. I cannot fight this. I will not fight this. This is for the good of society and the salvation of mankind. I bring to the world a future which goes undeserved. I give to the world a mercy.

Barr drove to work with his mind occupied by his new target. He had been watching for a while now, circling the neighborhood where the target lived.

His ability to be invisible right in the open was an asset. There was nothing memorable about his face; his features were dull and uninviting. No one felt the need to look at him for a long time. Sunglasses, caps, windbreakers, and coats with high collars— everything was to obscure his face. He had practiced the art of makeup and was able to give himself a different face whenever he wanted.

He had followed the school technician and, after two days, understood the man's patterns—how he worked, what to expect from him. He knew if he were going to capture the target—the one called Carter—he would need to enter the school undetected.

Careful planning was everything. Sometimes it took weeks—or in the case of Bingwen Zhou, *months*—to find the perfect moment to pick the target up. It wasn't something to be rushed. Failure would be the end of his run. Nothing was as important as not getting caught. Barr knew *if* he were caught, he would have to escape from the police. Take on a change of appearance. Move to another state, far from where he was.

All of which would impede the work.

The school technician was a burly, "All American" man. He kept a confederate flag on the back of his truck's and a registered twelve-gauge shotgun in the trunk. Before school began, he would park his truck in the school compound before crossing to the other side of the road to order Burger King for breakfast.

The man's gluttony was one of the reasons he needed to be cleansed, but Barr knew the technician was too far gone. His treatment would go to waste on the technician.

His best option was to remove the technician from the equation. A man who isn't important in the school's day-to-day running wouldn't cause too much alarm.

Barr sat in the Burger King, waiting for the technician to enter. The man arrived shortly before eight, as expected, and placed his order.

Switching tables to be closer to him, Barr picked up a bottle of ketchup from the table and shook vehemently, as though the content refused to come out. He waited until the technician looked up at him, then squeezed the bottle. The red substance flew across the table, landing in a huge splatter across the technician's shirt.

"I am *so* sorry. Let me get that for you."

"What the hell, man!" The technician set down his sandwich and pushed away the man who had doused him with ketchup. Ignoring the man's apologies and pleas to let him pay for dry cleaning, he went to the bathroom to wash off what he could.

In the end, he was left with a red stain and a wet patch across his chest. He decided to take the man up on his appeal to pay for dry cleaners but, when he emerged from the bathroom, the man was gone.

The technician returned to his sandwich, eating idly with no inkling he was being watched.

While he'd been in the bathroom, his sandwich had been dosed with capsaicin. He would feel the effect in a few hours—the pain of gluttony. His guts would reject the food and give him the pain of a lifetime.

Halfway through the school day, the technician rushed out of the building, grabbing at his midsection. The onset of intense diarrhea had begun. He drove quickly to his house, which was only a few blocks away. A small parking lot outside the apartment complex was where he left his truck before barreling out of the vehicle and running upstairs.

The kidnapper walked up to the car and found the technician had left the door wide open. The keys were still in the ignition.

He drove back to the school and changed into his handmade technician costume, topping off the look with a cap. He tucked a ladder under one arm and carried the man's toolbox in his other hand. As he walked down the hallway, he avoided eye contact with everyone, students and teachers alike. He had made up his face to have similar features to the man he was impersonating, but Barr knew he sounded nothing like the man.

Using the tools, keeping everything as casual as he could, he climbed up the ladder and unplugged the CCTV cameras which kept watch over the halls.

After returning to the parking lot, he went to the technician's office, which had been left open. The monitors showed the cameras which were turned off and could not receive a signal. Everything had been set up according to the plan.

He had given himself enough time to figure out which class Carter would be in and the location. He knew there would be a meeting in the gym by the close of school and he would be there to make his move.

Barr checked his watch. The technician would still need a few more hours to get his bowels under control.

The bell went off and the students hurried out of their classes into the corridors, heading off to buses or their parent's vehicles.

That was when he saw her—Tonya Carter—on her way to the gym for cheerleading practice.

* * *

Tonya joined the cheerleading squad because she needed something to keep her at school a little longer. As her family was beginning to fall apart, she was no longer interested in being at home. Momma had become more and more irritated by Dad. He came home only a handful of times for a shower and some clothes, then he would leave again without bothering to talk to anyone. He smelled of alcohol and sweat; he looked like he had been working overtime. Her father had bags underneath his eyes. His beard had grown completely flush over his jaw.

He didn't look at her when he came inside, merely mumbled to himself the entire time. One morning, Momma had stood right in front of the door, blocking him from entering the house. Tonya had watched as her father shoved her mother out of the way, stalked in, grabbed a bag and walked out again.

After that day, he did not come back to the house.

Thaddeus had followed his lead and started spending more time away from the house with his new friends, leaving Momma, Tonya and Shanice alone. Her mother was dealing with the immense heartbreak and in no mood for talking, especially to her emotional teenage daughter.

So, Tonya joined the cheerleading squad. She couldn't do flips or jumps, but she could still compete. In the end, she didn't care. She just wanted to be away from her scowling mother and her drunken father.

Tonya sat with the other girls, watching as the seniors gave their instructions. Tonya paid close attention, wondering how the white girl who was speaking could keep a straight face with the tight cornrows on her head. It was as though she was doing everything she could to appear cool, with the white strings attached to the dyed tips. Tonya laughed inwardly as she realized the cheerleader looked like a Barbie doll with a black girl hairdo. She was caught snickering and quickly averted her gaze, pretending to be busy adjusting her clothes.

As she did, she noticed a small steel ball—no bigger than a tennis ball—roll into the gym from the side entrance beside her. She gazed up and spotted the school technician, who appeared to be looking for the ball. There were a few others on the floor around him which he was struggling to pick up. Tonya collected the one closest to her and walked out of the gymnasium to the service entrance where the man worked.

"Here you go, Mr. Klop." Tonya placed the steel ball on top of the supply trolley.

The man turned. He was holding a spray bottle and wore a grim expression on his face. It took a moment for Tonya to realize the man she was looking at wasn't the one she had been expecting.

He squeezed the nozzle of the spray bottle and doused her face with two wafts of halothane vapor. Tonya fell forward and he caught her body with one hand, swinging her into the trolley and covering her with a dark tarpaulin material. Barr moved the trolley behind the gym bleachers, then injected her with just enough of the sleep drug to keep her unconscious until he was ready. He secured the trolley, as well, to avoid attention.

Barr left the school and returned the technician's car to where he'd parked it this morning; doubling back with the red Sedan he had left behind. He would wait for nightfall, then break into the school to grab her body.

Then, his work could begin. She would be cleansed.

It is easier to correct man when he is innocent, devoid of the evil machinations of the world which corrupt.

* * *

"Where's your sister?" Momma asked Thaddeus as he shoveled forkfuls of microwaved spaghetti into his mouth.

"Tonya?" Thaddeus asked. With his mouth full, the words sounded muffled.

"Yes. Shanice told me she didn't come home earlier and she wasn't with you."

"I'm not sure. She had cheerleading practice, but they take even less time than us. Maybe she went out with Emily?" Thaddeus guessed.

"Call me when she comes home. I'm heading to the store." Momma picked up the car keys and headed out the door.

Thaddeus used his newfound freedom to watch television. He wasn't bothered about Shanice, as she was playing alone in her room. She came out once to pee and returned without even taking a break to acknowledge her brother was there. The little girl loved her dolls and Thaddeus was happy she did; otherwise, she would have seen him watching Impact Wrestling, something Momma had seriously warned him against watching. But, when the cat's away…

Time flew faster than he could account for and, before he knew it, Momma was back home.

Thaddeus switched the channel and flicked off the television—a move he had practiced a few times in case she came home suddenly. Thaddeus was proud of himself. He had successfully evaded the scolding he would have received had he been caught. He was beginning to feel clever. He also had more money than he needed. Life was looking good for the boy.

"She's not still back yet?" Momma asked.

"Who?" The answer dawned on him the moment he spoke. Thaddeus cast a glance at the clock and saw the time was almost eight o'clock at night.

Momma picked up the phone and cycled through the logs for a moment before arriving at the number she was looking for. The line rang for what felt like an eternity to Thaddeus, who had begun feeling the first signs of panic.

The person on the line picked up. "Sarah, how are you?"

"I'm fine, Lana. Is Tonya with Emily?" Sarah asked, tamping down the panic which had crept into her voice.

"No, she's not," Lana replied.

"Has Emily seen her? Heard from her?"

"Is something wrong, Sarah?"

"She isn't back yet…"

Sarah heard Lana call out to her daughter. The sound of rushing footsteps. Then, Lana asked Emily if she had seen Tonya.

"I last saw her at school. She had cheerleading practice," the girl said. "I went home since she wouldn't be free for another hour."

"Emily, dear." The fear was now evident in Sarah's voice and she made no efforts to hide it.

"I need you to think. Did she mention somewhere she might be going? Maybe to see someone after practice?"

"No. She wanted me to wait, but I couldn't. She said she'd come home with Thad since his basketball game would finish around the same time. I thought both of them would come home together."

"Thank you, Emily." Sarah ended the call. Stumbling backward, she held her head in her hands.

"Thaddeus, get Shanice. Put on your sweaters and get in the car right now!"

Her hands shook. Her body was overwhelmed with dread. Every single possibility came to mind as she considered where her daughter could be. The murder rate was at a steady increase in Tampa. She could have been abducted. The community they lived in wasn't the safest place to live, but they were especially careful.

The phone clicked again—the principal picked up. It took all of Sarah's concentration not to scream at the man who he wasn't aware of when Tonya left the school. His response was lackluster and reluctant, like he was only interested because he had to be.

"Sir, my daughter is *missing*. She was last seen at your school. I'm heading to that building right now with the police and you better be there when I get there!"

She herded the children into the car and dialed 911. Then, Sarah paused. She hadn't called Nicholas. She tried his number and, once again, he allowed the call to go to voicemail. When the *beep* for the recording came, Sarah found herself speaking calmly and quietly, asking him to call her back if he had seen Tonya or was with her. The phone rang less than twenty seconds later.

Sarah answered before the vibration could turn to sound. "Is she with you?"

"No, I haven't seen her." Nicholas dropped the cigarette between his fingers. "What happened?"

"She's missing, Nicholas," The tears flow freely and without regard for the fact she was driving.

Thaddeus thought Momma was too quick to assume things. He knew Tonya. She probably had a date she didn't want anyone to know about.

Shanice turned toward the window to stare at the cars outside. Even the little girl could feel something was wrong.

"Our baby girl is missing and I don't understand. I don't know what to do, Nicholas. Is there someone you can call? I'm heading to school now. We have to find her, Nicholas. We have to—"

"I'll meet you at the school and we'll canvas from there," he said. "Don't call 911. They'll ask you to wait before filing a missing persons' report. I'll notify the precinct and have patrol officers lock down the roads in the area. We're going to find her, Sarah, just try to relax. What about Thaddeus and Shanice?"

"They're fine. Call me when you get there."

Nicholas arrived at the school five minutes after Sarah did and at the same time as the principal. The teacher representing Tonya's grade was also present. They headed into the school building together, Tonya's teacher staying behind with Thaddeus and Shanice, who had fallen asleep in the car.

It took a quarter of an hour to comb through the school twice. On the second scan, Sarah found Tonya's bag in the gym.

"She was here. Why did she leave her bag behind?" the principal asked.

"Tell me those cameras aren't just for show." Nicholas pointed to a set of cameras hanging in the corner of the hall. "Do they work?"

"Yeah. They're deleted every weekend, but we should have today's footage. I'll call the technician."

Sarah combed through Tonya's bag, checking each note for some clue as to where Tonya would have gone. She dumped out all its contents onto the hallway floor. Nicholas joined her, helping shake loose notes loose.

The technician picked up. "Sir?"

"Paul. I need you to head down here right now and pull up today's surveillance footage of the southwest hallway."

The man's disheveled voice came through the phone, which the principal had put on speaker for Nicholas and Sarah to hear.

"Yeah, sir, about that... I was going to ask, but I wasn't able. My stomach has been hurting today."

"Ask what?" Sarah shot back.

The technician was quiet for a moment before replying: "Sir, someone disconnected all of the cameras leading up to the hallway and exits. I don't know what happened. I guessed you called someone else for repairs since I was gone?"

"Gone?" the principal asked. "Gone where?"

"I came by your office and told you I had to go home."

"But then you came back a few minutes later."

"Uh... Sir?"

The principal exchanged glances with Nicholas and Sarah. "Paul, did you use the ladders on the cameras this afternoon?"

"No, sir. I was home all afternoon. Must've caught a stomach bug or something. I came back around six to grab my things. Who else was there on the cameras?"

The words the men exchanged seemed to breeze in and out of Sarah's range of hearing. She felt numb, like someone had dumped a bucket of ice water over her. Nicholas called her name. As she opened her mouth to answer, the world swayed, suddenly became horizontal. The darkness ate away at the edges of her vision as she crumpled in fear.

Moments later, she passed out.

Chapter
Twenty Four

Thaddeus did not hear a word from Adams or his gang until three days *after* the incident at Yola's Bar. The whole time he nearly drove himself out of his mind with worry. Regret plagued him. He should never have gotten involved in all of this in the first place. He should have listened to Jacob right from the start. Things were becoming insane and he wasn't sure they could be stopped. He couldn't talk to Jacob because he never told him he had accepted Adams' offer and, regardless of how close he was with Tonya, she was definitely out of the question.

"How's Adams?" He tried to ask Jacob as casually as he could—to conceal how nervous he truly was. Though he'd managed not to stutter the question, a patch of sweat grew at the base of his spine.

The same thought repeated endlessly in his head. If something bad happened to Adams… It would be no one's fault but his own. *His* inability to follow simple instructions.

"I don't know about Adams. Haven't seen him around since Wednesday. Why do you ask?" Jacob replied.

"Oh, nothing," Thaddeus said, too quickly.

Jacob shrugged and went on to talk about other things, but Thaddeus couldn't keep his mind straight. There was chaos in there. He knew there would be no peace until he found out whether Adams was okay.

A day after the incident at Yola's Bar, he'd seen Rosa on his way to his locker. She looked impeccably charming for someone who had endured the kind of beating she had suffered. She was dressed in her uniform and her hair was held up with butterfly pins. She hadn't been in class. Or, maybe he just hadn't noticed her there.

Lately, it has been hard for him to focus on anything. Momma had asked him to heat some food this morning and he had forgotten until the house began to smell like smoke. Momma had her temper with him; so had Father, though his anger was debatable. Despite everything going on in his life, he suspected his father must be going through some rough patches of his own. His father was always on edge lately, snapping at anyone who dared to test him. Thaddeus wondered what his father's anger stemmed from but did well to steer clear of his path.

Rosa called out to him first. He'd hurried over to her, wearing the warmest smile he could muster—a smile he hoped spoke nothing of the turmoil he was facing within. Only the smile of the girl he had spent most of his middle school fawning over and caring deeply about was enough to loosen the anxiety which had wrapped around him. By God, she was beautiful. Tendrils of hair had escaped the band around her head and formed wavy curls at the sides of her face. Her lips were cherry-colored and full. How often did he dream of kissing them? Of finding out if they tasted like cherry or only looked like they would?

She was fully recovered, with not a single scar on her body; for which, she made clear, she was incredibly grateful. She had only suffered minor injuries from the incident and no bones had been broken, she added, with a touch of humor. Then she laughed—a glorious sound. Something inside of him relaxed, releasing tension he had not aware had been building.

In another life, he hoped he would have the chance to make his fantasies come true. Because in this life, it was already too late.

***

He was back at home, doing his homework, when someone knocked on the door. It was a small boy. He was dressed in an orange tee-shirt and looked somewhat familiar to him. Thaddeus couldn't place where he knew him from. The boy spoke with a frightened voice, as though he were scared something would happen to him. Or, as though he were being forced to do something he did not want to do.

The letter he delivered read:

Garage. 4 pm. Don't be late.

–A.N.

* * *

Jogo knew right from the start that involving the boy had been a potential disaster. He'd known and it irked the hell out of him Adams didn't see it, too. Jogo thought Adams would change his mind about this plan after the other day at Yola's Bar. But Adams didn't seem fazed.

In fact, he didn't seem to think anything was wrong. Jogo could not wrap his head around it.

The police had come to the scene because the dumb ass kid—who was supposed to tell them if the police were around—had been the one to call them. Cops had been crawling all over the scene, trying to find out who was behind the shooting. Thanks to Yao Ming's reputation and the fear he instilled in people's hearts, no one had said a word. It was not like they knew enough to say anything, anyway. It was why they had chosen the restaurant. Small, but everyone minded their own damned business.

They were meeting Yao Ming about an important shipment. He needed their help obtaining some ammunition which was only licensed to the military personnel (i.e. banned for civilian use) into the country. They had no idea how they would perform this miracle, but he was paying them big bucks to get it done. Whatever he needed such high-caliber ammunition for was no concern of theirs. Their only concern was getting the job done.

Adams had a plan. He knew a guy who owned a ship and was doing business with the Italians—running cocaine from coast-to-coast in large quantities. He had been pitching this plan to Yao Ming when the boss received a call. None of them knew who the call was from, of course, or what was said. But, as he listened, Ming's hairless brow folded into a frown and his face began to redden. Jogo had the feeling something was about to go wrong. He knew Adams and Leo felt it, too.

Yao Ming had nodded to his men and the shooting had commenced.

They had escaped through an emergency exit in the kitchen. Leo was shot in the arm. He wrapped a shirt around the wound to prevent his blood from dripping onto the scene.

Jogo was furious when he found out what Thaddeus had done. He wanted to hold the boy by his scrawny little neck and snuff the life out of him. It would have been the easiest thing to do. Or have someone follow him on his way back from school, wait for him outside of his house. But then, if Adams caught wind, the act would easily have been traced back to him. There was no telling what Adams would do. So, Jogo devised a different plan. The plan was to ensure there was no chance in hell Thaddeus would go unpunished. He had given the boy a fair trial, in which he was both the judge and the jury. Unfortunately, the boy had no case.

The police were currently investigating the scene of the crime. What were the odds the whole thing would blow over? Leo had been careful not to bleed on anything, but they couldn't be certain of anything. The thought of going to jail and never seeing his son scared the living hell out of him. He would never hear him say, "Daddy." Never get to hold his hands or walk him to school. He wouldn't see his sick mother—who was currently receiving treatment in her hometown—again. *God.* The old woman would die if she found out he went to jail again. He'd made her a promise.

All this would not be worrying him if that fool hadn't called the police. If he had never been on the team in the first place. Jogo was filled with a rage which burnt his belly and turned his knuckles white.

His plan was bound to work. Thaddeus Carter would never cause trouble for anyone after this. He was solving a problem for Adams and the rest of the team. The fool had better be grateful.

The first part of the plan was accomplished. The letter he sent through his little cousin using Adams' initials had been delivered. Thaddeus would be there soon, and then the main event would be in full swing.

A package was to be delivered to Mr. Van Bough at four-thirty under the Lake Wobegon Bridge. The police never inspected the small warehouse due to the influence Mr. Van had. Maybe not influence, per sé, but *power*. Everyone feared Mr. Van. He was a top gang leader. Everyone knew what he was doing, but no one had the guts to pin anything on him. A detective had made it his duty to bring down Mr. Van. Initially, he'd appeared to be succeeding, until a subpoena for records was issued to Mr. Van. Two days after, the detective was found dead in his home, hanging from a ceiling fan. There were no signs of a break-in, forced entry, or struggle. The case concluded as suicide.

There were men at the top of the food chain in the pyramid of power. Men nobody dared to cross.

Dante Doyle controlled Palmetto Bay.

Salvatore Figaro controlled Coral Gables.

Antonio Wilson controlled Coconut Grove.

Christopher Thompson controlled Jupiter.

And Van Bough controlled more than half of Tampa Bay.

Anyone who dared to cross his turf never lived to tell the tale. He arranged for most of his victims' death to look like suicide, only "gifting" the heads of his victims to their relatives when he needed to send a message.

One thing was clear: Mr. Van Bough was a man of quick action. Certainly not the kind of man you double-crossed.

Which was exactly what Jogo planned on doing.

They were to deliver a bag containing cocaine to Mr. Van at said location at the pre-scheduled time. Jogo was supposed to be the one to deliver the package, but he had other ideas.

Before Thaddeus arrived at four, Jogo had already swapped the bag of cocaine for a bag containing wrapped talcum powder. It was going to be so easy. When Mr. Van found out what had come in place of the drugs he already paid for, there was no question he would execute vengeance on Thaddeus right then and there.

At the moment, Jogo had not thought about how—when Mr. Van found out he had been double-crossed—he would come for the rest of them, too. He was blinded by stupid pride and the need to seek vengeance for himself.

The fake package was delivered.

A day later, when Thaddeus visited the garage—alive and well—Jogo was shocked into silence.

When he regained his speech, he asked: "Did you not deliver the package to Mr. Van? How come you're... Well, here?"

"Something came up," Thaddeus replied, casual. "I went back home to grab something and Momma wouldn't let me leave the house until all of my chores were done. Jacob was around, so I asked him if he could deliver it instead."

Instead of going red with rage, Jogo grew ashen. His heart shrunk to half its size. "When was the last time you saw Jacob?" he asked, his voice in tatters.

"When I asked him to deliver the package. He never came back. I'll ask him how it went in school on Monday," said Thaddeus.

Jacob was not in school on Monday. Four days later, his head was returned to Adams in a box. Attached was a small note which read: *Joke's on you.*

Jogo was nowhere to be found.

Chapter
Twenty Five

His turmoil was not over yet. When Thaddeus returned home from school the next day, he knew immediately something was wrong. He stood on the doorstep, sweating, hands trembling.

Shanice's doll had been abandoned on the front porch, upside down. Shanice never forgot her dolls. They were the closest things she had to real friends. Now, Thaddeus stared at the doll and felt a strong sense of loss. He could not explain why he remained on the porch instead of going right in and announcing his presence.

He was remembering the look of intense hatred he had seen in Jogo's eyes. He would always remember the man by that look. There was no erasing the memory, no escaping from it.

Thaddeus knew, somehow, in his heart—Jacob was dead. And he knew, somehow, in his heart—he was the reason why.

Thaddeus glanced back at the police cars parked in front of his house and his breath hitched in his throat.

Steeling himself for the worst, he pushed open the door to his home.

Momma stood by the television. She wasn't unusually around at this time of day. By her side were Mrs. Matthews and Mrs. Craig, her friends. They consoled her with a comforting embrace and handed her a handkerchief as he walked by.

The room smelled of grief.
"Oh, Thaddeus!" Momma rushed over to him, sobbing gently.

He stood rooted to the ground, not saying anything. Not daring to move or even blink.
"Thaddeus..." Momma sobbed.

Thaddeus wished she would tell him instead of wasting so much time. If something tragic had happened, he wanted to know instead of going through the torture of waiting.

Shanice was seated on the sofa next to a woman he didn't recognize. The woman had black hair and beady eyes hidden beneath glasses. Her lips formed a smile more disturbing than it was comforting.

Shanice needed comforting. She was *wailing*.
"The police have nothing." Momma's voice broke off as soon as she said the words.
"W-what do you mean?" His heartbeat blocked out the sound of his own voice.

Momma tried to answer, but the words were jumbled. She stood there, shaking her head, trying and failing to convey her message. Thaddeus had never seen her look so broken and lost.

Mrs. Matthews came to her aid. "Hey, son," she said, watching his expression carefully.

Thaddeus wanted to scream he was not her son. He wanted to demand he be told what had happened to his sister. Instead, he stood there, limp and quiet.

Momma looked like she was going to pass out. Mrs. Matthews provided her with a chair.

Thaddeus could feel the air fleeing his lungs. When his breath returned, he didn't know how long he had been running. Five minutes? Maybe ten? His legs had become so wobbly he could hardly control them. Every part of him was shaking. He'd heard his name, but that may as well have been a distant memory.

He came to a stop in front of the Mission Hill Church. Its large oakwood doors were open. There was a different atmosphere inside. Thaddeus felt like he could breathe again.

He took a deep breath and the potent scent of burning incense filled his nose. A man in a choir gown sat at the piano, striking beautiful chords as Thaddeus stood there. He paused his playing to look up at the boy.

"Are you lost, child?" The man smiled a warm, comforting smile. The kind of smile Thaddeus imagined Jesus gave to everyone he performed miracles on.

Thaddeus was lost. Oh, he was incredibly lost.

"Come on in. No need to be shy," the man said. "You're in the house of the Lord."

Thaddeus staggered over to him, almost tripping once, which raised concern on the man's face. When Thaddeus reached his side and sat down beside the man, he did so without saying a word. Fascinated by the seraphic depictions on the colorful stained-glass windows, his mind settled into a semblance of peace.

"Did you lose your way?"

Thaddeus wasn't really listening to the man. All he could hear were the words he wanted to say. Once he began, he couldn't stop talking.

"It's my fault he's dead. He wouldn't be dead if I listened to him in the first place. He told me Adams was bad—good for *nothing*—and I didn't listen. I thought if I kept him by my side he would protect me. Keep me safe..."

The man said something like, "Only God can protect you."

"Now he's dead because of me. I miss him so much! He's dead and it's my fault! Now my sister... My sister…" He couldn't force the words out anymore and broke down into tears.

The man held him in a tight embrace, mumbling prayers over him. Thaddeus closed his eyes and lost all feeling. He was drifting; floating in a semiconscious state until everything was gone, every ounce of feeling.

He had no sense of how long he had been asleep but, when he woke and looked outside the window, the sky was so bleak he could barely see beyond the glass.

The man sat at the piano, playing 'Amazing Grace.'

Chapter Twenty Six

"It's been three days," Sarah heard her voice crack as she spoke. She sounded like she had gone an entire week without taking a sip of water. She'd barely slept, cried her eyes out each night and continued the search during the day. She passed out missing persons' posters everywhere, with Thaddeus and Shanice's assistance.

Even *with* the posters plastered over the streets, Sarah knew there was a minimal chance they would find anything. Tonya's abduction was not a simple snatch-and-grab. The perpetrator had carefully planned the abduction. They'd left no evidence behind. The police were still combing through the city, going door-to-door.

Now, she sat in the police captain's office, hoping he had information for her.

"Tell me there's something," she begged.

"Mrs. Carter, I'm sure you know what this case means to us here. One of our officer's children has been abducted. I'm not leaving any stone unturned until we find Tonya, I assure you. It's going to take us a little while, but we *will* find her and who took her. Our men are working hard and—"

"I can't wait. There has to be something else. Some other way. My daughter could be..." Sarah swallowed, refusing to say the words. "She's not—I know she's not—but every second she's away increases the chances."

"I don't think you understand, ma'am." Cosmo cleared his throat. "We are doing everything we can. There's no evidence or leads to follow."

The older man may have appeared battle-hardened but, at the moment, faced with a woman who had lost her daughter and was ready to do anything to get her back, he felt a bit cowed. Sarah Carter resembled a wild animal—one who wanted nothing but to rip him limb from limb.

"This is how it always is—" Cosmo began.

"What the hell do you mean by *always is*?"

"I'm sorry. I'm afraid I can't disclose the details of an—"

Sarah slammed both hands down on his desk, sending an ashtray sailing into his lap. Powdery white ash dusted his clothes as the steel *clanged* against the floor.

"If there is a suspect, I want a name and everything you know about him, Cosmo. *Right now.*"

* * *

The day after Tonya disappeared, Nicholas found himself standing by the gymnasium doors, only a few feet from where his daughter was taken. He tried to put himself in the shoes of the man who had taken her. Not to understand his motive, but to understand how he had pulled off the feat.

The captain of the cheerleading squad—along with a few others—had said they saw Tonya leave the gym on her own. None of them were close friends with her; no one knew exactly why she had left or seemed to mind when she didn't come back.

The exit she took was out of the field of view of both cameras which covered the hallway. Even if they had been turned on, they wouldn't have captured what happened.

Following the series of events, Nicholas and the other officers believed whatever happened to her had occurred in a very small window of time. Still, without the cameras, there was no way to know who had come or how she had been taken out of the building.

Nicholas prowled around the school premises for three days, watching for anything suspicious. As he surveyed the road in front of the school, he noticed a Burger King on the other side of the street. That's where the technician had eaten breakfast. As Nicholas approached, he saw the building had closed-circuit cameras. None of them pointed at the school, but they captured the parking lot.

Nicholas knew he could simply walk into the establishment and request to see their footage. They would oblige him the moment he flashed his badge, but that would mean interfering with the investigation. Cosmo had given him a strict warning—personnel were not allowed to investigate cases they were directly tied to.

Except, it was his daughter's life that was on the line and, even if he got in trouble, he would do everything he could to find her.

"Police." Nicholas held up his badge for the fast-food employee to see. "I'd like to view your footage from the past three days. The parking lot and inside."

After briefly explaining the situation to the manager, he was escorted to the security room. The video footage from outside was clear, but the footage showing inside was black-and-white and highly pixelated. The manager apologized, mentioned something about funds before rewinding the video back to the hour when the technician had walked in.

Nicholas watched with an eagle-like gaze, hoping to catch something, *anything*. Then, he did.

It was over in two seconds. The man who had spilled ketchup on the technician poured something into his food right after he turned away to wash up. His body was turned to an angle which blocked the camera, but Nicholas caught his hand sliding back into his pocket. Right after, he left. The video from the parking lot showed a red Sedan pull away.

The video was paused and Nicholas quickly scribbled down the vehicle's license plate number, then thanked the manager for his help.

He could not pursue the investigation as an officer, but it was his duty as a father to locate his daughter. Retrieving his cell phone, he called his friend who worked at the DMV.

"Stuart—run this plate number for me. Give me everything you can on its owner, including where he lives."

Chapter Twenty Seven

Tonya had stopped fighting.

If the first few days taught her anything, it was that she would not escape. Her bonds were too tight and, even if she did, the man who had caught her would just put her back in the chair.

She wasn't sure what he wanted. He didn't speak, didn't respond to any of her questions or pleas. Instead, he brought rice to her lips—boiled and unsalted rice. She had difficulty seeing the food because of the blinding lights filling her vision.

The spoon she was fed with was white. The man wore a pair of white gloves when he fed her. Everything Tonya had seen since she had opened her eyes blurred with the intense white lights. When she could no longer stare into them, she shut her eyes, a silent prayer on her lips.

But, even with closed eyelids, the low, steady hum of the lights pierced the silence, driving her insane.

She no longer had any idea what time it was or how long it had been since he took her. The lights left her in a constant sweat, which would then be replaced at random intervals with periods of prolonged cold.

Tonya had no idea who the man was. She couldn't remember anything other than his face, which did not belong to Mr. Klop. She had tried focusing on the face but, after multiple hours of the light burning into her eyes, Tonya could only see the white glow. It was all she could think about. The light burned her skin and clawed at the edges of her subconscious. Tonya was afraid she was becoming the light. If she did not do something soon, she would.

Chapter
Twenty Eight

"Carter!"

"Cosmo—"

"Don't do this. You know the protocol. Whatever leads you're pursuing, let us have it. We can help. Don't force my hand like this."

"Do you have kids, Cosmo?"

There was no reply.

"I'm going to look for my daughter," said Nicholas. "It won't be as a police officer. If that's what's important to you, I'll leave my badge here."

"What's important to me is the law and you're going to break it. Stand down, Carter."

"Can't do that, sir."

Cosmo had figured out he was working his way towards finding Tonya somehow, but his opinion didn't matter. Nicholas would deal with the repercussions once he was certain his daughter was safe.

His friend from the DMV had called back with an address and a name. Stanley Barr. A former soldier, he'd been dishonorably discharged for drug use. He'd settled into town five years ago for a life of quietude. Since he'd arrived, eight children had been abducted and were suffering from serious mental conditions when they were found months later.

Nicholas wasn't going to wait months to see his daughter again. He had an address and was on his way there.

It was a small house in the suburbs; so small he nearly missed it. He leapt out the car and dashed across the quiet street, bounding up the man's porch in two steps. Peering into the windows, he found the curtains were drawn closed on both sides, with only a tiny sliver left open to see through. It looked like no one was home, but that could be just what the resident wanted everyone to think.
  "Mr. Barr, open up! Florida Police Department!"

Nicholas banged so hard on the door the window panes around it rattled. After three knocks with no response, he shoved the door open with his shoulder. He held his gun out in front of him as he checked each room. He ensured there was no one in the house before returning to the start to look for anything which might give him a lead.

It was a basic house, one which obviously belonged to a single guy. He owned minimal clothing, only two furniture pieces, no television and enough cereal for a week. Nicholas went into the garage and discovered the car was gone. Only a few tools remained—shears, a rake, a watering can and a spade. The man lived a simple life without pets or any other obvious relationships.

A dark patch on the floor close to the garage door caught his attention. When he touched it, it blew through his fingers. *Sawdust.*

The connection hit him instantly—the woodwork shop he drove past on his way here.

Nicholas rushed back to his car. He did not slow down until he was right in front of the building. He'd noticed the place because of the huge clock by the window which kept the time, reminding him of how four days had passed since his daughter was abducted. The sign out front said *Closed*. A pair of secondary roll-up steel doors prevented thieves from entering.

As he left the car, his phone rang again. It was the captain. He tossed the phone onto the passenger's seat, slammed the door shut, and headed around to the back of the building.

At the rear was a steel door locked from the outside with a chain and padlock. Nicholas' instincts told him he was close to his daughter. He took a crowbar from the trunk of his car and went to work on the padlock, striking until the latch broke free. He pulled off the chain and, with a solid kick to its handle, the door flew open.

The lights were off in the back, sending Nicholas into a black labyrinth of furniture. His pupils tried to make sense of the shadows but were taking too long to adjust. After looking around frantically for a few seconds, Nicholas took a leap of faith.

"Tonya!" he shouted. "Tonya, are you here?"

The door behind him shut, drowning out all light. Nicholas wasn't alone.

"Mr. Barr, you're under arrest for the kidnapping of my daughter—"

The sentence was barely out of his mouth when Nicholas felt a nail gun press against his back and fire into him. He dropped to one knee and let out a cry before swinging his gun behind him and firing two shots blindly.

He heard footsteps behind him. They were too heavy to be Tonya's and sounded oddly hollow. Nicholas realized the shop must have a basement just as the nail gun fired into his arm, causing him to drop his gun.

He waited, listening, knowing the man would strike again.

The footsteps came from the left this time. A leg swooped in to kick him across the face. Nicholas caught the leg and the nail gun clattered to the ground. His hands took most of the damage, but at least he had made his move. Dragging Barr to the floor, he tried to climb on top of him and pin him down, but the nails sent multiple waves of pain through his body each time he moved. Barr landed a blow across his stomach before shoving him off and picking back up the nail gun.

He placed the gun against Nicholas' chest, looking to end the fight, but Nicholas drove his palm between the gun and his heart, catching the nail with his palm. It went straight through and punctured his chest, but didn't go deep enough to reach his heart.

Nicholas threw his head into the bridge of Barr's nose, knocking him backward. Barr recoiled, then dove in for another blow. Nicholas pulled the nail from his palm, caught the arm which held the nail gun and, pulling him close, drove the nail into the man's cheek.

Barr let out a cry, shuffling backward as tears blurred his vision. Nicholas' fist landed a right hook flush across the man's jaw, knocking him out cold.

Nicholas dragged his beaten body around the store until he found a light switch. He pushed over shelves and toppled cabinets until he found the hatch which led to the basement. Nicholas climbed down the narrow staircase and found his daughter gagged and bound in the middle of a storage room, three white lights searing into her face. Nicholas ripped the gag off, allowing her to speak.

"Daddy? Daddy, is that you? I can't see," she cried.

"Baby, I'm here. I've got you. I'll get you out of here."

Nicholas carried his daughter on his back, though his body threatened to give out. He held on until he had climbed out of the basement and placed Tonya in the car. She was crying—her cheeks sunken, her wrists and ankles bruised from the bondage. She shielded her face from everything, unable to look upon the bright, sunny day. Nicholas' heart broke for his daughter. Her hair was disheveled, her lips parched, and she still wore her cheerleaders' uniform. Her eyes—the same eyes which had looked at him with such discontent once—were blank. Nicholas locked Tonya in the car and retrieved his gun before going back into the store.

After a moment, Tonya heard six gunshots go off. Nicholas walked out and drove off, taking his daughter to the closest hospital.

Chapter Twenty Nine

A round the lower Tampa bay, there was a certain bridge Thaddeus liked to frequent. The time he spent there, in solitude, staring out over the brackish water, allowed him time to think. Plus, no one would come looking for him there.

On this particular day, there was a bit of rowdiness at one end of the bridge. Traffic had slowed down to a crawl. Several highway troopers stood along the edge, wearing long faces. A few cars had already pulled over—good Samaritans.

Reportedly, there was a jumper. Of course, there were jumpers from time to time on the "Sky Way"—another name the bridge was known for. With all the drugs and crime and gun violence, who hadn't been negatively affected? Thaddeus had met too many people who had lost their minds—and every last shred of hope—after all the shit they had experienced.

The media kept everyone informed of the vices of the society twenty-four hours a day. Analyzing and reanalyzing, studying and researching the worst aspects of life until one concluded there was no good left in the world.

A highway trooper approached the man about to jump.

It was a delicate situation. The trooper couldn't move toward the jumper too fast or he would spook. He had to walk slowly—one tentative step at a time—while the other troopers watched from a distance.

Once he was arm's length from the jump, the trooper called out to him.
"Talk to me. I'm here," he said. "You don't have to do this—"
"It ain't worth it! Everything's gone to shit" the jumper replied, sobbing. He was a middle-aged man. Around the same age Thaddeus' father had been. Thaddeus couldn't wrap his mind around that—speaking of his father in the past tense.
"How about we just talk?" the trooper reasoned. "Kindly do me a favor and step off the ledge. It's okay. Take my hand."

A small crowd was beginning to gather. Over the next hour, the trooper carried on a conversation with the jumper. He listened to him speak about his troubles, in vivid detail. And, when the man was done, they *both* jumped.

Thaddeus would always remember the trooper climbing over the guardrail. The way his colleagues had yelled for him to stop. He would never forget the image of the two men, holding hands. Jumping. Falling, together.

Though he wished he could have helped, he knew there was nothing to be done. Hopelessness was insidious and everyone was only a conversation away from stepping off of the edge.

Chapter
Thirty

A week had passed since Tonya Carter's return.

The day he rescued his daughter, Nicholas Carter went missing. He was now a miserable, wanted man who had lost his job and was on the run. Nicholas couldn't even call his wife. There was no doubt she hated him by now. He found little succor in alcohol, which seemed to take up most of his days. Someday, when the dust had settled, he would return. They could even leave Tampa if she wanted. For now, his life was a mess— one he needed to get back together.

Tonya's brother, Thaddeus, thought his sister's return would provide some sort of tranquility for him, but it didn't. Rage swelled in him every time he looked at her. He had wanted to find the bastard who did this to her himself, wishing he was old enough and strong enough to execute his vengeance. The past few days were utter hell for him. He kept thinking of Jacob and Tonya. Surely, he was losing his mind.

Tonya was in a state of mental paralysis. She saw the white light everywhere she looked. Momma would bring in a doctor to check on her twice a week and the doctor reported she was improving. Only, nothing was improving. Nobody said her father was gone, but she knew he was. The depth of loss was overwhelming.

Tonya's mother was going out of her mind but pretending everything was fine, like she had it all together.

And Thaddeus wasn't the boy she used to know. Something in him had changed. Her sister, Shanice, was fine as far as she could tell, but that did not mean something couldn't happen to her soon. Tonya imagined all these things as the burn of tears filled her eyes every night. Momma would come into her room and assure her she would be well soon. That everything was going to be fine.

Tonya had always known once the family portrait had broken, nothing was ever going to be the same.

Alphonso Williams, Jr

PART TWO

" For in every adult, there dwells the child that was, and in every child, there lies the adult that will be. **"**

*- **John Connolly**, The Book of Lost Things*

Chapter Thirty One

May 20th, 2015

A team of highly trained special ops soldiers waited patiently as their plane tore through the air, rattling as it hit low pockets of wind. Eight men and two women waited in the cargo bay, strapped with assault rifles and other tactical gear. Some prayed while others chatted, laughing loudly over the engines' roar and the plane's shaking. The commander walked to the front of the plane, speaking to the pilot before heading back to the hull.

"Alright, listen up! Drop zone approaching in two minutes. I want to see your game faces, people. Ten seconds to double-check before we roll out!"

The red light at the back of the plane turned green and the cargo door lowered, allowing the cold night air to rush.

When the commander gave the word, the soldiers rose to their feet and ran for the exit ramp. They jumped out and disappeared into the storm clouds below.

Thaddeus loved the feeling of the air on his face, the moistness the clouds left behind after he'd fallen through them. During those few moments, before they reached the ground, Thaddeus felt a peace he could not describe. He had done this enough time to know just how quickly things could go from peaceful to chaotic. Pulling his mind from out of the euphoria of free-falling, he moved into position with the rest of the team.

They descended like bullets, quietly, deploying their parachutes at the last moment before gliding to the ground. Landing in a ridge just south of their location, they balled up their parachutes, rechecked their weapons, and waited for the captain to finish recon.

They were in Al Jahrā'—a small city in Kuwait—attempting to extract Augustus Lindley, an agent working with the Central Intelligence Agency. He had been caught and captured by insurgent forces in the area while undercover. They had all reviewed the pictures and dossiers of the men who had captured him.

The building where Lindley was being held was a factory-style complex with men guarding the two entrances. There was one entry point to the east, with a single man on a terrace and another by the doors.

The one on the terrace held a cigarette between his lips, trying to find warmth in the frigid winter air. It didn't snow in Kuwait, but temperatures dropped low. The guard on the ground was feeding paper into a steel drum fire.

"Hamster, one on the terrace. Beaver, below him. Weasel, take Beta and move in from the north end. Make a clean sweep, neutralize, then rendezvous. Roll out once the target is acquired. Break on my mark."

The commander's words resonated with Thaddeus. Everyone on the team had been given code names of rodents, allowing them to maintain anonymity out in the field. The two snipers had been given orders to take out the men on the east side of the building, while he was tasked with breaching from the north with half of the team. The snipers had already set up position on the ridge, placing their high caliber rifles on hard, dusty soil which had endured years of eroding.

On the commander's word, bullets went off, both guns firing simultaneously. There was a low *whizzing* sound, followed by two thuds. The bodies dropped to the ground, leaving only a small splatter of blood on the walls behind them. One look at the factory's north side confirmed they were still undetected. The commander gave the word.

Thaddeus and the Beta team moved through the dark, ducking low behind burnt-out vehicles and barricades set up to keep vehicles out. They hopped over a short fence before snaking their way down. They were only a few meters from the south guard. The sound of a flash bang going off was the signal. Thaddeus stood and placed two shots in the chest of the confused man who had looked in the direction of where the flashbang landed. Once dropped to the ground, the soldiers moved past him and kicked down the side entrance door.

Thaddeus heard the shooting coming from the front and knew that most of the forces would head that way. The Beta team moved quickly and quietly, five of them spreading out into two teams of two, leaving Thaddeus to go through one of the rooms alone. The factory looked like it had been abandoned for a long time, with most of the equipment dilapidated and dusty. They had once weaved fabric in the heart of the building; most of the rooms were full of looms, blocks of wood and tufts of wool.

He swung his gun left and right, moving the weapon in sync with his eyes as he moved through room after room, searching for Lindley.

A door swung open behind him and a man dashed at him, holding an aloft machete. Thaddeus fell backwards, giving him enough space to rattle off three shots, killing the insurgent. He pushed the man to the side and entered another room.

A steel pipe hit Thaddeus between the shoulders, knocking him to the ground as his gun skidded out in front of him.

The attacker spun the weapon around, lunging forward with the sharp edge in an attempt to drive it into Thaddeus' chest. The soldier caught the man's arms and prevented the sharp end from penetrating his body. But, being on the ground, he was at a disadvantage. His arms would grow tired soon, and the man would win. So, Thaddeus pushed the sharp end of the blade to the right side of his chest; Thaddeus pulled out his handgun. The man let out a scream as he fired multiple rounds into him.

The sound of gunfire erupted from the front room's interior as Thaddeus tactically duck-walked deeper into the factory. As he approached the center of a corridor, he observed a man who had a hood draped over his head being dragged away on the opposite end. Thaddeus immediately raised his assault rifle, then lowered it in fear of striking Lindley.

The men carrying the CIA operative away fired at him. Thaddeus quickly ducked behind the adjacent wall for cover and was soon joined by two of his fellow special ops teammates. One man stayed behind to provide cover fire as the insurgents retreated.

"Sir, I've located Lindley. We're being pinned down on the east end of the building. He's being taken away in a vehicle," Thaddeus radioed.

"Weasel, stop that vehicle by any means necessary. That's an order!" The commander's reply came over the sounds of bullets flying.

Suddenly, a grenade landed mere feet from Thaddeus and his colleagues. Thaddeus dove as far away from it as possible and hit the ground just as the explosive went off, sending debris and roofing material down on them.

Another soldier, hurt by the explosion, groaned in the corner.

Thaddeus knew those men would return to finish the job, believing the grenade attack was successful. Thus, he waited, groaning alongside Hamster as he heard footsteps approaching. When he saw the man's boot, he fired a shot in the leg and another to the head.

Thaddeus quickly rushed over to Hamster. Meanwhile, he could hear the engine of a vehicle pulling away.

The grenade had hit Hamster with its full force, severely injuring him. A bit of shrapnel was lodged in his neck and blood trickled from his mouth.

"Go... Go get 'em, Weasel," said Hamster, with a painful smile.

Thaddeus lifted Hamster's arm to his neck and pulled out the piece of metal before applying a tourniquet to the affected area. He then exited through a hole in the wall. He saw the vehicle in the distance, trying to maneuver its way through the blockades. A dirt bike sat in the middle of the road. Not too far away, its driver suffered from multiple gunshot wounds to his body. Thaddeus jumped on the bike, ignoring the pain radiating through his arm.

The motorcycle roared to life, firing forward and propelling him towards the vehicle carrying Lindley and the insurgents.

The sound of the motorcycle alerted to his presence. One of the insurgents in the back of the vehicle had a gun pressed to Lindley's neck. The front seat passenger leaned out the window and observed Thaddeus following behind. He pointed his pistol through the back glass and fired off two shots which both missed Thaddeus by inches. He struggled to maintain balance on the dirt bike.

Lindley heard the shots and head-butted the insurgent.

The man recoiled, pulling his hand back inside the vehicle. Thaddeus used the distraction and rode up to the vehicle's side. Gripping the handle, he pulled the door open, causing the man in the back to fall out.

Looking over his shoulder at Thaddeus, the driver swerved the vehicle to the right in an attempt to hit the bike. The soldier locked on the brakes and allowed the dirt bike to pull ahead slightly. He retrieved his handgun and steadied the bike with one arm.

The CIA agent in the back seat managed to remove the bag from his head. The first thing he saw was Thaddeus riding on the bike behind them, a Beretta pistol aimed straight at him. Lindley ducked, and Thaddeus saw his chance. He fired four rounds at the driver seat's headrest, causing the vehicle to swerve left, into a ditch.

Thaddeus leaped off the bike and rushed down to the vehicle to pull Lindley out.

The man had been beaten badly, but he made it out of the enemy camp thanks to his military friends, who gave their all to rescue him. Hamster and Ferret—who had also been shot—also managed to survive the incident. A helicopter had been radioed in right after Thaddeus pursued the fleeing vehicle and arrived shortly after he returned to the rendezvous point with Lindley in hand. The chopper airlifted the squad back to the Camp Doha Army Base in Kuwait Bay.

***

Two months after the extraction hit, a young soldier walked up to Thaddeus while he was working out. His damp, dark hair clung to his skin. His formerly lanky frame was now hard, lean muscle.

"Sir, the commander wants to see you," the young soldier said with a salute and a look of affirmation—one which came from being in the presence of such a well-decorated soldier.

Thaddeus returned to his quarters to grab a clean shirt from his locker before stepping out.

A photo of Momma and Tonya stuck out from the mirror in his locker. Their faces smiled at the camera, but their eyes were blank and lost. It was taken thirteen years ago, a year after Tonya was taken and life in the Carter household began to fall apart. Thaddeus rubbed a thumb over their faces, making a mental note to call soon and let them know of his plans. Then, he walked briskly to the commander's office.

It was a small room in one of the few buildings on the base with no air conditioning. Behind the commander, a shelf was decorated with an assortment of trophies and medals, which he had earned over the years in service to his country. Thaddeus had nothing but respect for the man as he had been the one who requested he join his unit. It had required Thaddeus to dedicate his entire being to the missions and duties which had impressed the man. The commander was responsible for shaping his military career. He had built Thaddeus, trained him twice as hard as he had everyone else with the hopes he would become the best to ever come from underneath him.

He'd been successful. Not only did Thaddeus become an excellent soldier, he was also the chief of his team, a leadership role which he had groomed him for. Which was why the letter on his desk had come as a surprise to the commander when he received it a few months ago. He had expected Thaddeus to stick around for much longer, but apparently the soldier had other things in mind.

Thaddeus knocked twice before stepping into the office. "Sir."

"At ease. What's this on my desk, Thaddeus?"

"Sir, I believe it's time I went back home to serve my country in another capacity. It has been an honor Sir, but I think it's time I begin the next chapter of my life."

"Is that so?"

"Yes, sir." Thaddeus, swallowed hard as he stared at the man behind the desk.

"And what do you want to do after this? How do you want to keep serving? Become a firefighter?"

"A police officer, sir," Thaddeus replied without missing a beat. "I believe the neighborhood around Tampa where I grew up should be policed by someone who has lived there."

The man rose his feet and stared at Thaddeus through cold, calculating eyes. Then, his right arm shot forward, shaking Thaddeus, "Son, I never knew the day would come when we'd have to part ways. But I respect you and I respect your decision. Seven years in a combat unit is no easy feat. I've got a few contacts who can help make your transition smoother. I'll put the word out, make sure you get the job you want,"

"Thank you, sir."

It was hard leaving the army behind—the friends he had made, lost and shared with. Thaddeus felt stricken from leaving the men and women who had become his family behind, but the blow was softened by the fact he was going back home to his mother and sisters.

Chapter

Thirty Two

*May 20th, 2015

Gilbert was the old doctor who came once a week to check whether Cyrus was getting better or worse. Either way, his face kept the same blank expression, for the sake of his patients. Once, he had treated a man suffering from acute diarrhea. Although he told the man's obese wife he would be fine—when he sure as hell would not—she had slumped on the spot when she saw the look on his face. It was a look of utmost sympathy. After a few separate cases, Gilbert decided he needed to work on his facial expressions if he was going to keep his patient's guardians intact.

In the case of Cyrus, he was not certain whether the young boy would endure, but he did not have the heart to break the news to his family. He had not entirely given up on the boy, anyway, even though several physicians before him had done so.

Cyrus had been admitted into three different hospitals; but, in the end, returned home because his family could no longer afford the fee. That, or because his physicians had resigned him to a closed case.

His situation neither worsened nor improved.

Gilbert could not imagine the agony both the boy and his family were going through. He knew, most likely, it would be over soon.

Whether he was going to recover miraculously or die peacefully, and the eventual relief would come.

As he waited for the worst to happen, still, wished there was something he could do.

Cyrus laid in bed, covered by a brown sweater. His body was rail-thin beneath the clothes, and so appeared as though a rag had just been draped over his body. His bones jutted out from every conceivable angle; his cheekbones were defined to an almost skeletal degree. In recent months, he had lost nearly fifty pounds. All his former clothes now seemed like they belonged to someone else.

Each month, Ebony went down to the thrift shop to buy clothes for him—it was the only way to keep up with his rapid weight loss. Gilbert said if he kept losing at this rate much longer, Cyrus could suffer arrhythmia and many other big named afflictions Ebony had neither the heart nor intellect to remember. She saw her brother every day and every day it took self-restraint not to burst into tears.

Cyrus hardly spoke now. He offered a word or a mumble now and then, as though he were only trying to assure them he was still alive. Ebony wasn't sure how much longer he could keep on fighting; or even if he was going to make it out of this battle.

Today, he was wearing yellow Tom and Jerry shorts underneath his big sweater. His face lacked color.

"What do you think, Doctor?" Ebony sat by the sofa, sipping coffee, barely tasting the drink as she watched him lie on the bed. Dr. Gilbert stood over him in a white suit and a cobalt blue tie, like some sort of guardian angel. She knew he was not Cyrus' guardian any more than she was and, when the time came, there would be nothing either of them could do to stop the inevitable.

Dr. Gilbert's face held its blank expression, but his eyes twitched as though they were trying to communicate something he was unwilling to. How bad could things be?

I'm sorry, Ebony. I don't think he's going to make another birthday. I think you're wasting money, time, and effort. Don't you see how it's affecting your peace of mind? You barely eat. You're losing weight, and if you keep up with this—whatever hunger strike you're on—Cyrus isn't the only one you'll need to be worried about.

I'm sorry to break it to you like this, honey, but someone has to. Go out. Have fun. Stop thinking there'll be some sort of miracle with Cyrus. God knows best, eh? If he brought him in only to take his life after a few years, I'm sure he must have his reasons.

If there is a cure for your brother, I don't see it yet. And, believe me, I practiced for over thirty years before I finally retired. I have seen a whole lotta things. You have to stop holding onto whatever hope you have. The sooner you let go, the better it'll be for you...

And him. Have you thought about him and how he feels about all of this? No shit, he can't talk much, but if he could, he'd tell you how much he hates himself for putting you through this stress for all these years.

The treatment just isn't working, Ebony. The only way out...Well, you know the only way out.

For a situation which is uncertain—with only a slim chance of him making it out alive—I'd say a whole lot of money is being thrown to the wolves. A whole lot of money that you don't have and I don't see you having any time soon unless you plan on robbing a bank.

Let go, girl. Everyone else has.

But Dr. Gilbert didn't say any of the things she was expecting. Instead, his eyes were asking a question of their own: *Do you want to know what I really think or do you just want me to say what you want to hear?*

Ebony didn't know. It didn't matter how many times she braced herself for the inevitable heartbreak—she was never ready. She couldn't allow him to go just yet. She wasn't sure she'd ever be able to. Cyrus was more than a brother to her. Tears welled up in her eyes and she felt like if she didn't let them out, she would fucking explode.

Dr. Gilbert sensed her distress and stepped closer to her, wrapping his arms around her as she started to cry. Her shoulders trembled; the sound of her cries were muffled against his chest but still loud enough to be heard by the person in the adjoining room. Dr. Gilbert stroked her hair in a gentle, fatherly way.

She wondered if he had a daughter, He never spoke of his personal life. Maybe, if he had a daughter or a son or anyone close to him suffering the same fate as Cyrus—he would understand better. But Ebony didn't wish Cyrus fate on anyone.

She only wanted to cry until she could no longer feel.

The doctor was whispering something in her ear, but she could not hear the words. It might've been a prayer or words of consolation. She needed consolation and for him to say her brother would be okay, even if she knew it was a lie.

"Do you want me to stay for a bit longer?" he asked.

Dr. Gilbert's voice was hoarse and tired, like after a deep drag from a cigarette. His chest felt strong. He was comforting in many ways. Yes, Ebony would find the utmost comfort drifting away on his chest, in a world where there was no pain and no hurt. Where she was not constantly scared, exhausted, or anxious. She did not know whether she had spent ten minutes resting on him or only a couple of seconds, but she was already starting to feel better.

Cyrus stirred on the bed, groaning softly, and she turned instantly—a move that was more a reflex than it was a conscious decision. A transparent tube filled with blood connected to his wrist. Once, she had asked the doctor if it was really necessary. Couldn't he see the boy was dying and needed every bit of *him in him*? The doctor explained he was infusing blood, not taking his blood away.

Ebony believed he meant well, but she wasn't taking any chances. There were stories of doctors taking their patients' blood in exchange for money.

Ebony walked briskly to the boy's side. "Hi." She tried smiling, but her lips curved into something resembling neither a smile nor a frown. "How you doing, little man?"

Cyrus was sixteen, but he could pass for fourteen with his small, emaciated frame and boyish voice.

"Fine," he said, though only the first syllable had been pronounced.

Ebony completed the rest of the word in her head.

He didn't turn over much as the movement seemed to cause him a great deal of pain. When his eyes met with the bright lights, he squinted and turned away sharply.

She pressed her fingers to his neck, checking his temperature and pulse. Everything seemed normal.
"He's a strong boy," said Dr. Gilbert.

Ebony jumped a little, she had completely forgotten about him.

His blank expression was gone, replaced by a smile. It wasn't a full-on, clearly-defined smile, but she could see; his lips tilted in a fairly unusual way, which made her want to return his grin.
"He has your eyes," he said.

Ebony chuckled, despite herself.

Dr. Gilbert noticed the sparkle in her eyes. Her black brows lifted in a quizzical arch. He thought she was beautiful. The moment reminded him of one summer he spent at a grand hotel in Albany. He would walk through the garden every morning just to smell a whiff of the flowery fragrances, just to see the sunflowers glisten and dance under the sun. She gave him the same sense of serenity he had experienced, breezing through the garden and he knew he would do anything to see her smile unendingly.

Hell, he would put his life on the line for the boy if necessary.

He had already put his career on the line. He'd retired years ago but was still treating Cyrus. Most of the drugs and equipment he used for her brother came through rather discreet means. If he were caught practicing without a license, he would end up in jail. But he was risking this for Ebony.

She stood by Cyrus and watched him close his eyes again. He looked so peaceful, as though nothing on earth could ruffle him. Ebony bent and planted a kiss on his head, lingering for a long minute. He smelled of olive oil and strong herbs.

When she turned back to the doctor, his face suddenly seemed years younger. The streaks of white in his hair gleamed brightly under the room light. One hand was thrust deep in his coat pocket, while the other clung to his briefcase. Ebony felt his fatherly compassion towards her, I knew he cared for her and that was why, after two months, he'd only charged a pathetic fee to look after her brother. She didn't know how she could ever thank him, but she tried in her own way, in the little things she did to show her gratitude.

"Do you mind if I walk with you a bit, doctor? Seeing you're on your way out and I could use a little fresh air."

"Oh, no. Absolutely. That's fine with me." He held out a hand, gesturing for her to lead the way.

"Shall we?"

Ebony reached for her beanie from the couch. "Yes, let's go."

Across the living room, she could hear the sound of furniture bumping into the wall, her mother giggling and whispering. The stench of cannabis floated in the air. Her deadbeat boyfriend, Nico, was undoubtedly there. The both of them were probably seeing who could down shots of tequila faster, then doing whatever dirty shit he could muster up.

Ebony hated Nico. No, *hate* was too gentle of a word. She *despised* Nico with every ounce of her being. He was everything a woman should run from in a man, yet her mother opened the door for him each time he came knocking. Didn't she see he was bad for her? Truth be told, she was already wasted before she met him. The thought of the two of them together filled Ebony with such intense nausea she swore, if she put a finger down her throat, she would throw up a week's worth of food.

"Love is a drug," Dr. Gilbert said, bringing her back to the moment.

They strolled through the streets. It wasn't as busy as usual and the evening was closing upon them.

"Sometimes, it can be a good drug and sometimes it can be a bad drug. The problem is we never know which it is until we're knee-deep, already addicted. Then, it becomes all that you need. You feel ecstasy, or you feel your mind and soul being eaten away, destroying you bit by bit, but you still can't stop. You come back for more every day—even though it's hurting you, you come back. People don't know this," he explained. "They think it's an emotion. That you can *decide* to feel it—and, sometimes, I suppose you can." Gilbert remembered his wife before she died and how the act of loving her still was such a painful, deliberate thing to do. "But in the end, it all boils down to the things we can't control. You can't tell a person not to love who they choose to love."

"Maybe. But she doesn't love him. Or, more precisely, he doesn't love her. They are just using each other and don't even know it. Or maybe they do and they're just fine with it," said Ebony, shuddering.

"It's the *maybes* that scare us the most."

"They don't love each other," she repeated fiercely.

"Maybe," he whispered. He wore a faraway, thoughtful expression and Ebony had the feeling he was not talking about her mother and her mother's boyfriend anymore.

"Have you ever been in love?"

Gilbert chuckled. "I've been married."

"Yeah, but that doesn't answer the question, does it?" Her eyes were calming, not intending to unsettle him the way they did.

"No, I suppose it doesn't." He twirled his finger around a vacant spot on his forefinger. How quickly he had disposed of the ring after Diana's death. No, it was not the same thing at all. "I did love my wife. She was a lovely woman. Kind, caring..."

As he spoke, Ebony realized that he wasn't just saying the words because it was what any decent man would say of his wife, but because he actually meant them. She also couldn't help but notice that he spoke about her in the past tense.

"She was the kind of woman any man would be proud to have as the mother of his kids, the kind who could address a crowd, and you'd be proud to call yours." He froze, and she waited for a continuation, but he did not say anything for a long while. Minutes passed. When he finally spoke again, it was after a deep, long heave. She did not want to talk about it if he was uncomfortable, but it seemed that he wanted to continue, so she let him take his time.

On both sides of the street, shops were beginning to shut down; women took in their umbrellas and trays of fruit that they displayed on the street that led to the central market.

"Things don't always go the way you plan. Now you see, Diana... Diana couldn't have any kids, for no reason explained by science. Every test result showed that her reproductive organs were fine, and I... I'm as fit as they come. But something somehow was wrong, and she could not have any children."

Ebony knew what he was going to say. She knew how men treated their wives for not giving them children, how quickly they changed. She couldn't see the doctor as that kind of man, but then, you never really knew a person. What's more, she was only barely acquainted with him in the first place.

"You wanted a child. The marriage couldn't work because you wanted a child."

"Oh, no, no. Far from it. The marriage was working just fine—I was just fine. I mean, it was obviously not her fault, and I was fine with it. It was Diana who wasn't."

Instead of asking what he meant, she let him go on when he was ready.

"She began to blame herself and became insecure, bitter, spiteful. She started drinking, and then it became an obsession. Every day when I got home, there were empty bottles all around, or burnt-out cigarettes, or something else destructive. I tried to stop her, tried to convince her that I still loved her, but she just wouldn't have it. She was punishing herself severely, and as much as I couldn't stand it, one day, I just snapped. And I yelled at her.

"At that moment, I realized that I'd actually stopped loving her. The next day she upgraded to drugs. Hard drugs. And it went on that way until... until she died. Sometimes, I blame myself. Perhaps there's something I could have done to help. Perhaps I could have tried harder, then maybe she would still be alive... maybe I would still love her." Subconsciously, he repeated to himself, "It's the maybes that scare us the most."

Ebony didn't know what to say or if there was even something she could say to make him feel better. In his voice, there was a lingering of the old hurt, despite how hard he tried to disguise it. There was an unusual quiver in his words. Is this what it turns you into when you lose someone you loved?

"I don't want you to have to get too far off. Thank you for walking with me, Ebony. I really enjoyed your company. Perhaps we could spend some time together some other time. We could talk about the sunset, roses, and all that ladies your age read about in romance novels if you like. What's your favorite place for lunch?"

Ebony was genuinely flattered. "De Trio." She had never been to it because the restaurant was very expensive, but she had been dying to go there.

"Alright, then. Whenever you're ready, you let me know?"

It was as much a question as it was an invitation. She nodded. Friday was good. She could manage to get away from the office on time since her boss usually left early to catch a bus or a flight to wherever she was spending the weekend with her lover.

He turned down another road and left, tapping her on her shoulder in that fatherly way again. He was a strange man, she thought, resting against an old wall. Then she remembered his voice as he talked about his wife and thought of Cyrus. It would break her to lose him. No, it would destroy her. He was the only family she had left—her mother could rot for all she cared. Ebony knew what she had to do. With tears dripping from her eyes, she knew that it was inevitable.

She would visit Mr. Toliver and tell him that she had accepted his generous offer.

Chapter Thirty Three

On an abandoned dock off the Delaware River stood three men staring down into the darkness. One of them sat in the car behind them on the road, engine running. It was a cold winter morning, a few hours past midnight. The slapping of the waves on the docks and boats, along with the low hum of a nearby port, reverberated through the wooden dock.

A small boat quietly moved through the waters, coming to a stop by the edge of the docks. The driver was a man with greying hair and eyes full of discontent. The man was angry, and the emotions in his face couldn't be hidden, regardless of how dark the sky was. He stayed out of the direct path of the single streetlight, remaining in his boat rather than stepping on board. The men waiting at the docks stared at him, unsure of what to do.

"You boys work for Reed?" the man in the boat asked, his voice sounding tired and weathered.

"Yeah, we work with him," the oldest of the bunch fired back. "They say you got something for us?"

"Depends on if you can give me the intel I want." The man on the boat pulled a small pouch from his pocket and poured some of its contents into his palm. It glistened under the streetlight before he returned it to the pouch, then he tossed it on the dock, equal distance from both parties. "Your diamonds. Where's Reed?"

One of the men began walking towards it, but the man in the boat quickly pulled his gun, aiming for the man's face. He froze, like a deer in headlights, before backtracking and moving away from the diamonds. He did not know who the man was or why he was paying handsomely for a retired police officer's location. Reed had become a big name in politics, and he had a huge sway with the local government in Tampa.

"Tell me what I need to know first." The man in the boat spoke in a controlled manner like counting every syllable that left his lips. Seeing the intent in his eyes, the man on the dock recognized the threat in front of him and took another step back. "Then you can get the diamonds. Not a moment before, otherwise we have no deal." He gestured at them with his handgun as he spoke.

"What makes you think we won't take the diamonds?" the eldest one spoke up. He was in his late twenties, maybe early thirties. He spoke with a certain confidence that only came from years on the job; he didn't seem to care that a loaded gun was pointed at his face. He stepped forward, walking past the one who had stopped, and slowly approached the diamonds with his arms by his side, raised to show that he was unarmed. "There's three of us and one of you. You have a very slim chance here."

"I'm the only one pointing a gun."

"All three of us have guns. At most, you get a shot off on one of us, and the others will put you down. I'm sure money from the diamonds is more than enough to take care of a simple gunshot wound, eh, boys?"

The men laughed, regaining their composure and willingness to take what they wanted from the man in the boat. He wouldn't fire because he needed information they had, but they could fire because they would take the diamonds from him either way. It was a win-win situation until the first shot went off. The man on the boat had fired so quickly that none of the men were able to get their fingers into the triggers.

He shot the eldest first, knowing that he would be the one responsible for rallying the others to do his bidding. He then placed one round in the right leg of the guy on the left and another round in the man on the right. All three men hit the ground in a matter of seconds; the man got off the boat, hurrying over to them.

He kicked the guns away from their arms and stomped into their injuries. They screamed a sound that echoed in the silence of the night. He knew the police would only be minutes away, so he had to act fast. He took his gun and drove it into the opening of the bullet wound of the man who had attempted to grab the diamonds. "I'm going to ask you this question once. Answer it wrong, and I'll put a bullet behind the bullet that's already inside you. Get it right, and there's a chance I'll leave the diamonds behind. It's more than enough for three bullet wounds. Am I right, guys?"

"Alright, alright, wait. We don't know what room it is, but he's at the Seminole Hard Rock Hotel for the next few weeks. He's there with security. He had a meeting with some Senator, but I'm not sure who. It's supposed to happen within the next two weeks, but that's all I know, I swear."

Nicholas listened through the sound of the man's labored breathing, hearing the wailing sound of sirens in the distance. He whipped the back of his gun into the man's temple, knocking him out. He picked up the diamonds and jumped into the boat, soaring away into the night as the police arrived on the scene. As the waters of the river sprayed across his face, Nicholas tried to remind himself of what it was all for. All those years ago, he had shot the man who kidnapped his daughter, and that had set him on the path of a criminal.

Since then, Nicholas had lived on the run, becoming a completely different man. The police placed him on their wanted list, making Nicholas a target throughout the country. He had spent the majority of the first few months after the incident hiding from the world.

He couldn't return to Sarah and his family because the police had men stationed outside of his home. Nicholas had considered going back many times, but even before Tonya was taken, he had left the house, leaving his marriage in the gutter.

He'd gone from an officer of the law to a homeless, wanted man within two months. He had taken the brunt of the first winter living on the streets, but Nicholas was a survivor. He fought the worst of it and came out on top, finding his way out of Tampa and away from the police's main buzz.

Nicholas found work with a moving company in Miami and was able to rent a place to live with just enough money left to keep food in his stomach twice a day. The men from the moving company were kind, with stories similar to the one he had told them. He was on the run from the police for a crime he committed, even if it was justified to him. They had all been homeless at some point and tried to help out one homeless person every night before they parked the truck.

But as fate would have it, they were not as clear-cut as they had seemed. One night as Nicholas slept, the men approached him with an ultimatum he couldn't say no to—mostly because they had a gun pointed at his face. They were looking to rob one of the houses they had helped its occupants move into. The men had swiped a key to get access to the home.

Nicholas had agreed and took part in the robbery. They took anything that they deemed to be of some value—everything from expensive upholstery and paintings to china and silverware. The items would then be shared amongst them and sold on the streets of Miami. Nicholas started out feeling guilty, being forced into a life of crime and becoming a man he knew he wasn't. But it made more sense to him with each passing day. He needed to survive, and certain things had to be done to survive.

Everyone he knew considered him to be a criminal, and everyone he'd previously worked with was looking to arrest him. The men who had taken him in were not any better, looking to make his life better by making him an even worse person. Nicholas had had it; there was no stopping what he had become. He would no longer fight it because there was no way he could ever win. Not against a fate that made him go from family man to wanted man. He would embrace what was being thrown at him and make sure he was the best at it.

That night, Nick was born. The persona that was no longer a homeless man who worked with thieving movers. He had become a man who offered his services for pay—a consultant for the criminal underworld. Every few years, he would expand this new career, getting hundreds of criminals to trust and rely on him. A police officer turned criminal, advising others like him, helping them out with their plans, and pointing out flaws.

Life was going well until he fell under the radar of the man who had originally filed a warrant for his arrest. Cosmo Reed had become a well-celebrated officer in the years after he had left, eventually becoming the police director. Cosmo heard that Nicholas was back in Tampa and wanted nothing more than to catch him. But Nicholas was tired of running, especially from the man who had constantly berated him over his career as a police officer. Cosmo would be a problem for Nicholas, and eliminating him from the picture would be the only way to move forward with his plans.

* * *

The dark prison cell was dank with the smell of urine and sweat. It wasn't cleaned as regularly as other cells, and the man locked inside wasn't allowed to go out for exercise. He'd plead guilty to the murder of nine women, among other crimes, and was sentenced to spend the rest of his life rotting away in the cell. He had been incarcerated for twenty-five years so far; his hair became a deep gray and his features wrinkled with time. The inmate was in his early sixties but stayed in tremendous shape by exercising regularly, including doing dozens of push-ups every night.

Other than his constant workout routine, which the guards had described as disturbing, he had been a model prisoner for the last two decades. He spoke minimally with the guards and his attorney, but other people enjoyed conversing with him because he was a delight to talk to. He spoke calmly, in a tone that was jovial or playful. Even the meanest guards found it hard to stay mad at him.

Over time, the guards and warden grew complacent. The prisoner wasn't looking to make trouble; he only wanted to live out the rest of his sentence. They soon allowed him to spend time with the rest of the prisoners in the mess hall and general population. The man could go outside to the rack yard once in a while, where he would simply sit and lift weights until the period was over. Then he would return to his cell without making eye contact with anyone and doing as he was told.

But those trips he made allowed him to piece together what he needed. In two and half decades, he had memorized every guard's rotations, every camera in all corridors, every guard tower, and every entry and exit point. He had a plan formulating in his mind while he clanged away at the weights until he was satisfied. Stealing a screw, he took it back to his cell and sharpened it into a blade, using it to carve a solid black brick he had found.

The day of his escape began like any other day when he would be allowed to go out for exercise. There were no handcuffs, and the guard engaged him in a conversation about the state of the cleaners; he had grown fond of the guard. He would be led right where he needed to go—a range of corridors that served as the intersection of all wings of the prison facility. There, he politely spoke to the warden and convinced the man to bring in his attorney.

Believing that the inmate was looking to provide information on the case, the attorney was called and arrived at the prison, where the inmate was given a chance to meet with him in person. That was when he used what he had crafted from the black brick. It resembled a gun and looked enough like a semi-automatic to pass for one. He hid it behind the attorney's neck and walked up to the guards who were instructed not to shoot in a bid not to hit the attorney.

The inmate used his sharp screw and slit the guards' throats, taking one of the men's shotguns. He took the lawyer hostage, shooting people randomly to make sure the warden agreed with his simple demand to let him go. Jon killed five people on his way out and injured five others. He needed to do one more thing before he died, and he would walk back into the cell himself once it was done.

He had a single, simple mission—one that involved vengeance on the man who had put him behind bars.

Chapter
Thirty Four

"You like that?" the girl asked, giggling as she teased him.

Lucas Toliver let out a low groan, holding the call girl's hair and pushing her head towards his groin. It was so good that he could hardly breathe. He loved the girls from The Crib Hotel. They were experienced, gentle, and passionate—more passionate than the regular call girls from any other place in town. It was almost as if they were trained to act like the job they did was more than what it was—pure business. A mutual exchange.

He wasn't fooled. Maybe they went the extra mile for him to please the mighty Lucas Toliver, so he might fall in love with her and make her his mistress. But there was only one woman in the world he was interested in—Ebony Houston. He didn't care if he had to flip the heavens and the earth over, but he *would* have her. But for now, he guessed he would have to make do with the girls from The Crib.

They were outsourced by Madame Roots, an old busty woman who owned a large restaurant next to the hotel. Lucas Toliver had never dined at the restaurant because it wasn't really his taste—or for men of his social status. There were rooms inside the restaurants for the call girls and their customers; it was also said the Madame trained the girls herself. Exactly what that training consisted of, he had no interest in knowing.

This one was a beautiful brunette who spoke French. She had oversized breasts and a small, firm ass that bounced in Lucas's hand like a roll of dough. A wave of electricity coursed through him. Perhaps, after this, he would go down to Madame Roots' restaurant to thank her in person and maybe even have lunch there for once.

She rose to her feet, walked to the blinds, and let them down. There were two heavily-armed men in the lobby and two more on the roof.

She stood in front of him in her pink flare gown with ruffles in front and a deep cut in the middle that just barely covered her nipples and joined at the waistband. With her eyes on him, she cupped her breasts and bit her red lips.

Lucas gawked at her navel ring and felt himself grow even harder. In one swift hungry move, he drew her to himself and sat her on him. She giggled, drew her hands around his neck, and whispered, licking his ears. "You're strong, Mr. Toliver. I love that." He didn't even know her name. She rose and sat back on him in a slow rhythmic way. Lucas Toliver shut his eyes tightly as he felt her hands going around his buttons, undoing them.

"Christ," he muttered. She was so fucking amazing that he didn't hear his phone ring. He only realized it when she slowed down, letting him decide if he would take the call. He wasn't.

"Don't stop!"

And so she went on, her breasts jiggling in his face while he struggled to bite her nipples. He grabbed onto her back tightly, pressing her body to his. God, he could spend his entire day on this one.

The phone didn't stop ringing. It rang the second, third, fourth, fifth...

"Fuck it!" he growled, veins popping out of his head. "Get me the damn phone."

She obeyed. When she brought it, she sat back on him slowly, with the telephone in her hands. He moaned, closed his eyes for a deep breath, and popped it open again when the telephone rang for the sixth time. If it was not an important call, he swore to God that someone would suffer for it.

"What?" he snapped into the line. It was his receptionist. Her voice was fast but unsteady, as though she was scared of disrupting him from whatever he was doing. She was desperate to get her news across to him.

Lucas listened, disinterested and impatient until she said the one name. His eyes widened. He pushed the woman off him so violently and quickly that she almost fell to the ground.

"Get dressed quickly! Get into one of the rooms upstairs, and for the life of you, don't come out until I tell you to."

She looked confused, maybe even slightly offended, but she didn't ask any questions as she obeyed.

He knew she would eventually come around. When the receptionist said hastily that a Miss Houston was there to see him, he was about as surprised as he would have been if he found out his mother—the fucking crackhead—was dying of cancer.

"Send her in," he spoke into the receiver, smiling. His pretty girl was here for him, had decided that he was a righteous man fit for her after all. She had come to her senses. He almost laughed out loud; he knew she would.

By God, he remembered how feisty she had been when he first offered to help—how she had literally spat in his face, claiming she would rather watch her brother die than accept help from a man like him. Now, it turned out that her brother *was* dying, and, contrary to what she said, she would rather come to him than watch him die. That was the thing about humans—they were always so predictable, so easy.

Easy for them to choose themselves over everyone else. Easy for them to choose the option that best suited them—well, in this case, it suited him, too, and there was no way he was going to let the opportunity slide. What the hell was taking so long? If that stupid receptionist were still interrogating her after Lucas had given the word that she was free to come in, he wouldn't take things lightly on her. Lately, she was beginning to get on his nerves.

He buttoned his shirt quickly and finger-combed his hair, making sure the sitting room was in order and that there were no signs any woman had been there. He saw the pink panties on the floor, cursed, and threw them underneath a couch. If anyone had told him that he, Lucas Toliver—The Don to the underworld circles—would be trying so hard to impress any woman, he would have laughed himself into a coma. No, he would have put a bullet through his head for such an insult. But this was Ebony Houston, and she was not like any other woman he had ever met. He just knew, by God, that he had to have her.

Lucas was deep in thought and was almost startled to look up and find her there in a black, loosely-fitted gown that exposed fine, shapely legs.

A thin, rusted necklace hung around her neck and settled just above her breasts. He appreciated the view and was even flattered that she made an effort to look good for him. God, he was willing to give her the whole world if she only just asked; his entire empire.

"Why come on in, Princess there's no need to feel shy. You should feel at home."

There was no way in hell that she could feel at home, Ebony thought, looking around the white mansion. Everything was spotless, as if the whole place was scrubbed daily. It was flamboyantly furnished, with furniture and artworks that looked like they cost a couple of million dollars each. She tried not to be obvious about taking in the surroundings, but it was hard not to be amazed. Everyone knew the man was swimming in money, but she hadn't expected the house to be *this* big.

She walked in slowly, her eyes darting upstairs when she saw a curtain move. She was distracted by the gold balustrade. There was no doubt that this man would really do what he said—help Cyrus to get well if she agreed to be his—but she was not sure how willing she was. This was a man who has killed people, embezzled money, kidnapped, and directed all sorts of unmentionable crimes. In fact, it would be harder to think of a crime he hadn't committed.

Yet, here she was in his living room, about to make a deal with the devil. Her hands trembled, and she fought with herself. It was not too late to just turn and leave, but somehow, she knew there was no turning back now. She had come too far.

"You can help my brother get better? Send him to the best hospital?" she said without ado, holding his gaze, which was tirelessly moving across her body, stripping her bare. He hadn't even touched her, and she felt so dirty.

Lucas laughed and walked over to the bar. "Why don't you have a drink? I trust you must be in need of something. There's wine, champagne, brandy, whiskey—"

"I'll have water, please."

He shot her an amused look. "You're not scared I'm going to drug you, are you?"

"If you wanted to, it wouldn't make a difference if it was brandy or water."

He smiled warmly, and for a minute, she could almost have been fooled that he wasn't the devil he was.

"You know what I love about you? It's that smart mouth of yours." He imagined that smart mouth moving all over him and his pants grew painfully taut.

He rang a bell, and a second later, a tall young woman wearing chef's attire appeared from a door.

"A glass of water for the lady." He turned to her. "Anything else?"

She shook her head and hugged her arms; winter was here, both inside and out.

A moment later, the lady returned with a tray holding a cold glass of water. She placed it on a stool in front of Ebony and left.

She took a deep, long gulp, avoiding his gaze for as long as possible. If it were anyone else, she might have considered him to be a rather handsome man. His dark eyebrows and smooth brown hair and his strong, muscular build. His skin was spotless and his hair, fairly golden under the light, twinkled. There was a tattoo of a small heart on his neck that might otherwise be enough to make her fall in love, except that he was Lucas Toliver, and it would be madness to feel anything besides unabashed hatred for the man.

"Cyrus is dying. The doctors... they don't know what it is. They say it looks like he got a hole in his heart, like a very rare form of blood disease. They say they can't help him here. That he would have to be moved to a bigger hospital... meaning more money. If he doesn't get treated soon, I might... I might lose him. There's a doctor who comes to check on him. He does what he can, but then, it's just what he can. He's retired and doesn't have access to anything that could be helpful. *He* has been really helpful. I don't know if Cyrus would have made it this far without him."

Lucas looked thoughtful and, at the same time, relaxed. "This doctor who comes to look after your brother... what's his name?"

"Doctor Gilbert. Doctor Gilbert Schwartz. Why do you ask?"

"Nothing." He waved dismissively. He sat beside her, close. Too close. She could smell his cologne and the scent of his aftershave. She considered moving a couple of inches away, but that would be indirectly accusing him of something he hadn't done. Instead of fear, a thrill ran through her, a sense of danger that heightened her senses but also excited her.

"Are you sure you don't want some of this wine? I received it as a gift in Italy, straight from the brewery. My dear old friend, Jermaine, was having some, well, troubles with the government that I helped him to take care of, and for all my results, he gifted me all sorts of... things." He laughed. "Jermaine is such a dear old soul. Are you sure you're not going to have even a taste?"

"Are you going to help my brother?"

"If you're not going to have a taste of the wine, you should at least taste this pie my boys got downtown. I don't know *how* they make this thing, but you have to try it, please."

"He doesn't have much time left. I can see it. He's dying."

"And then, of course, there's the Spanish dish of—"

"Please, Lucas."

He smiled, and she knew he was purposely screwing with her, waiting for her to say the word. To acknowledge that she needed him. Damn him.

"I have just one request, my dear." He placed the wine flute next to her glass of water and trailed his finger over the side of her face, caressing her cheeks softly. She held her breath as he touched her, feeling her skin grow cool and pale. He drew in closer and kissed her on her neck.

"You're mine."

It wasn't a request. It was an order, and anger rose inside her. Just who the hell did he think he was? And a small voice said, "The man who was going to save your brother from dying." She tried to relax.

Then his hands began exploring her body, creeping beneath her gown, beneath her underwear. She turned her face away, but he turned it back to him, covering her lips with his, forcing himself on her. His grip was strong, almost painful.

"Relax."

She realized he was used to giving orders and having them obeyed. He gripped her wrists and pinned her down against the couch; his hands savagely parted her thighs and drew down her underwear.

Breathing became harder. She couldn't do it—this man was a monster. She could not allow him to touch her this way. Coming here was a huge mistake. She would find some other way around it; there had to be another way. If Cyrus got well—no, *when* Cyrus got well—and he learned that she had sold herself to this man for his sake, he would either loathe her or loathe himself, and she could not live with either of those.

She cried and tried pushing him away. For a moment, he still pressed his weight on her, going on as if he did not notice the struggle. Then, when she became insistent, violently shoving at him, he pulled himself off. Lucas stared into her face, his eyes wide with passion. No, not passion... hunger. And she realized he didn't think of her as anything more than an end to a ravenous desire. He could have just picked up any whore to please his insatiable libido. Why did it have to be *her?* She fought back the tears as he turned from her.

"I know what you think of me." He took a sip of his wine and frowned. She doubted he tasted it.

"It's the same thing everyone thinks of me. That I'm this ruthless, heartless man who goes around killing people, building casinos, masterminding prison breaks, and funding whorehouses." He chuckled and took another slow gulp. "I'm certain you think the worst things about me."

"And aren't they true?" She was openly crying now, hoping he would deny it with reasons tangible enough to make her believe him. "Tell me they aren't true, then."

"At this point, nothing I say would matter to you," he said bluntly, which was not exactly a denial or a confirmation.

"You've killed men to have your way, done despicable things."

"Everyone has."

She realized how easy it was to fall under the category of "everyone" if she agreed to this terrible thing she had considered doing. She thought of her mother and her boyfriend and laughed at how much of a hypocrite she was.

She stood up, drew her underwear back up, and smoothed her hair, trying her best not to look at him. Half of her expected him to pull out a gun and threaten to shoot her if she moved, or stand up and force her back down, *ordering* her to stay. Instead, he watched as she pulled herself together; from the corner of her eyes, she thought she saw him smiling.

"You'll be back," he said as she walked out. "You'll see that there's no other way, Ebony, my love. You'll be back..."

She couldn't hear him anymore. She was running and crying. The girl at the desk gave her an almost sympathetic look as she snatched a tissue on her way out.

Damn Lucas Toliver. Damn the stupid hospitals. Damn her mother. Damn them all to hell.

Chapter Thirty Five

"Friend said they saw you going into that Toliver mansion yesterday," Mrs. Houston said, watching her daughter write in her diary.

Ebony hated that her mother popped into her room wherever she pleased—even though she was her mother—and dragged in the smell of cigarettes with her. She hated that she dared to do whatever she felt like. She hated it so much.

"Yes," she said simply. She drew at the top of the page—something that made no sense but was a way to keep her fingers busy until her mom left.

"What business do you have with the man?"

Certainly not any of yours.

Ebony looked up at her. She stood by the doorway in checkered shorts, her hair held loosely by a band, with one hand thrust in her pocket and the other holding a can of beer. Disgust flooded her each time she looked at her mother. Ebony wanted to scream, *your son is dying, you witch! Do something!* But each time, she held back, and lately, all of that holding back was killing her. She wanted to cry and scream at God. Anything that could help the pain.

She began to laugh, and then she couldn't stop, thinking that she might laugh until she passed out. Her mother stared at her strangely, neither moving nor saying a word.

"He wants me to be his woman. His mistress," she said quickly.

"Well...?"

"Well, what?" she shot back at her.

"He's got a lot of money. And he *wants* you."

She made it sound like a surprise, like no man could ever want Ebony. At that moment, she was overcome with a rage that threatened to eat her whole.

"So? His money is all that matters?"

"Stupid girl," she hissed. "You sit by your brother every damned day, wishing he got better. A man comes up to you with an opportunity worth gold, and you wanna throw it away like this? Well, you go ahead. Just don't think you're gonna be spinning a single penny off my ass."

Her eyes were filled with tears, a recurring theme lately. "He's your son."

She took a long gulp of beer, belched, and waved her fingers in the air. Ebony thought she was about to say something, but then her mother turned and left quickly, as though a wall was coming down and she didn't want her daughter to see.

Ebony went to check on Cyrus and found him fast asleep, his skin as pale as snow. She inhaled sharply. There had to be a goddamn reason for it all.

* * *

Dr. Gilbert did not show up the next week or the week after that. For a month, he didn't show, and she did not know what to do with Cyrus. Ebony was losing her mind. She knew where he lived, in a small house down Main Street. Maybe something had happened to him. And then the thought had filled her with terror—what if something *had* happened to him?

She visited him the next Saturday morning and stood by the front door for two minutes before getting a response. He was dressed in his pajamas and peeked past her into the street. He looked scared and restless.

"Come in." He practically tossed her inside.

His sitting-room was a mess. There were books and pens and study lamps scattered here and there, and a cat stretched lazily on the rug. He didn't ask her to sit or offer her something; he just began speaking in a rushed tone.

"I was going to visit you, but I haven't had the time. I'm afraid it's bad news."

Ebony's breath caught in her throat. This was it. He was going to tell her that Cyrus was a lost cause and if all those doctors had been unable to identify his problem, that he was giving up, too.

"I can't visit any longer. I'm sorry."

So, it was just as she suspected. She gazed at him through blurry vision, and in a way, she couldn't blame him.

She got up to leave, not bothering to ask why. She was on the brink of tears. Then he said something, perhaps out of desperation to make her stay or because he truly had her best interest at heart. "You should let Mr. Toliver help you."

She froze in her tracks, turned back, and looked at him. The old doctor looked like a ghost of his former self. Her stomach dropped. "He got to you," she said, almost in a whisper.

The man's hands and lips trembled. From the look in his eyes, she saw he instantly regretted mentioning the man's name.
"Please... he'll kill me."

Ebony was genuinely sorry for putting the doctor's life in danger, but she was blinded by such fury that she didn't remember reaching the gate of the white mansion. She didn't realize she was screaming his name and pounding on the gate until an angry-looking guard appeared.

* * *

"Where is he?" she fumed as she paced in his living room, unable to stay still. She had underestimated the bastard. How could she have ever considered accepting the proposal of such a ruthless, despicable demon?

A menacingly huge bodyguard covered in tattoos and holding a gun said, "He'll be with you in a minute." Except for the receptionist, everyone was dangerous and unfriendly, but she was too angry to feel fear now.

Lucas Toliver descended the staircase, hooking his cufflinks, a silk burgundy tie slung lazily across his neck.
"I've been expecting you, Ebony." There was a sinister look on his face. "You've changed your mind?"

Ebony stormed up to him with a speed she hadn't known before, and the sound of the slap resounded in the next room. Then she was restrained by two hefty men, one swearing in Italian and pressing a gun to her side. Maybe he was saying he would shoot if she moved again, but her rage refused to settle.

Lucas held his cheek in shock, then he laughed and told them to let her go.

"Feisty. Just how I like it."

"You're a monster," she spat.

"I've been called many names."

She burst into a fresh bout of angry tears and jumped when his hand touched her shoulder.

"All you have to do is say yes."

"I'd rather die!"

She shot him a fiery gaze and raced out.

"With time, you'll see you have no other choice! With time..." he called after her. She didn't hear the rest.

Chapter
Thirty Six

The Seminole Hotel was the definition of top-notch luxury and security, at least that's how it was advertised. Nicholas was certain about the luxury—he'd seen the cars driven into the hotel and knew they weren't the types of vehicles one would drive working a nine-to-five as a Chipotle clerk.

He had changed into the only good suit he owned, one that was incredibly inexpensive. Nicholas remembered something a friend of his had once said, "It's not the price of the suit. It's how you wear it." It was a dull yet enthralling burgundy color made of cheap, satin fabric that shimmered intensely under any light. Nicholas would have preferred one in black to draw the least attention to him, but it was all he had.

He walked into the hotel lobby, fighting the urge to look up and admire the marvel at the architecture. It was most certainly the finest hotel Nicholas had ever been to, and he wished it was under better circumstances. He kept his head low—just out of sight of the security cameras, but high enough for the guards watching not to think anything of him. He walked up to the front desk, where an elderly man with a warm smile stood behind the counter.

Nicholas spotted the camera fixated directly behind the man and knew that it would get a good shot of his face if he went straight at it. So, Nicholas tilted to the side and stood with his body angled against the counter, hiding his frame behind the man behind the counter. Nicholas was a fugitive, and if he were caught on any cameras, the police could trace his last whereabouts.

He couldn't afford to be caught. Nicholas had successfully evaded capture for decades on end, and while he knew that the police were no longer actively searching for him, he continued to practice caution. He smiled at the man at the desk before speaking. "I want to see the manager."

"Do you wish to file a complaint? I'm terribly sorry. How can I assist you, sir?" The man replied in what sounded like a Native American accent.

"No, I just want to see the manager," Nicholas restated, watching the man's jacket on the chair behind him.

"I'm afraid that won't be possible. He is a very busy man, and you'll have to get an appointment. Now I can get you through, but that will still be a few weeks of waiting. Which is why I think you should talk to me. I'm sure whatever it is, I will be able to help out in one way or another, sir."

"You don't seem to understand," Nicholas continued. "I don't want an appointment. I want an investment."

Nicholas held up a single diamond between his index finger and thumb, allowing the man to see it clearly. "I hold the entire collection of these flawless stones. Forty of them in total, about twenty grand each. That's where I want to start the negotiation process. I'm sure your manager would appreciate you bringing my matter to his table discretely. Perhaps you might even get yourself a nice little raise if you play your cards right. Who knows. So, I'll ask again..." Nicholas trailed off, pretending to peer at the name tag on the man's shirt. "Mr. Arun, can I see your manager?"

"Yes, of course. I'll be back in a moment. Please, sir, there are few seats available for you to wait in."

"I'd rather stand, thank you."

Arun dashed off, leaving his station empty. Nicholas knew greed and self-interest were traits every human possessed to some extent, and he knew just how to extort them. In a building as big as the Seminole, everyone expected everyone else to be where they were supposed to be, even with all the security. Nicholas stepped around the counter and donned Arun's jacket before sitting down at the computer and vanishing behind the counter.

Nicholas knew Cosmo was in the hotel. Even though he had been informed that someone was coming for him, he wouldn't leave. He would, however, have doubled his security and would rely on the hotel's additional security to protect him. But Cosmo Reed did not know *who* was coming for him, which would be the advantage Nicholas had on his side. The first element known to man—the underrated element of surprise.

He went through the bookings, looking for a single group that would require multiple rooms at once, likely taking up an entire wing of the building. There were two of them. On the fourth floor, the entire left-wing had been taken by a Mr. Youssef, and a Ms. Leslie booked another on the seventh floor. Nothing under the name Reed, but that was expected. Nicholas knew Cosmo would never pay for the rooms in a way that could be traced back to him. Youssef seemed like the most likely one, with one of his guards handling the funds and paying under his name.

Nicholas stood gracefully and walked away from the counter, noticing something heavy in the jacket pocket, which he now wore over his suit. Inside, he found four hundred dollars in cash, a pack of mint gum, and a can of hairspray. Nicholas returned everything to his pockets and entered the elevator, keeping his head low. As he exited on the fourth floor, he looked to the right, using the chrome reflection of a no-smoking sign to check out the side that had been paid for by Youssef.

A single Seminole employee stood by the door, tapping away at his phone. Nicholas took a corridor to his left and walked up the stairs until he found an abandoned steel bucket and some ice in a room marked for personnel. He took it and walked backward, heading for the room. As he approached, the man by the door looked up at him, then the steel bucket, before opening the door and letting him in wordlessly.

Behind the doors were nearly thirty people, ranging from Americans to Middle Eastern. Both men and women, all drinking and dancing horribly to the music playing out of hidden speakers. There were drinks everywhere, and men and women snuck off into the adjoining rooms. In the center of the small hall was a Middle Eastern man, eating what looked like a cake, with a birthday cone-hat on his head. Nicholas stifled a laugh. Seeing a grown man who would have passed for a terrorist or some other stereotype having a birthday party in Tampa was one of the few things he hadn't expected to see.

"Yes, you. Over here! Bring the ice!" he called out to Nicholas, his accent and intoxication slurring his words.

Nicholas walked over to him, picked up the wine bottles, and slid them into the bucket. Apparently, Youssef was just a man who wanted to have a birthday party. Ms. Leslie must be the name Reed was hiding under. It made sense for him to use a female alias, throwing off suspicion even more. The birthday boy laughed and squeezed a hundred-dollar bill into Nicholas' chest before taking a huge swig of the bottle of wine.

He left the room abruptly, dumping the bucket and heading for the elevators; it parted as he pressed the button, and inside was a man in a suit. Nicholas kept his head low and away from the man's gaze, but he could tell from his posture that the man had a concealed weapon. Nicholas paused, allowing the man to pick which floor he was heading to. The man hit the sixth, and they began ascending.

"We're going to need some new sheets by evening on the sixth. Who do I need to talk to?"

Nicholas froze for a moment, thinking of the appropriate response, but his pause and refusal to look the man in the face gave him off. "I'm sorry, I didn't hear you, sir."

"I said we needed sheets. Where do I go to get them?"

"We have a laundry room; I could make the call and get someone to come up. The number is also on the phone inside the rooms. You could place a call from there."

"What's the number?" the man asked, his hand moving in Nicholas' peripheral vision, heading for his weapon. "I asked you a question!" his voice became more demanding.

Nicholas reached into his pocket, the one out of sight of the guard, who was now openly reaching for his gun. Both men pulled at the same time—the guard had his pistol, and Nicholas had the hairspray. With his free hand, he smacked the guard's arm with the gun to the side just as the gun went off in the enclosed space, rattling their eardrums.

Nicholas drove the butt of the steel can into the man's throat, causing him to gag and grab at his neck.

Nicholas sprayed the contents of the can at the guard's face, directly into his eyes, and the man fell backward, his gun falling from his grip. Nicholas picked it up and whipped it into the side of the man's head, knocking him out. He quickly searched the man, pulling out the small radio on his belt buckle and taking a pair of keys.

The elevator doors parted to reveal an older couple staring at both men in disbelief. Nicholas acted quickly. He pretended to talk into the walkie-talkie he took from the guard. "Command, we've got a man down in the east elevator, lock down the sixth floor. Over."

"What happened?" the older man asked.

"I can't tell you, sir, but I need you and your wife to head down and exit the building in an orderly fashion. It will be taken care of. Just get to safety, alright?"

They obliged, taking the elevator down after Nicholas pulled the body out. He put the jacket he had stolen from Arun over the guard and tucked the gun into the waistband of his suit, putting a piece of gum into his mouth. The harsh minty aroma filled his nostrils as he breathed and walked towards the door. He listened through it, hearing footsteps but not voices, realizing that the wing was noise-proof, just like the one on the other side of the hotel.

He had no way of knowing just how many people were in the room and couldn't risk charging in headfirst. If he did and were outnumbered, he would be gunned down before he'd be able to do anything. It was now or never. Nicholas opened the door and caught the attention of one guard.

"Hey, is this guy with you?" Nicholas asked before shutting the door and standing beside it.

The man opened the heavy mahogany door as he walked through. Nicholas shoved it backward, knocking the door into the man's head, knocking him out. He turned and ran, hearing footsteps rushing in behind him. Nicholas ran towards the stairs, knowing the elevator was a death trap. As he ran past it, he hit the button, calling it to open. As the men came charging out of the room, they saw the elevator doors close, so they took the stairs, with two peeling off to take the elevator. Nicholas ran down two flights of stairs before jumping over the banister, then holding himself flush with the wall.

The guards ran down to the next corridor. As they rounded the stairs, Nicholas pulled himself back up over the railing behind them. If they had looked up, they would have seen his shoes going over the top. He doubled back, heading towards the doors. As he got there, he spotted one man standing next to it and instantly looked away to hide his face.

"Hey, he doubled back! Did you see him? He came back this way!" Nicholas called out, looking backward over his shoulder.

"No, no one has come through. Wait, turn around—"

Nicholas was already close enough to land a right hook, punching the guy out of the way. He expected the blow to knock the guy out, but instead, he staggered to the side, grabbing his jaw. To Nicholas' surprise, the man ignored the weapon he carried and chose to attack with his bare hands. He caught Nicholas around his legs, lifting him off his feet and driving him into a nearby wall. The man returned the initial blow, hitting him across the face before grabbing his neck with both hands, cutting off his airflow.

He knew he had just a few moments before he passed out and a few more before he would be dead. Nicholas reached down and grabbed the gun, firing through the waistband three times. The man fell limp on top of him, dousing his shirt with blood. Nicholas shoved him off and checked his pulse, confirming that the man was dead. He took the man's gun, pulling out the magazine and tossing it to the left end of the corridor before he turned back to the door.

He opened it just enough to hear the blast of a shotgun slamming into the wood from the other side. Nicholas moved away from the door, standing to the side as the man behind fired another round. He took the hairspray can and rolled it into the room, then fired twice at it. The contents inside quickly erupted, burning small hairs on the hands of both men. Nicholas jumped first and tackled the man to the ground.

He pulled the shotgun free from the man's hands and drove the butt of the gun into his face before he turned the barrel back at the shooter. The smoke cleared enough for Nicholas to recognize the shooter as the man he came for. On the ground below him was the former captain of the police department where he had worked decades ago, Cosmo Reed.

"Carter?"

"Cosmo, you're a hard man to reach these days. You won't mind if we had a little discussion in private? There are a few things I've been meaning to ask you."

The gun smashed into his skull again, knocking him out. Nicholas went back to the door, locking them in. He had gotten to Cosmo. The issue now would be getting what he needed to know out of the man. Nicholas had only a few moments before the door would be smashed in, and the place would be full of police officers and security personnel.

He took a cup half-filled with brandy and splashed a bit of it over Cosmo, jerking the man awake. In the brief time, he was unconscious, Nicholas had restrained him with duct tape, rendering him immobile. Cosmo tried to shriek, but his words were muted by the tape over his lips. He appeared to be in a storage room, with Nicholas being the only other person in it. His captor dumped the rest of the drink on Cosmo, ignoring the man's pleas.

"I'm going to ask just once, and I want a detailed and truthful answer. Otherwise..." Nicholas pulled out a cigarette and lit it, holding the lighter towards Cosmo's face. "Governor Sanders. Details."

Chapter Thirty Seven

Stories are powerful tools. They share something that has been vital to all of mankind since the beginning: information. Our early ancestors told stories about their adventures while hunting for food in the wilderness or their interactions with other people. They use stories to teach their young how to cook, what to eat, and what to fear. Even today, stories of the boogieman are still used to terrorize naughty children. The power of story-telling is, many times, overlooked...

Tonya sighed and rubbed her temples, staring at the laptop in front of her. The cursor flashed expectantly, waiting for her to input the next letters. It blinked in and out of the screen as though it was taunting her, daring her to keep writing. She looked at the sides of the monitor and noticed the margins were off. With a heavy sigh, she shut the laptop and lowered her head to the desk, wondering why her music wasn't drowning out the outside world as she had expected. Pushing the earphone cord out of the way, she stared at her phone and saw she'd missed a text while she worked.

She swiped up on the lock screen, opening the text message that was a simple, *Come see me today* from her mother. Tonya visited her mother a few months before when she was in the area pursuing a story. It had only been for a day, but she loved the moments she spent with her mother. Tonya made a conscious effort to call every week, regardless of how much work she was drowning in.

After college, Tonya went into communications and soon after got a job at Bay News 9. Her persistence and excellent writing skills ensured she always got her scoop. In a few years, she had gone from a measly intern to a top reporter who her peers highly respected. She'd led some of her colleagues to uncover a story about the kidnapping and selling of children into sexual trafficking run by the Bay area and the theft of a small bag of diamonds worth over four million dollars.

Tonya didn't just find the stories; sometimes, she made them. Writing pieces that got thousands of views and responses—one making headlines as her outspoken nature got her a response from the secretary of state, commending her work. She worked nine hours a day, and while she absolutely enjoyed her work, it could sometimes feel like hell, especially on the slow days where she had to wait for a lead or sift through paperwork. She was working on a new piece, and it had fallen flat to her, coming off as a bit too stoic.

"You ever think that you might just be walking over to the elevator, bump into some nerd with glasses who drops the books in his hands, help him pick them up, and five hours later, he's back at your place with you, drinking tequila and laughing at your jokes while asking you what you looked like under your work clothes and layers of fatigue induced by this job?"

Tonya smiled before looking up at her friend and owner of the next-door cubicle, Francine. She was a burly woman with deep brown eyes that resonated with her strict "I will bite you if you step on my toes" demeanor. Francine waved her black curly hair to the side before peering down over the cubicle wall at Tonya, eyebrows raised.

"What did you do last night, Francine?" Tonya asked, laughing.

"Oh, you don't want to know," she replied with a smirk.

"Dear Lord, this woman. Did you even know who he was? Did you use protection?" Tonya looked over her shoulders. "Was he cute, and has he called?"

Francine threw her head back, laughing heartily. Tonya chuckled too, then noticed the cup of coffee on her table that had gone cold. She put it to her lips, taking a sip of the dark liquid. She regretted it instantly and swallowed heavily, trying to hide the pained look on her face. It had been nine in the morning when she got the coffee—the current time on her phone read four pm. Francine giggled at her before sliding back down to her seat.

"For real though, sister, you've been working your ass off for months now. When was the last time you got some pipe? There's literally a bomb-ass selection of clerks downstairs, and I'm sure you've noticed the looks. Go for Clyde, the skinny one. You know how it is. If they got no meat on their bones, the meat is the bone."

"Thanks, but I'll pass. Besides, there's too much work to do. Come on, I can't start some relationship now, especially not a workplace relationship. They always end up with one person being fucked up."

"That was one time, T. Don't play me like that, come on."

"Just saying. Besides, that literally can't happen to me today. I have to go see my mom."

"How's she holding up? It's been what, three months? She doesn't come around here anymore. I miss her stories about your annoying ass growing up."

"What I haven't missed is her being on my ass about a boyfriend. I swear, if that's the reason she's asking me to come home, I will go to the adoption clinic myself. Like, I get that you want grandkids, but calm down. I want to do my thing a little."

"You're twenty-eight," Francine said matter-of-factly.

"And you're turning thirty in a month," Tonya shot back.

"But I'm black, and can get myself a baby daddy in a week if I wanted, so own it, sister."

Both women laughed, catching themselves as their voices climbed a bit louder than they should. In her peripheral vision, Francine spotted the editor-in-chief scurrying towards them. The woman had her glasses balanced so precariously across the bridge of her nose. A small nudge would be enough to send them flying, just like her temper.

Tonya and Francine turned back to their desks, pretending to be engrossed in whatever it was they were working on. But they were too late—the older woman spotted them. She shuffled across the floor, moving silently, with her face etched into a constant look of disappointment. Everyone had to learn early on to ignore the look and do their job or lose morale and quit. Tonya was the first to get a peppering by the editor. One thing Tonya couldn't get over was how much the woman's voice would constrict when she was stressed, and today, she was extremely stressed, so her voice came out in a squeak.

"Carter, I expected your paper on my table this afternoon. Why haven't you sent it?"

"Oh, well," Tonya stifled a laugh. "The paper is almost ready, but the printer ran out of ink. I sent for someone to get some, that's what I'm waiting for. It'll be on your desk the moment the ink is put back in this good old desk jet." Tonya smiled wryly, hoping the woman would bite. She did and turned her attention to Francine.

"And you?"

"Nah, it ain't done."

Tonya burst out laughing, using her hands to cover her mouth. Francine didn't care about lying; she had never worked well under pressure. The woman was a maverick, never listening to anyone and doing what she wanted. In every single case where she went against what she was told, it had turned out that she had the better intuition, and Francine would rub it in the faces of everyone who had tried to force her into doing something else. But that didn't stop the editor from unleashing her fury on her, just because she could.

"Francine Jones, I hope you understand what exactly it is we do here? It's not some place where you can do what you want when you want. For this organization to work, every single one of us has to put in our best. You keep slacking off like this, and I'll have no choice but to reconsider your position here. I understand that you've done good work, but it's no excuse for you to act out like this. I'm watching you. You have until noon tomorrow to have it ready. You too, Carter."

Both women watched the editor walk away noiselessly—perhaps she wore rubber-soled shoes. Francine rolled her eyes and sat back in her chair, sighing to herself, but just loud enough for her friend to hear. "Well, now I know I won't be sleeping early."

"Sorry, I have to work on these opening paragraphs, and I should be done. I just can't work on it now. I'm exhausted, or should I say coffee-deprived."

"Girl, I bet the reason you ain't seen a man is because you're probably too drunk on that stuff. You drink it black and complain that it tastes bad. Who are you trying to kill?"

"Go away." Tonya laughed, her mind heading back to the first time she tried coffee. Her mother had taken her to see a shrink. While the adults talked, Tonya spotted it in a mug, its soft aroma wafting into her nostrils, calling to her tenderly. It was black, strong, and tasted bad. But Tonya instantly felt a connection to it. It tasted like her, bitter yet strong.

As she grew, she had tried other combinations, but nothing had worked out for her as much as black did.

"You leaving?"

"Yeah, I have to if I want to get to my mom's and be able to make it back to my place tonight." Both women instinctively looked at the large clock on the wall; it had the loudest tick Tonya had ever heard. Everyone agreed that they could hear it as they worked, a loud reminder in the back of their mind that time was money, and it would keep counting on them, literally. There was talk about the clock being so bothersome that a man with OCD had quit after being overly discomforted by it.

"You know she's going to kill you for clocking out early," said Francine.

"Which is why I won't. You'll help me out. Thanks," Tonya replied, picking up her purse and pushing the essentials into it haphazardly.

"No way, Na-uh. I'm not doing that shit again," Francine protested, but Tonya was already halfway down the corridor, smiling to herself as her colleague looked over the cubicle in time to see her leave.

Tonya walked out into the lazy evening sun that blanketed the building's entrance steps in a beautiful golden yellow. Hundreds of photos were taken there every day, making an amazing backdrop for all kinds of shots. She got into her car, considering going home for a shower before heading over to her mom's place; she still had a bed in the house and could spend a night there. But Tonya quickly halted the idea formulating in her head.

As much as she would love to stay with her mother, it would hurt in the long run. The house was a full hour away from where Tonya worked, and the morning commute would be horrible.

Also, she knew that seeing her mother would stop her from making the decisions she needed to. She wouldn't do her work. Instead, she'd begin doing chores around the house, like she normally would have when she was a lot younger. She couldn't bring herself to leave her mother alone most times, and she knew she'd be unsuccessful if she tried. She had been Tonya's rock during the most trying periods of her life, times when she needed her family, and a major part of that family wasn't there. She had held Tonya steady, guiding her through the difficult times with unrelenting perseverance that Tonya had come to feel entirely indebted to.

She took the highway, heading along the path the navigation app said would leave her with the least traffic. The streets had changed—the roads were different, and many of the families that lived there were new. Tonya parked behind the same fire hydrant her father had used to on Sundays, just before they would go to church. Tonya smiled as she remembered herself and her brother running out of the house towards the vehicle, trying to get into the front seat first.

As she sat smiling, the front door of the house opened, and Tonya spotted a face she hadn't seen in much longer than just a few months. It had many features similar to hers, with the same dark brown hair as herself and her father's and a sharp smile that could brighten anyone's day with ease. Shanice had grown into a beautiful young woman over the years and was in college, pursuing her medical career. Shanice's face erupted into a smile as she crossed the driveway to her sister.

"How's my favorite doctor doing?"

Shanice's eyebrow arched in mock surprise. "You have another?"

They hugged tightly before giving each other a once-over. "Where's Mom?" Shanice asked.

"She's not home?"

"No, she texted me to come to see her. I thought she was home. Came back, and it was locked. I used my key to get in. Let's go call her,"

As they walked into the house, the sound of another vehicle came from down the street, one which both women recognized as their mother's. She barreled out of the car, crashing into both her daughters with a long hug; Tonya watched her closely, trying to get a good look at her.

After Nicholas had left, their mother had taken on the role of both parents. The sheer weight of taking care of three children had left her with loads of stress, and worse still, her husband's disappearance had broken her. She never admitted it, but she was shattered. She began smoking and drinking herself to sleep at night. Tonya would stay up with her during those nights, unable to bring any peace, as she sought the peace. In the end, she had gotten some help for her depression, but Shanice and Tonya could see it in her eyes.

Her voice was full of life, but her eyes were the pathway to the hollow emptiness of her heart.

"You girls are a sight for sore eyes. I know it's not my birthday, or Facebook would have told me. Why are you here? You should have called before coming. I would have gotten more food."

"Wait, you didn't know we were coming?" Tonya asked.

"No," she replied, looking back and forth between her daughters.

"You texted me to come to see you," Tonya added, showing the text to her mother. As they peered at the screen, another text popped in.

*Look up.

Standing by the only window in the attic, holding her mother's phone, was the only boy Tonya had ever truly cared about, the same person who had taught Shanice self-defense. Thaddeus peered down at them, grinning. His plan had worked better than he expected. Shanice let out a scream, dashing into the house and running up the stairs to collapse into her brother.

There were hugs all around. Thaddeus had snuck into the house and taken their mother's phone after she went to pick up food. Then he texted his sisters to come home, bringing everyone together as he wanted. Shanice and Tonya fired questions at Thaddeus, who responded with a smile, realizing how much he had missed his siblings. Their mother watched her children through teary eyes, feeling the weight of all she had done through the years coming off her shoulders. She had a beautiful family, one she was especially proud of and loved with every part of her being.

"Why didn't you tell us?" Tonya almost screamed, shoving Thaddeus.

"Then it wouldn't be a surprise, now would it?"

"But we can't stay!" Shanice cried. "I have a test tomorrow that I can't miss. I have to head back today!"

"Me too, well, not a test. But I can't stay either. Let's reschedule because we definitely have to celebrate. I should be free by Friday evening. Shan?"

"Yeah, I'll be free too. If I'm not, I'll find a way around it. My brother is home!"

"Is it true?" Momma asked. "Are you home?"

"Yes, I've done all I can on that front, so I came back here to serve my city."

Chapter
Thirty Eight

Cyrus' health did not improve; if anything, it got worse. His body would grow extremely hot and then become cold. His eyes would pale and then fill with redness. There was nothing she could do—nothing she *knew* how to do. Ebony cried way too often, but that was futile, and she prayed, but her words were minced with anger. *If God had allowed him, given him this nameless illness that could not let him live, would the same God answer her prayer and remove the strange plague?*

For a few days, he seemed to be getting better. His temperature was normal, he talked a bit, and his eyes twinkled when he smiled. On Sunday, three days after his supposed recovery, he passed away.

Ebony got home from working at the store and found him lying lifeless on the bed, his eyes closed in eternal rest. And he looked peaceful, as though he was sleeping. For two hours, no tears had come. An emptiness swirled inside of her that she could not express; it just sat there in the pit of her stomach. She smiled. Cyrus would wake up at any moment and tell her he felt better. Then she would peel some oranges for him and tell him about her day. When Cyrus did not wake up, she went on peeling the oranges and telling him about her day, anyway. She left the oranges on a tray beside him, and she sat there until morning came, writhing in an agony she had never known before.

His funeral was simple. Their mother was there, but only briefly; also, there was a neighbor and a doctor who had previously looked over Cyrus. Towards the end, Dr. Gilbert showed up, and he looked twice his age. His eyes were sunken and low. Ebony embraced him and said quietly, "It's not your fault." And she truly did not blame him. Cyrus would likely have passed on much sooner if it hadn't been for him.

* * *

In all her life, Ebony had never felt so alone. She met Thaddeus in Oak Lawn Cemetery one Friday evening when she was paying her respect to the departed, and it was as if they were destined to be together. Maybe it was because she was in the midst of a desperate time in her life, or maybe he was sent by God, but she had connected with him on a deep, personal level. He told her of his time in the army, and she told him everything. It was like she was waiting for him her whole life.

Ebony had no idea if he was only a temporary way to ease her grief, but she looked forward to her meetings with him. He had the most beautiful brown eyes she had ever seen, and he made her laugh so hard that sometimes, she forgot she was ever sad. Some nights, they snuck away to a beach house where they watched the moon cast on the surface of a glassy river. Other nights, they danced in The Castle or listened to music. Their bond tightened quickly, and she told him things she had never shared with anyone. All the while, she kept telling herself that misery needs company because it excused how much she needed *him*.

Her mother had been the first to notice the signs. The extra weight, the recent fatigue, her eyes, her swollen feet.

"You're pregnant," she stated.

Ebony had only found out two days earlier when an extra line had popped up on the pregnancy strip test. She bit her lip and said, "Yes."

Of all the things she had expected, it was not the light that twinkled in her mother's eyes or the smile that stretched her lips. "So, you finally came to your senses. Have you told Mr. Toliver that you'd be having his baby?"

Ebony's belly filled with disgust as her realization dawned on her. "He's not the father."

The smile on her face slowly vanished and was replaced with a sneer. Her eyes stopped twinkling and filled with deep-seated hate. When she spoke, her voice was venomous, heavy with disgust and rage.

"You stupid whore," she said, a cigarette pressed between her fingers, and she stormed out.

Ebony knew her time had come to leave.

Chapter
Thirty Nine

Ebony Houston's Diary.
June 12th

I don't know if I'm making a mistake with Thaddeus Carter. My mother hardly even talks to me lately, not that I care much, but I can't help but wonder if there is something she sees that perhaps I do not? Does she think that Thaddeus is not the right man for me?

Hell, why am I even thinking this? It's not like she makes the best choices herself when picking partners. She chose a drug addict and gangster to be the one she lies in bed with and tells all her secrets to, and that's definitely not the kind of person I want to take relationship— or any—advice from.

I would rather make the mistakes on my own and learn from them than have them facilitated by that crazy woman (Lord, forgive me, I know you don't like it when children disobey their parents, but you of all people should know if you have the kind of scrutiny you are perceived to have, that she has not been doing such a great job of being a parent recently. She has not been doing a great job at being anything aside from a pain in the butt, and I just wish... I just wish that you would take her life?

No. No. That would be murder on my conscience. I'm sure you know what's best for her.)

Do you know what's best for me, also? Do you have some genius plan in store for me that I do not yet see? Cause I've been dying to know where my future is headed and not just my future but also the present. Where all of this is taking me to, 'cause I get fucking tired sometimes. I get tired of holding my breath underwater, waiting for some miracle or an answer to come.

Do you know what my mother said when she found out that I had turned down Mr. Toliver's offer? She told me that I was a fool. And it did not just stop there. The next day, when she saw me having oatmeal for breakfast, she said that I was a bigger fool, and then she gave the most sadistic laugh I had ever heard, and it was laced with bitterness. I was angry, drained of appetite, and felt slightly miserable. And then her boyfriend walked in, drunk and laughing.

Nico was all forms of crazy, but they were fit for each other, so I really was not going to tell her that I thought her boyfriend was crazy like I did not tell her about the time he had touched my breast and begged to have sex with me. Do you even know how fucked up that is? If he were not my mother's boyfriend (which is not even on the list of reasons he disgusted me terribly), I would have still turned him down.

For the life of me, I cannot imagine his hot stinking breath on me, nor can I imagine the taste of alcohol on his tongue, his rotten hands on my face... No. Those are not thoughts I want to write down now or thoughts I want to tell anyone. My mother can keep on fooling herself with him. I would not interfere in their matter.

But he came into the kitchen that day and laughed at me, too. Laughed so hard that I could see his rotten tongue, surrounded by cigarette-charred teeth. If I had leaned in a bit closer to him, I would have probably dropped dead from the stench that surrounded him.

"You know you're really stupid," he said, wagging his finger at me. "You know who Lucas Toliver is? You know who tha' mutha is? He's not your average man, is what you should know. Who goes 'round turning down an offer from God himself? Who spits away sugar?"

"Diabetic people," I said drily.

He laughed. "Some sorta joke to you, is it, 'bony? Some sort of fucking joke to you, is it? You could have made us rich, you know that? You could make us rich."

I couldn't help but notice that he was using 'us' that he had included himself in the family, and it filled me with greater disgust. He is such a bastard, that Nico.

"If I were you, I would go back and accept the kind man's generosity."

"Well, you're not me, and that's a fact, so why don't you shut the hell up and move out of here? Don't you have better things to do with your time? Well, if you don't, I do. So, if you don't mind..."

I did not finish the sentence when Nico started towards me with an angry blaze in his eyes. An anger that I knew would lead to something ugly, so I grabbed a small knife from the cutlery rack, waiting for him to do whatever he was going to do. Then my mother stormed into the kitchen, holding her lighter. Nico was only inches away from me.

"What's going on here?"

Nico paused, his left hand folded in a fist in the air and my knife aimed at his belly, and the both of us had stared at each other with so much hate flowing in our eyes, and then he turned to leave, smiling, and shaking his head. A gesture that read: You're lucky.

And mother stared at me—even after seeing the scene with her own eyes—and it was an angry, hateful glare. Both of them could burn in hell for all I cared.

They could call me stupid and act like I had made a mistake, but Thaddeus Carter walking into my life is not a mistake, and the way I feel about him is not a mistake.

I know deep within me that it was predestined, and I do not care what anyone else has to say about it.

* * *

**June 20th*

Thaddeus took me to a little river today outside of town. I don't know the name of the river or if it is even inside of Tampa, but it was so beautiful. And Thaddeus was there holding my hand all through as though he was scared that I would get carried away by the waves or something of the sort. I felt like laughing, and I felt so... Oh, diary, I felt so safe and really happy. So happy that I don't even believe I deserve to be that happy. When last have I been that happy?

Since junior high, when my crush back then, Dexter, told me that he loved me, too? Or when I got an A in a subject I had anticipated totally failing? Or the one time when Cyrus told me about a girl he thought he was beginning to develop feelings for? Maybe then. Because nothing made me as happy as seeing Cyrus happy, and boy, I wish you could see the light in his eyes as he spoke of her.

The way they glistened. Like two precious stones buried in his irises, the way his lips stretched into the most beautiful smile. Yes, that made me so happy. And then, Cyrus told me about the first time he had fallen sick in school and was admitted into the school medical facility, and the girl had designed a get-well-soon card for him.

He said she drew little roses around the corner and designed them with a blue and pink glitter pen, and as he talked about it that day in his sickbed after Doctor Gilbert had just finished checking on him, he was unable to keep the emotions out of his voice. I felt so happy then. It was the same kind of happiness that I felt as I sat beside Thaddeus, watched it grow larger—if that was even possible—as he held my hand and told me his little stories.

"Growing up wasn't so easy for me," he said, barely smiling. He stared straight into the river as he spoke, as though there was some sort of answer on the glassy surface which reflected the sunny horizon. Two flamingos were floating on it, side by side, undisturbed, as though they were lovers sneaking off to a location known only to them.

One dipped its head into the river, and when it raised it back up, there was a ring of leaves hanging over it. The flamingo did not shake it off. It swam gracefully with its partner, and I called that one with the leaves over its head, the female flamingo and the bald one, the male flamingo.

"What do you think? They're off to get wed?"

"That's a thought," I laughed and turned to him. "You were going to tell me about your childhood?"

"Yes." He stopped and looked at me like he had just remembered something. "Would you like to meet my family? I've told you about my sisters."

There was such hope in his eyes, such desire that I would agree to his invitation, and I couldn't bring myself to say no. I found that you could hardly refuse a man like Thaddeus Carter; the man was irresistible when he wanted to be.

When Thaddeus told me about his father, I was so sad for him. I wanted to talk to him about it, but deep down, I did not know if he was willing to face his past again, and I did not want to pry. What if it still hurts to think about his father? What if he blamed himself for everything that happened even though it was obviously not his fault?

When he talks about Jacob, his childhood friend, the one whose grave he had been visiting on the day we met, I can hear the guilt in his voice. I know that he blames himself for what happened to him, and as much as I know it was not his fault, I do not want to keep telling him that. I want him to outgrow the guilt as the years go by, to discover for himself that it was, in no way, his fault.

And I keep finding out that in more ways than I would like to admit to these pages, that Thaddeus is not in my life by coincidence. It was fated

Last week, I received a letter from Lucas Toliver. I did not read it. I did not need to. What could he possibly have to say that I would want to read or even know? The man is a shameless, ruthless, and brutal beast, and as far as I am concerned, I want nothing, absolutely nothing, to do with him!

Showing up at his house was a huge mistake, one that I would not repeat for the life of me. I shredded it into tiny pieces and threw it down the street on my way to work so that there was no way that mother would catch wind of the situation.

Yesterday, another letter came. And just as I was about ripping it to shreds right in front of the man who had delivered the message, he warned me that it had something to do with my boyfriend, Thaddeus

Carter. Or rather, something that would happen to him if I did not read the letter and reply.

The letter asked me to meet him at the park so we could have a small chat and talk things out. He promised to offer me help—whatever help I needed, and while I was sincerely moved by that sort of chivalry and had a little fear for what my response would mean for Thaddeus, I told the stoic-looking man that I had no intentions of meeting with his boss. He staggered for a moment as though he was waiting for a different kind of reply, but then he left.

This morning I met with Thaddeus. He took me for lunch at Stoney's bar, and we had a good time. No, it was always magical each time that I was with him. I kissed him after lunch, and on our way home, at the last minute, he booked a room in a small motel, and we made love for two long hours.

It was beautiful! I've only been with one man before Thaddeus, but he is like nothing I have ever known. When he makes love... he is demanding and giving with equal fervor. He is passionate and rough. He is kind and savage. He switches up the tempo each time, and I have never felt the way he makes me feel.

I would never really tell anyone this, but I love how he makes me feel like a woman, making me feel wanted. We make love all the time. After work, during our weekend getaways, whenever we meet. It's always amazing.

He makes me forget my grief.

* * *

August 3rd
Thaddeus doesn't know that I'm pregnant, and I don't know if I should tell him. I mean, I know that I should, but what would he say? I don't

even know if he's ready to become a father. No, I don't think he is. Who would be? Things are moving too fast. Mother has already noticed that I am carrying a child—and hates me for it, as much as I don't care—but I'm starting to wonder how long it would take for the rest of the world to notice? For Thaddeus to notice. What would he think?

Oh my God, I feel like I am going out of my mind, and I just need to breathe. The letters keep coming, too. Mr. Toliver is restless; everyone knows that about him. He would stop at nothing to make me accept him, and I would stop at nothing to stay as far away from him as I possibly can.

Maybe I see it now. I did not see it before, but maybe I do now. I don't know if I have the heart to do this, but I'll have to. For Thaddeus' sake and for mine. What we have is beautiful, and though I have never admitted it before, I care for him in a way I have never cared for anyone else. Which is why I must do this.

I love him and always will.

What I want to do might hurt him—would definitely hurt me—but then I do not want to know the odds if I did not go through with this plan.

I can't believe I won't even get to say goodbye to him.

* * *

*August 29th

I did not run away. I could not run away, from him, from any of it. I stood by the train station with my ticket in my hands, immobilized, frozen. And an old lady walked past me with her luggage and asked if I was not getting on. A young boy told me the train would soon be leaving. Another old woman asked if I was lost. I was. But I could not tell her this.

Tears began to fall from my eyes in slow progression as though it was a practiced march, and then my belly began to ache, and everything began to spin in front of me. I held on to the rail for support, but I might as well have been holding onto a straw. I had never felt so devastated all my life. I was stuck between two roads.

If I chose to leave, to leave this man whom I had already fallen deeply, and irrevocably in love with, and everything behind, then a new life would be waiting for me at the end of that train. A new life for me... and the child in my womb. I was not sure if I was ready for that. To do this all alone. Thaddeus still did not know that I was pregnant by him, nor did he know that I was planning to run away.

If I did run away, it would be the best thing... wouldn't it? The letters would stop coming, and I would not have to put Thaddeus in such an awkward situation of making him want to choose what he wanted when it was obvious it wasn't... well, this. And what if he wanted me to do an abortion? I can't possibly do that!

So, I stood there in front of the train as it filled up, and I took no notice of the world around me.

"Why don't you go home, dearie?" A voice said, accompanied by a hand around my quivering shoulders. I did not want to fight it off. I needed comfort. But what is home? To the terrible shack where my mom puts up with her good-for-nothing boyfriend?

The only home I ever want has Thaddeus in it.

So, I go home. To the construction site where I know Thaddeus spends most of his afternoons for now. The pay is fair. And I break the news to him in front of a dozen workers, all dirty, sweaty under the sun. But it was extra hot in there because of the heat from the equipment, like a fucking sauna!

And Thaddeus lifts me right in front of everyone, happier than I have ever seen him, his brown eyes twinkling like far-off stars, and he kisses me. We get a loud applause from the men.

Later, we go to Yuri's Corner and have celebratory drinks to enjoy the news, the men from the construction site, Thaddeus, and I.
"I thought you'd be mad," I lean in to whisper.

Thaddeus laughs, pulls me closer to him, and kisses the tears off my cheeks.
"You make me the happiest man alive."

He later takes me home and introduces me to his family. He has the most beautiful family ever! They are such wonderful people. Tonya hugs me as soon as Thaddeus introduces me to her, and she's laughing. She rubs my cheeks and speaks to me as if she has known me her entire life. My God. Could this really be happening? She acts like we are best friends and keeps mentioning how we will have a lot of fun together in the years to come, and she gives a strict warning to her brother that he should not do anything to hurt me, and we all laugh.

I trust Thaddeus never to hurt me.

Shanice is beautiful and young, and perhaps, shy? She doesn't talk much when she sees me. She just stares at me in this interrogating kind of way... I don't know, but she stares at me somehow, a dry smile on her face. And then she tells me that she hopes I'd be great for her brother. I guess she doesn't like me, but Thaddeus later tells me that Shanice is usually skeptical of people, especially when they are strangers to her, and I relax. With time, he said, she'll come around.
"You don't have to go back home, you know? Stay with me. We'll get married, raise a beautiful family, we'll be happy—"
"Yes." I cut him off with a kiss.

At that moment, I did not know if I said yes to running away, or marrying him, or being happy, but now, as I write this, with tears of joy rolling down my eyes, I realize that it is neither of those, per sé.

What I'm really saying yes to is Thaddeus Carter.

Chapter
Forty

When Brielle was born, Thaddeus held her in his arms—his baby—and he had never felt such joy before. It was like he was a whole new person. He saw himself in every single yawn, in every stretch, in every giggle... Oh Lord, when she giggled, a part of him came alive that he didn't even know existed.

"You give me so much joy, sweetie," he said to her one evening, rocking her to sleep. She curled her tiny baby fingers around his beard as though she understood what he said. Everyone who held her commented on how beautiful her eyes were. They were neither brown like his nor black like her mother's; instead, they had taken on a greyish shade, which Thaddeus could not explain.

Her eyelashes were long, dark, luscious hairs framing those glittery pebbles. He could hold her in his arms all night, sing to her, dance for her and with her, and not feel an ounce of fatigue. He loved Ebony, and he loved her with all his heart; but this... this was a kind of love that he could not describe or categorize, a kind of love that he had never felt before.

He looked at her, and most times, almost broke into tears. She was so pretty, and she was his daughter. And to think that Ebony had thought of not telling him about *his* daughter. He would not have been able to live with himself if he found out sometime in the future that he had such a beautiful daughter and that she was away from him.

When he wasn't working at the office, he spent time with Brielle at home, talking to her, playing games with her. She was still a baby, but she heard all the things that he said to her, and when she liked them, she giggled; when she did not, she gave a soft purr-like sound.

Brielle became even more beautiful as she grew. She had long, sleek, curly brown hair, and her eyes grew in sharp contrast to it. The dimples in her cheeks deepened, and Brielle laughed a lot—she was such a pretty sight when she laughed.

One day, his mother and Shanice visited them in their apartment. Brielle was just three years old.

"Mama!" Ebony yelled when she saw Mrs. Carter's car pull up in the driveway.

Sarah Carter was aging, but she still looked beautiful and younger than her age in a flowing yellow gown and black, three-inch stiletto heels. She never saw her mother-in-law as a heels kind of person, but it had given a certain flair to her steps.

"Hi, Ebony!" She grinned and drew her daughter-in-law into a hug that lasted for a long minute. Ebony inhaled the scent of fenugreek and aloe vera off Momma's hair.

"You grow more beautiful each time that I see you!"

"I could say the same about you, Momma. You make me look forward to growing old." They laughed, and then she saw someone else.

"Shanice!"

"Hi, sister!"

Shanice looked absolutely ravishing in a pink tank top and slim-fit denim jeans. Her hair was braided into cornrows, and Ebony noticed her nose piercing.

"My God, you look so beautiful."

"You don't look so terrible yourself."

"Is that a compliment?"

"Nah, it's obvious I'm the most beautiful woman here. I'm just tryna be modest."

"Modest, my ass." Ebony laughed. "Come on in, come on in."

She held the door open for them and helped Momma with her bag. Whatever Momma was carrying in such a huge bag were probably gifts for Brielle.

"And where's my little angel?" Shanice asked, settling on the brown sofa.

"Aren't you even going to ask where your brother is first?"
It was Thaddeus, appearing behind a curtain.

"I don't give a damn about you." But she rushed into his open embrace and gave him a hearty kiss on both cheeks.

"I've missed you, baby sister."

"Oh, damn you, you're still the asshole," she groaned, and he broke into laughter. She hated being called "baby sister," and he knew it.

Brielle was upstairs in her room, scribbling away with her crayon in her coloring room. Thaddeus served them chips and dip while Ebony went to call her down. Brielle had to be restrained from running so she didn't trip down the stairs. She was just as excited to see her grandmother and aunt as they were to see her—perhaps even more excited.

"Grandma!" Brielle jumped on top of her, and Ebony shrieked as everyone else laughed. Ebony was scared she would break a bone, but Momma assured her that she wasn't *that* old and her bones were still quite strong.

Shanice talked about school life and the hurdles she was going through to get her degree. There was a name that kept popping up in her stories—Brandon Sturgeon—and Ebony made a mental note to ask her about him later. Her eyes were filled with glitter as she spoke but sparkled even more when she mentioned his name. Ebony knew there had to be something more to it, even though she was willing to bet that Shanice would deny it if she *did* ask about him. Shanice was the kind of person who kept things to herself until she had arrived at a particular level of certainty.

They played a game of Monopoly later—Ebony won one round, and Momma won the second round. Thaddeus knew that his wife would not let him hear the last of it, so he was going to challenge her to another game when they had more free time.

It was evening, and Momma had just finished her tenth story, but everyone's attention was still held captive. No one was ever bored when Momma was telling a story—she was a natural.

"I think I must have seen your father last week," she said. It was already evening, and Brielle was asleep in her arms, exhausted from all the jumping around and activities.

Thaddeus tried to keep a straight face. From the lack of expression on Shanice's face, he could tell that she had probably already told her.

"Where?" he asked coolly, careful not to let anything slip in his voice. Even after all these years, he could not decide what to feel.

"He was outside the hospital. I mean, I *think* it was him, but I can't exactly be sure. I just wanted you to know... I don't know. I have the feeling that he might be around. I don't know if I'm ready to face him yet." Her voice was smaller, unsteady.

Ebony offered her water, and she reached out and took it with pale hands.

***

Some months later, Shanice called Ebony, and her voice was unsteady as she spoke; she was crying.

"What's wrong?" Ebony asked, alarm rising inside of her. "Just tell me, Shanice, talk to me, please. What happened? Is it something with school? Something with..." Ebony had run out of guesses. She was just hoping that Shanice would open up to her.

Shanice agreed to meet her at a breakfast café next to her street in thirty minutes. When she arrived, she wore a white cotton gown, no makeup, and her eyes looked red and swollen.

"He's getting engaged." She broke the news suddenly and without ado, falling into her sister-in-law's embrace.

Ebony was going to ask who, but she didn't really need to ask the question to know that it was the guy whom she had spoken about in her stories. Shanice sat in silence. Ebony assured her that it may not seem like it now, but she was going to be fine in the end; she *had* to be fine. Tonya was hardly around lately, so she told Shanice that she could always visit if she needed a shoulder to lean on.

Shanice visited often after that, whenever Ebony was around. They would play games together, have heart-to-heart conversations, and exchange skincare tips. Thaddeus was often at work, fighting to reduce the crime rate. Shanice was fun to be with, and she helped a lot with the chores, especially when Ebony fell sick and had to take a leave from work.

Ebony didn't know what was wrong with her; she didn't feel much like herself. She was always tired and easily nauseated and had suffered a fever some days back. Shanice advised her to go to the hospital, which Ebony did. After she was evaluated, Dr. Frontier gave her the results a week later, smiling broadly at her.

"Congratulations, Mrs. Carter. You're expecting a baby."

There was a big celebration when Jonathan was born. Thaddeus had a son. Momma invited many of her friends, who invited a lot of their friends and made for a merry party.

Jonathan had barely begun talking when his sister, Augusta, was born. Ebony announced with a laugh that she was not having any more children.

Two years later, after Thaddeus picked up some pictures from the photographer, he stared at one for a long while before he finally hung it on the wall—high above Brielle's reach. In some recesses of his mind, he was still being shaped by his childhood and could hear Tonya's voice saying that it was a bad omen for a family portrait to get broken.

He didn't know if she still thought that way, and he wasn't a superstitious sort of man, but he was not willing to take any chances.

Chapter
Forty One

"No, Mom. I don't want to learn how to play the keyboard when I get older. I want to be a drummer like old Geoffrey in the church that plays for the choir," Jonathan said with a small frown on his face. Ebony looked back at her son and smiled. He was so beautiful, even with those little frown lines drawn across his forehead. Such a wonderful child. She was going to scold him, but then she had forgotten what she was going to say when she saw the pout on his face.

"You want to be a drummer?" Ebony poured soap on her hands, transferred the lather on the sponge, then onto the white ceramic, cleaning both sides before dropping it in water for rinsing.

"Yes, I want to be a drummer," Jonathan said, smiling with pride.

Brielle was playing with some peculiar-shaped toys with magnetic backs that stuck to the fridge. Three of them had gone missing in the last month, and she could never seem to leave them alone.

"Let him be, Mom. I'm sure he'll change his mind soon. Last year, he wanted to be an astronaut, and now he wants to be a doctor."

"That's right." Ebony giggled. "Maybe next year he'll decide to be an artist."

"Or a circus clown."

"Hey! That's not fair. And I still want to be an astronaut. Because I *can* be an astronaut and a doctor at the same time, right?"

Ebony and Brielle both laughed.

"No, son. I'm afraid that's not possible."

"But Reverend Cook said it in church on Sunday that nothing was—*is* impossible, and then you nodded your head and said 'Hallelujah.' You agreed to it."

"Yes, but—there are some things that are just outrageous, wouldn't you agree?"

"What's outrageous?"

"Crazy, looney."

"Thank you, Brielle."

"So, things like wanting to be an astronaut and a doctor is outrageous?"

"Well, it is quite crazy when you think of it, isn't it? Let me tell you how it works—how I *think* it works. When you're a doctor, you'd be busy every minute of the day saving people. You might get a call at two am, in the middle of the night, saying that your attention is desperately needed, and someone may be dying. So, you do what you must. You have to sacrifice your precious wee hours and get to work— by two am!"

Ebony paused, studying their faces. "That's how dedicated you have to be if you want to be a doctor. You have to put your service to your job first, before your own self. Now, tell me. If you're doing a job that gives you barely enough time to take care of yourself, what time would you have to do another entirely different unrelated job, huh? None. And that's why I say it'd be impossible to be those two things at the same time."

Jonathan didn't interrupt her. He listened with rapt attention, and when she was done, he said stubbornly, "That's not what Daddy said."

Ebony paused, amused. "You told your father already?"
"Yes."
"Well, what *did* he say?"
"He said that I can be anything that I wanted to be if I really wanted."
"Of course." His mother smiled. "You know what? You can. But why don't we have this conversation when you're much older, huh? We'll discuss everything about who you want to be and how many jobs you would like to have, and if you still want to be an astronaut or a doctor, or an astronaut *and* a doctor. Is that okay?"
"Sure," he said, nodding. "Sure, we'll talk about it when I'm a big boy. But... I don't want to learn to play keyboard!"
"And why not?"
"Because it's too boring! I told you, there are a million other instruments to learn. I'll learn the drums first, and then the violin and then the saxophone, but not the keyboard. Brielle is learning the keyboard already."
"Yeah, but I don't see the problem if you and your sister play the same instruments."
"Maybe, but I don't want to."
"I don't want you near my keyboard, either," Brielle chimed in.
"Don't start, you two. And where's Augusta?"
"She's upstairs watching one of those boring cartoons like always. I don't see how anyone enjoys those crappy things!"
"What if I told you, you enjoyed the same 'crappy' cartoons when you were young like her?"

Jonathan laughed. "That can't be true."

"But it is true. Why don't you ask your father when he's back, or ask your grandma whenever you see her?"

"Yes! But when do we get to see Grandma again? I miss her so much, Mommy. Can we go see her this weekend? Please? Please?"

"I don't know about that. You know I don't like you leaving when you still have homework to do."

"But, Mommy, I promise I can do it before leaving. I *will* do it all before leaving."

"We'll see about that then."

"Yes!" they both cried.

"That isn't a yes, yet. But neither is it a no."

"Oh, at least you're thinking about it," Brielle said, twirling around in her pink knee-length dress.

"Yes, I'm thinking about it. Would be nice to see your aunt, Shanice, too. I haven't seen her in a while."

"Mommy?"

"Yeah?"

"Is Aunt Tonya getting married?"

"What?" she laughed. "Where did you get such an idea?"

Brielle shrugged as though she had asked just about anything: *when was the pizza delivery guy arriving? How many hours were in a day? Who's the president of America?*

"My friend says he sees her on the internet, posting pictures with a guy."

"Your friend is on the internet?"

"Oh, he isn't. But his older brother is. So, he uses his phone when his brother falls asleep."

"And how does your friend know your aunt?"

"I showed him a family photo we took last Christmas. And there's the last name, Mom. Did you forget?"

"No, of course not."

"So? You didn't answer the question. Is she getting married to that man?"

"His name is Tim, darling. You can stop calling him 'that man.' And I don't know, Brielle, but they are engaged."

"Does that mean they'll get married?"

"I hope so. See, when you are engaged, it's simply a promise that you want to marry that person, and if things go well and nobody changes their minds, then comes marriage."

"Oh. So, when Daddy wanted to marry you, he had to engage you first?"

"That's right, baby. He engaged me first before marrying me."

"Did you want to marry him?" The question came from Jonathan.

"If she didn't, then you wouldn't have been born, silly."

"I wasn't even talking to you."

Ebony tried to hide her laughter.

"Then that means that Aunt Tonya would marry the man who engaged her then?"

She wanted to say that sometimes things don't go according to plan, that something bad might happen, and the engaged couple might end up not getting married, but she just nodded.

"I can't wait to be the flower girl!"

"And I can't wait to be the bellboy!"

"Whose wedding is it?" said Thaddeus, sneaking into the kitchen.

"Daddy!" They both turned and ran to him.

Thaddeus had a hard time deciding who he was going to lift and spin around first. But he chose Brielle, laughing and kissing her on her forehead as he lifted her. When he sat her down, he picked up Jonathan and repeated the process.

"And where's the last musketeer?"

"Augusta's upstairs watching cartoons."

"If she's not busy turning the room into a circus ground by now."

Ebony hung the pots and frying pan and closed the oven door. Then she walked over to her husband to welcome him.

"Hello, sweetie. You're back early today."

"Didn't think it would be such a bad idea to spend some extra time with the family now, eh?" He grinned and hugged her, kissing her on both cheeks. "Let me go see what that adorable devil is up to."

"You better. Before she sets the house on fire. I'll be busy fixing up dinner. Make sure you get a shower, too!" she called after him. "You smell like something took a piss on you."

"Thank you very much, my darling wife! That's such a comforting thing to say."

"You're welcome!" she responded, grinning.

The kids followed Thaddeus upstairs, leaving her alone in the kitchen. She felt a little betrayed, but the bright side was that she wouldn't have to answer silly questions every five minutes. Finally, some peace and quiet. She giggled to herself, knowing somewhere deep within her that she would not change this for anything in the world.

At the last minute, Thaddeus suggested they go out for dinner instead, and she was grateful for it. She was too busy in the kitchen to start cooking, and when she *was* done with her work, she was too tired to start whipping up anything. Once again, he came to her aid. She loved and appreciated how he always knew when she needed some help.

They had dinner at The Eight Club, a small restaurant on the south of town, famous for its French wine and pepper soups. But they weren't there to have pepper soups—the kids, especially Jonathan, couldn't handle peppers. Instead, they had spaghetti and meatballs with garlic sauce and apple pie.

There was always someone singing, and that is what Ebony found most inviting about the restaurant. She loved music. It was either someone playing the organ or a beautiful siren on the dais, swaying from one side to the other.

This one was dressed in a full, sequined black gown, her lips covered in black lipstick; her hair, in a long, fuzzy, brown afro, fell down the sides of her neck. She was singing a song by Mariah Carey, whose title Ebony could not remember until she got to the chorus. It was *Angel's Cry*.

"You remember this song, don't you?"

"Of course," Thaddeus said with a wince. He once had a friend who had his heart broken by a girl whom he had sworn to give everything to—no, that wasn't quite right. He had his heart broken by a girl to whom he *had* given everything, including his two estates, money, and everything he owned.

Thaddeus never knew the full story because it was too painful for Edward to talk about, but the song soon became something of a comfort to the broken man. He would play it every single day until it began to get on Thaddeus' nerves, and he ended up hating the song.

"Are you okay?"

He laughed and took a slice of pie. "Yes, it was just a memory."

They got back home an hour later, stuffed and tired but happy. Thaddeus said something about a case that he was working on and how he might have to leave home very early the following morning.

"You're working so hard lately," Ebony said, massaging his shoulders.

He loved the way her hands worked; it was like she had been a professional masseuse at some point in her life, but he knew she hadn't.

"A lot's going on in the office lately."

"Today was good."

"Yeah, I'm glad you liked it."

"Do this again soon?"

"I suppose so. I mean, if I get the time to, then I suppose it's fine, right?"

"You're always saying that these days. I know that your job is important to you and that you have big cases you're working on, but, babe," she paused and turned to face him. "I feel like you don't spend enough time with us, with your family. I mean, when was the last time we went to see a movie? Or went to an exhibit?"

He groaned. "You know how much I hate those exhibits."

"I know, but you also have to admit that we don't get to spend a lot of time together lately. And the kids need their father around more, you know? Babe, look. I know it's hard for you, but you need to find a balance in all of this. For me, for the kids... for you. I miss you and our little games and the times we spend together. I know you need your job to support us and because you, well, love it... but I'm sure you get my point, don't you?"

"Of course," he said with a thoughtful sigh. "Of course, I understand what you're trying to say. I'm sorry if it feels like I don't get to spend enough time with you guys. I want you to know that you're all that really matters, babe. You're all I have, the reason I do all of this, and I love you very much. I don't want you ever to forget that. You're what comes first regardless of how swayed up I might be with my job."

"Yes. Yes, I understand," she said quietly.

For some reason, Thaddeus was thinking about his father now. Hadn't he started out this way, too? He was always busy in one case or the other and hardly ever had time to be home with his family. And when he did come home, he was short-tempered, easily triggered, and angry about one thing or another from work. This was the exact way he started, and, as much as he was related to the man, Thaddeus wanted nothing to do with the way he turned out in the end.

He didn't want any of that for himself. He wanted to grow old with his wife and children, telling them how much he loved them every day. Eventually, he knew he would have to find some sort of balance because he wasn't giving his family the attention they needed.

He wanted to be there for her at all times, but there was just so much activity going on all the time, and he couldn't find a way to make everything pan out as he wanted. There was going to be some way that he could do it; there *had* to be. But for now, he was confused.

"Penny for your thoughts?" Ebony said, touching his shoulder.

He smiled. "Just thinking you're the most beautiful woman ever and how lucky I am to have you in my life and as the mother of my kids."

Whether or not the lie had sold, he didn't know, but she smiled and kissed him. Then they made love with wild, unrestrained passion.

The next day was a Saturday, so she didn't have to bother getting up early for work or getting the kids ready for school. But when she woke up, Thaddeus was already gone.

Chapter
Forty Two

The sun's rays poured in through the east window of the room, bathing Tonya in the soft yellow colors of morning. She rolled over in the bed, letting out a breath and suddenly becoming aware of the hand wrapped around her waist. For a second, she was alarmed but relaxed as she remembered. Her boyfriend—no, her fiancé. Tonya still couldn't believe it, nor had she gotten used to waking up with someone else in her bed. Even when she shared a room with Shanice, Tonya had always gotten a bed to herself. But at that moment, she wanted the bed shared; she loved that it was, and she loved the man behind her.

"Morning, baby," Tonya spoke in a soft voice, one she didn't know she had until she met him.

His name was Tim, simple and ever-loving Tim. He looked at her, his lips turning up in a dreamy smile that she found dorky yet mesmerizing.

He stared at Tonya for a moment, turning her body, so she was face to face with him. His finger crawled up her arm, pulling her hair away from her face. His thumb trailed her lips for a moment before stopping at her chin and pulling her face closer to his.

"Morning, love." He kissed her on the lips, full and hard in a way that ignited the dormant emotions Tonya kept hidden. Her hand crept up into his curly hair, pulling the face of the man she was engaged to closer to her. Their tongues met, exploding with passion and a flagrant disregard for breathing. All that mattered was that they fed off each other, a thirst filled with lust that was never quelled. Tonya allowed the clip-buttons of her nightdress to slip off as she became one with him.

As the sun found its way behind a cloud, Tonya returned to bed, full of exhaustion and a feeling of heaven. Her face was flushed, and her cheeks hurt from smiling. Tim planted kisses on her body—the small of her neck, behind her ear, on her lips. He kissed her without a lack of resolve, determined to cover every inch of her torso with his lips. Tonya giggled as he got to her hands, kissing the back of her palm softly.

"It's alright, I get it, Tim. You love me!" she laughed, trying to pull her arm away.

"Are you sure?" he asked, his brown eyes big and glaring as he stared at her maniacally. She knew what was coming next and began to pull away. "I need you to be certain," Tim continued in a high-pitched, animated voice, dragging her hands towards him as she tried to fight him off.

"No, leave me alone! You're crazy." Tonya laughed, managing to break free and roll towards the edge of the bed. He caught her with a single arm before she was able to escape, dragging her back into his embrace, smothering her neck with more kisses.

"I am Count Dracula, and I will suck your blood... without teeth," Tim spoke in a mock accent, breathing heavily down her neck.

"Get off me!" Tonya grabbed his arm from behind, twisting a few fingers till he let go. Then she dropped off the bed, allowing her feet to reach the floor, ran around the corner of the bed behind Tim, and grabbed him in a full nelson. She licked the back of his ear, playfully, before speaking into it. "Well, Dracula, say hello to Drusilla. You're mine."

"Drusilla? No way."

"Yup, all seven seasons of it."

"It's like you find ways to make me fall in love with you every single day."

Tonya kissed him, slowly and passionately, before pulling away and putting on her pajamas. She laughed at the look of disappointment on his face before she turned and shuffled down the stairs. Tonya took her toothbrush and went to work, pausing as she stared at herself in the mirror and broke out into a laugh. Tonya never dreamed she would be married; it was too surreal to her.

Since her father left when she was young, Tonya had thrown herself into what was expected of her. Schoolwork and chores at home, taking care of Thaddeus and Shanice. Tonya felt a need to step up and fill her father's shoes who wasn't there—a father whose absence she blamed herself for. For a long time, Tonya thought that relationships were always destined to end badly. But she denounced her previous assumptions when she met Tim. It was five years in the making, right after the day she had been forced to flirt with a random person downstairs.

She met Tim in the elevator, and, in the time it took the steel box to get to the bottom floor, Tonya was sold. His hazel brown eyes were his most distinct feature, one she couldn't get enough of. She felt the radiation each time his eyes were on her. Tim had taken his time, coming on as a friend at first, one who was just the right amount of flirtatious. He was always there, giving her the attention she wanted, and after that, the love that she desired.

"I was going to make breakfast in bed, but you woke up before me!" Tim called from upstairs, making her laugh. "If you think about it, we sort of already had breakfast."

That was another thing she loved about him. Tim was willing to do anything to see her smile. On one occasion, she had caught him telling a joke to himself just before he said it to her.

"Just don't go into the kitchen. You'll kill us all. I'm going to make breakfast!"

"I'm making toast, want some?" he asked.

By the time Tonya made it out of the shower, two slices were left on a plate with some mayo on the side. She frowned; she had been trying to avoid mayo for some time. Tim stretched out an arm and took a slice off the plate, sticking it in his mouth. He smiled at her and grabbed her phone, holding it up in her face as he chewed. She reached out for it, but Tim pulled away, keeping it out of her reach. She hugged him, reaching out for his arm as he stretched away until both collapsed under each other's weight, throwing the last slice of bread on the floor.

"Now, whose fault is that?"

"Mostly yours. I just wanted you to kiss me for the phone, but you just had to go and feel entitled, didn't you, T?"

That was what Tim had begun calling her on their first "date." It came with his dorky awkwardness that Tonya found ridiculous and adorable. He had dressed loosely so that it wouldn't seem like an official date, but then he had brought a rose and told her she looked beautiful more than once. Since then, the name has stuck.

"It's my phone. If anyone is going to feel entitled, it's *me*." Tonya snatched the phone from one hand and the rest of the toast from the other. She walked over to the kitchen counter and pulled out a box of cereal; the box was full, unlike the half-eaten one she had left after her previous bowl. "Did you eat my cereal?"

"Did I do what?" Tim asked, doing his best to feign being distracted by something out the window.

"I had... never mind."

She flicked open the lock screen on her phone and saw that she had two missed calls from work. They came in during her morning "routine" with her fiancé. Tonya smiled, biting her lip as she was hit with the thought again. Even saying "my fiancé" to herself sounded so foreign, yet that had become her reality. The calls had been from Francine; she hit redial.

"Hellooo, Missus," Francine spoke in an excited tone, her voice pitching in exaggeration.

"What do you want, Francine?" Tonya asked with a laugh.

"What I want is to know if pretty-boy is looking to have some fun the night of his bachelor party because I know a good spot!"

"Stop it; I'm off today. Why are you calling from the office?"

"Because it's office stuff. You got a delivery. It's very shady—no names, no tags, nothing. Just a small envelope with your name on it. The delivery guy said he got it from the mail and was called to pick it up. Whatever it is, it's real damn important love." The sound of pages turning crinkled through the line.

"What do you think it is?"

"I got no idea, but either you come down here to find out what this story is, or I'm ripping it open myself. Also, once you're on your way here, let me know."

"Why?"

"So I can go over there and rip Timmy-boy open!"

"Francine!"

"Bye, babe."

"Thought you were off today," Tim spoke from behind Tonya, doing his best to hide the disappointment in his tone. She had promised him that they would stay home all day and only leave the house together if it were important. Tim was an engineer at the solar power station and finally got a day off that coincided with Tonya's. He wanted nothing more than to spend it with her, but apparently, the news was never satisfied. There was always a story to catch, breaking news at each turn.

"Babe, I know. Just give me thirty minutes, and I'll be back. I just need to get the story. Someone sent it to me, and it could be something big. Thirty minutes tops."

"I don't like tops." He grabbed Tonya's shoulders and pulled her in for a kiss. She let herself feel it down to her toes, breathing slowly before she blinked rapidly, pulling herself away. "Dammit. Almost made you forget."

"Don't get too cocky. I'll be back soon, alright? How about I get a season of Buffy on my way home? We could binge-watch all night?"

"We both know we won't get past five episodes."

"Six, we do six."

Tonya quickly put on a blazer, then paused, looking at the piece of clothing. She hadn't bought it, but it was clearly feminine, so it didn't belong to Tim. She was about to ask him when she remembered Ebony gifted it to her a few days prior. Tonya couldn't believe the pace at which life was moving. It was like something happened with every turn of the page, but while she was there for every one of them, she couldn't grasp how quickly the time went by. Which was another reason she was happy finally to have someone in her life.

She started the car and pulled out of the driveway, turning on the radio. She immediately noticed the country music playing; it was Tim's preference, proof he had been in the car at some point. Tonya loved those little moments where she found random things pertaining to the man she loved. They were often things that made her laugh, but occasionally he would leave the toothpaste cap open and offer a teary, puppy-dog face as an apology.

She got to the office building and bounded up the stairs. The stairwell's reflective steel surface served as a mirror for her to do one final check of her hair before she stepped into the office. She got a few nods from her coworkers, people who knew her personally, and those who knew her from her achievements. She smiled and nodded back, hurrying to her desk. It would be quick—grab the folder, look at its contents, and then store them for when she was back at the office and ready to work.

"I see that glow girl. Work that strut!" Francine screamed from behind her before covering her mouth with her hands and looking around embarrassingly. "Sorry, guys."

"I will kill you one of these days, Francine. I swear to God."
"Shut up and tell me how it went down. I want all the juicy details. Come on, tell me."

"Later. I just want the file." Tonya looked at her desk, expecting to find it in the center.

"Where is it?"

"At my desk for safekeeping, duh." Francine pulled open her drawer, giving Tonya a moment to see into the bottom, a moment she could not take back. Francine looked up at her. "Hey, you got your boy-toy, I got mine. Except mine fits in a drawer. Here we go."

Tonya took the envelope and pulled the small thread seal from the lip, yanking it open. She stared inside but found it empty. She cast a glance at a confused Francine before turning the envelope over and shaking it. A single piece of paper fell out, slightly bigger than her thumb. On one side, "Call me" was written, and on the other side was a phone number.

"Okay, this should be interesting," Francine said as she walked around the wooden board that separated both their desks, coming over to Tonya's station to sit and listen. Tonya pulled out her cell phone and dialed the number. It rang for fifteen seconds before disconnecting. She was moments from hitting redial when her phone rang, the call coming in from a different and unknown number. She picked up and held the device to her ear for a few moments, listening to see if she could hear anything. When Tonya didn't, she spoke.

"Hello?"

"Hello, is this Ms. Tonya Carter?"

"This is her. Who am I speaking to?"

"A man who would like his anonymity to be maintained. I have a story for you. One, I'm certain your job wouldn't be able to pass on."

"I'm listening."

"Oh, not here. Not over the phone—too many people could be listening in to our calls. There's a restaurant on the corner of 4th and Lincoln, a really nice place with the best tea in America. Come alone, or there is no deal."

"How do I know that I can trust you?"

"We're meeting in a public place, but still, you shouldn't trust me or anything. What you should trust is the story I have for you. It's about your father."

Chapter
Forty Three

"This one is very beautiful, ma'am, and it would look just perfect on you. Would you like to try it out?" The lady with the light French accent, Fiona, asked Shanice. She ran her fingers over the blue floral gown hanging on the pole. It had ruffles in front, small, tiny stones pressed into the neckline, and drawstrings around the waist.

"The necklace you selected earlier would suit it perfectly, don't you think? There, you can go into that little room and change. You'll look fabulous!"

Fiona was a short, animated woman with blonde hair, large eyes, and full, red lips that Shanice knew were natural because of how many times she had licked them already. A rather awkward habit, she thought. Fiona had said the word "fabulous" four times already, jumping up and clapping when she thought something looked nice. Shanice liked her;

she was a kind and lovely woman, and her gestures were nothing short of hilarious.

The woman was right, Shanice thought as she changed and looked at herself in the mirror. She looked absolutely stunning in the dress; it complimented her eyes and the small butterfly necklace she picked out from the jewelry section. The necklace came with two small gold studs and a hairpin that could also be used as a brooch.

"Excellent! You look magnificent in this. Don't tell me you're not going to take it. It would be a pity to put it down."

"She's right," a customer in another aisle said. She was pushing a baby in a stroller. "You look great in it. Almost like it was made for you."

Shanice smiled and looked at the gown again, nervously. "It does look nice. How much is it?"

"Oh, you don't have to worry about that."
"What? Why not?"

"The kind gentleman over there has already paid for everything. All you have to do is pick what you want."

Shanice followed her finger's direction, and when she saw who the woman was pointing at, she froze in her steps. Her throat dried as she clutched the sides of the dress, which had already been paid for by the *kind gentleman*. He smiled at her and waved, but Shanice did neither.

Instead, she stood there, her knuckles growing white and her heartbeat erratic as she stared back at him. Fiona said something in that high-pitched voice of hers that sounded like a bird's squeal, but Shanice didn't hear the words. All she could focus on was the man standing at the other end of the store; his hands were thrust in his pockets, and a cheesy grin overtook his face.

She turned and stormed towards the exit, still wearing the dress he had paid for. Fiona was begging her to come back, but she ignored her until the gentleman stopped her as he met her at the door.

"Shanice," he said, holding her hand atop the door handle. She took hard, unsteady breaths, aware that her eyes were growing teary, and her hands were shaking. She hated that she was incapable of controlling how she felt and how she wore those emotions on her sleeve.

"Please, I saw you when you walked into the store. I was just parked by the sidewalk, waiting for—" he paused, changing his mind at the last minute. "I was waiting for someone when I saw you walk in. What's going on, Shanice? You just sort of... vanished." He gave a nervous chuckle and looked at his watch as though he was late for something.

That's good, Shanice thought. She wouldn't have to put up with him for more than a few minutes. She felt sick and lightheaded all of a sudden. How on God's green earth was she supposed to talk to him now? She looked at him, and her stomach churned all over again.

"Can we go somewhere and talk? For a little while?" he added desperately.

She looked away into the busy street, where a boy was dragging around a paper kite, and a little girl was plucking purple orchids from the sidewalk. Her gaze landed on an old man sitting on a bench, reading the day's news. For a moment, she thought of her father.

He had enjoyed reading the newspaper every single morning. Sometimes he would even tip the newspaper delivery guy when he had some change to spare. When he became extremely occupied with his job, of course, his reading habit was affected. Most days, he would barely even touch the paper, and it would end up stacked beside all the books on his shelf.

Brandon cleared his throat, reminding her of his presence.

She looked at him and nodded slowly, with a smile that appeared from nowhere and was shocking to both of them.

He drove her to a nice restaurant that she had never been to before. In her anxiety, she did not even look at the name, but she knew it was the sort of place where even a glass of water would cost an arm and a leg.

The interior was mostly white, with ornaments of gold, and a touch of bright red, lilac, and blue from the flowers inside the vases that lined the walls.

Classical music was played from a far corner by a man wearing a funny-shaped hat. The workers were dressed in blue dress shirts and black trousers.

"It's been a while. How have you been? *Where* have you been?"

"Around," she said, intently watching the servers carry food from one table to the other.

Brandon nodded, observing how much she had changed since the last time he saw her. She seemed to have added a few pounds, which suited her, and was wearing makeup, something she rarely did before.

"How is she?"

"Who?"

"Your fiancé."

He sighed and leaned back in his chair. "I'm sorry you had to find out the way you did. I didn't mean to hurt you. I didn't think it *would* hurt you. You never told me—" he broke off and called a waiter to take their order.

She wanted scotch. Just scotch.

"So how are things?" she asked again, eager to know, despite herself.

"We broke off the engagement."

Somehow, Shanice wasn't shocked to hear this. And somewhere, in the deeper recesses of her mind, she wondered *why* she was not surprised. She could not find the words to respond to him until several heavy seconds later.

"Why?"

"Because she got engaged to someone else."

"I see." She took a surreptitious glance at his finger and found that it was void of any ring.

They finished their drinks in awkward silence. Then he made a joke, and she laughed, and it managed to break the ice between them.

Two hours later, they were making out in the backseat of his Mercedes when he got a call from his director.

"Are you free this weekend?"

"Are you?"

He kissed her, and they had a date.

Chapter
Forty Four

Sarah walked down the aisle, picking out groceries. She pushed the cart with her hip as she considered what type of shrimp to get. She wanted to invite Thaddeus and his family over for the weekend and planned to make a big meal for the five of them. Her lips curled as she felt a bit of pride in herself. She had raised the perfect children and had become a grandmother. Sarah put in the more expensive option, hoping that it wasn't one of those premium purchases that weren't worth the price. She looked for her friend but gave up and moved on when she didn't appear.

"Hey, wait for me."

She turned to see Candice heading towards her. The once fiery red hair had become a dull grey that flowed quite gracefully. Candice was Sarah's oldest friend and a woman she was willing to give her life for—

in the same way Candice had sacrificed herself to save Sarah's life a long time ago.

Candice's arms expertly rolled the wheels of her chair as she moved towards her friend with a small cart in her lap. As always, there was a big smile on her face, though Sarah often couldn't understand how or where she found the strength to smile so much. By the time Candice woke from her coma, Sarah was married to Nicholas. But even then, she was unable to speak and was forced to stay strapped to her bed for a little over a year.

During the recovery process, she was able to get feeling back in her arms and regained most of her motor and speech control. The doctors had called for Sarah when Candice requested her, using a piece of paper and a pen. Sarah and Nicholas had rushed over to see a weak and shriveled woman in a wheelchair. Candice stared up at her friend and her husband, and after three and half years in a coma, her first sentence was, "Russian dolls are so full of themselves."

Even then, when she had just escaped the clutches of death, Candice found a reason to smile, and that was something Sarah needed desperately when Nicholas left. She would occasionally see her friend at the hospital, and Candice would give her the best comfort she could, join her in crying, and help her pick herself up. Sarah had no idea how she would have gotten through that period without Candice.

She had made a full recovery with no issues, except for the obvious, but even still, Candice did not want to be treated as less. She would often joke about being lazy because all she did was sit around all day.

"I thought you were leaving?" Sarah asked with a laugh.

"Look, the doctor has to go to work in a few hours, and I don't want to be left to rattle alone in that house. So, we're heading to yours. Haven't heard from Officer Thaddeus in a while, you know. I keep wondering if he could help me out with a ticket issue? I mean, not that I don't want to pay, but I don't usually have time when I'm driving."

"You can't drive, Candice." Sarah laughed, dropping a cabbage in the cart. "Look at the price on this. What's the world coming to?"

"Cabbage to garbage, eh? I know, I've been there. So, about the ticket..."

"You don't drive!"

Candice spun around in her wheelchair, dancing left and right as much as she could before rotating back to face her friend. "I don't know what? I'm a certified wheelie. Don't even try me."

Sarah laughed again, pushing her cart towards the registers while Candice followed close behind, chattering away about the cooling temperature. Winter was on its way, and everyone could feel the cold coming, but Candice seemed to be overly anxious about it, dressing up in sweaters in the middle of the still-warm day. Sarah helped her reach the top shelf for some deodorant on their way to check out.

"I know you're going to need help cooking."

Sarah looked at her friend as the man behind the counter scanned her items, the low beeping sound interrupting her thoughts. "Candice, you just want someone to talk to, huh? You left your husband, told him that I would take you home, and now you want to help me 'cook,' which we both know is code for, you just want to bother me today. Don't you?"

"Oh, come now. Are you saying I never helped you with cooking back at school?"

"We almost entirely ate out, all the time!" Sarah laughed.

"Yeah, but at least I helped," Candice added with a wink. "Plus, you honestly can't leave me here. I won't be able to get a taxi."

"I'll call you an Uber XL. Some things make life easy these days, hon."

"I'm certain some do." Candice placed her basket on the counter, and the man behind it went to work.

Sarah carried both bags to the minivan and dumped them in the back before going around to help Candice into the car. She folded up the wheelchair and put it on the back of the vehicle. As she got into the driver's seat, a little kid ran up to the window. He couldn't have been any older than fourteen. His brown hair and vibrant eyes reminded her of Thaddeus when he was young. She smiled at him before rolling down the window. "Hey, kid, where are your parents?"

"They let me go out on my own now. Uh, there's a man who wants to talk to you, ma'am. He says it's important."

Candice and Sarah looked over the boy's shoulder at the man sitting on the only bench in the vicinity. Even with his back turned, Sarah didn't have to look twice to recognize him. It was his distinctive pose, one which he couldn't undo, even after so many years. He'd always sat as though he was a minute away from leaving the chair, even if he wasn't.

"What's your name?" Sarah asked.

"Kenneth," the boy replied without missing a beat. "Kenneth Long. My friends call me Kenny."

"Kenny, look. See that man who spoke to you? If you ever see him, walk away. Don't talk to him, don't look at him. And if he comes close to you, tell your parents. You need to be careful about who you speak to. I know you're a big boy, but there are some really bad people out there, and you wouldn't want to get hurt now, would you?"

"No, ma'am."

"Good. Now head home."

The boy pushed off on his skateboard, rounding the corner and disappearing. Candice looked on, trying to understand what had just transpired, but it clicked when Sarah turned to face her. The man sitting on the bench was one she had not seen in almost two decades—her husband and a wanted fugitive of the law, Nicholas Carter.

* * *

Nicholas had done his best to stay away from his family. In his early days as a wanted man, he went back home one night, sneaking past the officers stationed out in front of his home. He got in through an open window in the garage and made his way into the living room. He had expected to find Sarah asleep in the bedroom, but instead, she was in the living room, a bottle of whiskey in hand and tears on her face.

It had been five weeks since he was charged with murder; five weeks since he had seen her. At that moment, he felt all the shame and anguish come rushing back to him. He wanted to apologize. He wanted to make things right with her, but before he could speak, Shanice appeared at the top of the stairs in her nightie, screaming his name with pure joy. Nicholas smiled, then realized that the officer outside had heard it.

He was forced to leave that night, and when he came back the next day, he saw they'd added additional men to keep a closer eye on the house. Men who Nicholas had worked with. It was as though Cosmo was doing everything in his power to make life as difficult for him as possible. Nicholas had to stay away from then on and spent his time living the life of a man on the run until he found a photo of Sarah.

He had kept it in his wallet—the same wallet that held his badge as an officer of the law. It was the only thing he had that could remind him of his wife. He would drop money off for Sarah to find, never leaving a note. But she knew it was him, because each time she saw it in the mail, she would hurry to the window and look outside, as though trying to find him.

Nicholas did not want to be found, at least not as he was. He had become a criminal, a man hated by the average individual—not the best look for his children. He wanted them to remember him as he had been, and the best way he could think of to make that happen was by leaving them with the impression of a father who loved them dearly. He was there in the crowd when Tonya and Thaddeus had gone to college. He had even sat next to Shanice the day she got into med school. She had been too young when he left to recognize him so many years later.

He watched his family, loving them as he always did. Nicholas would do anything to protect them, and that was why he had come back. Five years ago, he had spoken to Sarah for the first time in decades. It wasn't what he was expecting or why he wanted it, but it was something she had to know. A man he'd put away had escaped from prison. Nicholas didn't know if he were a target; he expected to be, as most criminals would want vengeance.

He knew that there was little chance that he would be found living life on the run, but the same couldn't be said for his family. Nicholas broke into the house that night, found Sarah asleep in the bedroom, and woke her. His words were heavy, full of regret, and so many unsaid things. But he held them back, knowing that it was too late. So much had happened, and the chance at a mended relationship was long gone out the window.

He instructed her to call the police and tell them that he had come to the house, knowing that Cosmo would send officers again. By the time they arrived, Nicholas was long gone. The police were there to arrest him, but Nicholas had drawn them there to protect his family. They stayed on the scene for nearly a month until they were called out. In that time, Cosmo had been promoted to the police commissioner, and Nicholas uncovered a plot to undermine the local election, one which a senator had sponsored.

Cosmo and the senator were both stripped of their positions. It caused the police to look closer into the family, but he had killed two birds with one stone from Nicholas' perspective. He'd gotten 24/7 surveillance for his family and had gotten rid of corruption within the police department. Deep down, Nicholas wanted nothing more than to look his family in the eyes and apologize to every one of them. Thaddeus had gone off to the army, and Nicholas had never been prouder; his boy had become a man, married, with children, and now even an officer, just like he had been.

Nicholas once considered visiting Thaddeus, hoping the boy he had deeply connected with all those years ago would somehow forgive him. But the night before Nicholas made his move, he had a dream so vivid, he was sure it was a vision of the future. Thaddeus was furious at him, blaming every bad thing that happened to them on Nicholas, threatening to kill him if he ever came back to the house. It was the worst nightmare Nicholas had ever had, and since then, he was somewhat shaky whenever he saw his son.

But in the end, the family was the one force he couldn't escape. After all the years he had spent away from them, yearning for his wife and children, Nicholas could not fight it anymore. Damn, whatever got in the way—all he wanted was to sit down with them one more time and make things right. But that would only happen if he could get through to his wife; if he could get Sarah to listen to him, then maybe she could reason with Tonya, Thaddeus, and Shanice. He watched as she stepped out of the vehicle and walked over to him.

He put the phone in his pocket and stood, turning to see Candice in the car. He smiled at her and waved but got no response. Sarah stopped a few feet from him, giving him a once over. His previously black hair had turned a fitting grey, and lines began to etch the corners of his eyes. It was the first time they had stood face to face in the open in what felt like ages. The wind blew silently around them as they stared at each other, Nicholas looking for the right words to say.

Sarah moved quickly towards him, her arm raised in the air, causing Nicholas to shut his eyes, waiting for the slap. Her arms wrapped around him in a tight embrace, one that almost made him fall. He was weak in the knees and unable to speak, so he kept quiet and hung on to his wife. The tears came, but he didn't fight them; instead, he took a step back, staring at her for another moment before he finally spoke.

"I'm sorry for everything, Sarah. I don't deserve your forgiveness, but I just wanted you to know that I'm sorry I wasn't there."

Chapter Forty Five

The man got out of the car and walked into the diner. He looked around anxiously but kept a prim smile on his face. Asking for a cup of coffee while he waited, he smiled at the waiter in a manner that would charm anyone. He looked good for his age and hoped he could still be a hit with the ladies. Jon smiled at himself on the table's reflective surface; it was his first date since he escaped prison. Although his date didn't know it, she was most certainly going to have a fun time.

He made sure every single woman he had ever gone out with had the time of their lives when he took them back to his place. Sadly, his old house had been seized and destroyed by the city while he was in jail. Jon had kept a low profile during his first three months on the outside. He played a game of cat and mouse with the police, usually evading them in the nick of time.

But after a while, he had gotten used to the game; it was like a dance that had to be practiced and perfected daily to ensure one had full mastery over it. He'd hardly had any issues with the police. Though he had been stopped for routine checks, he always had everything in order. License and registration, a working address—all the necessary details to prove that he was Flynn Osterman and not the man responsible for the deaths of several women.

He looked at his watch and noted the time. Six minutes left until she was late—plenty of time. He sipped on his coffee, thinking about how lucky she was. When Jon had gotten out of prison and finally faded under the police's radar, he put his plan in motion. The entire reason for his escape in the first place was vengeance on the man who had put him in that little corner of hell in the first place. The first thing he discovered was that Nicholas Carter, the officer who had stolen his life from him, had been charged with murder and went on the run. Just like Jon currently was.

It surprised him to no end. The man who had arrested him had become a fugitive himself. Jon spent months trying to find Nicholas, but the man didn't want to be found. One night, he had decided to draw him out. The cop had married her, the woman called Sarah. He remembered having lunch with her before it all went to shit. Then they joined in matrimonial bliss and even had three children for their efforts.

At first, he wanted to attack the house; burn it down with the hopes that one or two of them would die, bringing Nicholas to the surface. But Jon had to change his plans when he realized that the house where the Carter's lived was swarming with police vehicles for months on end. The cops were also looking to catch Nicholas, and Jon knew they would succeed if he weren't careful. So, he kept his distance, waiting and watching. It took five years, but he finally did it.

Tonya entered the diner, looking around for the man she was supposed to meet. Jon waved and got to his feet, allowing her to walk over to him. Jon saw the striking resemblance—a clever head held on strong shoulders, the straight to the point and no-nonsense attitude. She had his hair and eyes and a lot of his tenacity as well. He could have so much fun with her, but then Nicholas wouldn't know, and that was the whole point, wasn't it? He wanted more than anything for Nicholas to know exactly who he was and what he would do.

"Ms. Carter?"

"Yes, Mister... Anonymous?"

Jon smiled, pulling out a chair for her. "Please, I only choose to stay anonymous because, in this day and age, one can get canceled for doing just about anything. While I don't think an old-timer like me can be, I still won't take chances."

"Well, that sounds fair. Can we get right to it then?" Tonya asked, setting her purse on the table and pulling out her notepad. Jon knew that she had secretly started recording on her phone. He counted on it because he knew someone would listen to that recording, and hopefully, one of those people would be the man who had caused the waking nightmare he was trapped in.

"Nicholas Carter," Jon began ominously.

"My father."

"Yes, your father. You know, it's hard to see someone like him these days. I mean at the office. Very few policemen have the same gusto and resolve for truth and justice your father had. It was one of the few things I respected most about him."

"Were you an officer?"

"No, but he did work with me for a short period. In that time, I realized that I'd never known a better man." Jon took a sip of his coffee. "Where are my manners? What can I get you?"

"I'm fine, thanks. Already had breakfast. I just want to hear what you have."

"But this diner makes the finest steak and ribs in the entire state!"

"I'll come back to try it some other time." Tonya fired off, her voice bordering on irritation.

Jon smiled at her. There, in her eyes, was that fire he expected. The same one he'd seen in Nicholas.

"Something to drink then?"

Tonya gave in. She was trying to get back home as soon as possible, but whoever the man was, he had a story, one which was personal to her. She wasn't going to let it go. Tim would understand. She ordered a salad and a cup of water. Jon brightened up instantly, as though he really wanted to have lunch with her. He ordered a Reuben and a milkshake—not exactly what he would have preferred, but times had changed, and so did he.

They ate in silence, Tonya doing her best to ignore her phone while gulping the salad. Jon took his time, enjoying the food and savoring each flavor, only looking up occasionally to smile.

Tonya gave Jon a once-over. The man seemed around the same age as her father, maybe older. His hair was cut incredibly low, but she saw a few remaining strands of blond in the mass of white hairs. His face was weathered with time and had a light scarring just above his eyebrow. He must have been quite active during his younger days.

"Well, that was delightful, wouldn't you say?"

"It was really something." Tonya smiled, her lips pulled tightly together.

"Ms. Carter, I know I've taken up your time, and I'm terribly sorry about that. I'm old-school, as they say, and I would not feel like I've truly been a good host without dining with the people I've requested to see. Thank you for paying me that courtesy."

"The salad was lovely, thank you. Now that it's out of the way, you said you worked with my father." Tonya drew in a sharp breath. "Do you know where he is?"

"No, I don't. I'm sorry, I wish I did. However, it is about him. Your mother, too, around the time they first met. Did they ever tell you about it?"

"Well, only a little."

"I was there on the scene. Not when they first met, but when she helped him catch a criminal. You see, there was a man who had been abducting women and liberating them in his basement," Jon began.

"You mean mutilating and killing," Tonya added.

"Yes, that's what he called it. Your mother was a brave woman— the bravest I've ever seen. Did you know that she sat right across the table from him, just as you are now, and stared fearlessly at the man? A killer who knew no mercy. Sarah Carter is a true champion. I can't imagine what she went through. He tried taking her hostage. That's when Nicholas noticed it."

"Noticed what?"

"A flaw in his perfect plan. The man had a dead man's switch, but somehow, he had taken his finger off the trigger by mistake. I'm not sure what, but something tipped Nicholas off, and he knew there were broken splinters of a mop stick, not actual dynamite."

"Look, Mr... what do I call you?"

"Whatever you'd like," Jon replied with a smile.

"Are you just here to give me a history lesson? Because I'm sure if it were somehow important, I could have easily gotten the details from my mother."

"Oh, of course not, but I'm afraid that's all the time I have for now. I have to get going. Perhaps the same time this weekend?"

"I'm afraid I'll have to decline. I'm quite busy, and I can't just leave like that. I'm sorry. If you do have a story, you can call me,"

Tonya placed her card on the table. "Here's my card. Thank you for the salad."

She dropped two twenty-dollar bills on the table and stood, nodding at the man before walking out. Jon picked up the card and stared at it thoughtfully until she left. He watched her through the window and waited until she had gotten into her car before he paid the bill with the money she left on the table, telling the waiter to keep the change.

***

Tonya shook her head as she left the restaurant. The day had been a complete bust. The man was probably an old partner of her father's, looking to relive the "good ol' days" at her expense. She normally wouldn't mind too much, but she had taken too much time away from Tim. She jumped in her car, mulling over the mystery that was this man. He said he wasn't an officer, but he knew a lot about the case with Jon. Perhaps he was there? Or maybe he worked at the diner where everything went down.

Tonya sighed, starting her car. At least she had Tim and the rest of her now-happy family to look forward to. What had she wanted to get from him, anyway? She didn't care anymore; her father had left them. They'd grieved and taken the time to heal. They didn't need to go around opening old wounds.

Tonya was startled by the buzzing on her phone. She'd forgotten to stop recording when she left the restaurant. She paused the recording, answering the unknown number.

"Hello?"

"I said I had a story."

"Yes, and I appreciate you reaching out to me. I understand you did so because he was my father, and you felt it was best to tell me. Thank you."

"But that wasn't all I had to say, Tonya. There's more to the story."

"Perhaps another time," Tonya replied, moving to end the call. She heard him whisper something and put the phone back to her ear. "What?"

"The man from the story, the man who your father shot..." Jon said, trying to hide his excitement.

"He escaped from prison five years ago, I'm aware."

"Correct. You just had lunch with him, and he loved every moment of it."

Tonya hit the brakes, causing the car behind her to slam into her, throwing her face into the steering wheel, and her phone to the floor. She groaned as she sat up. She knew she was alright, but her heartbeat had tripled, and her breath hitched in her chest. Jon was a man she had been told about when she was much younger, a name sometimes used to scare Tonya and Thaddeus straight. It had always felt unreal to both of them, but Tonya had just unknowingly been sharing a meal with him.

She picked up her phone and saw the call had ended. She began scrolling through her contacts, forgetting she had Thaddeus on speed dial. As she did, the man who rear-ended her jogged over to her car and yanked the door open, trying to see if she was okay. But she wasn't. Tonya felt naked, like she had been put in a cage for everyone to gawk at.

"Tonya, what's up?"

"I just spoke to him. He's here! He was in the diner with me, but I didn't know it was him. He said he had a story, so I went there, and we ordered food, and we talked. I didn't know. He might still be in there, Thad. He might be there!"

"Slow down. What are you talking about? What's going on?"

"Jon, the man from prison! He found me... I..."

His voice tightened. *"Where are you?"*

"I'm not sure. My car... someone hit me after I left."

"Are you okay?" Thaddeus asked.

"Yes, I am. I... I'm just shaken up. Um... Seventh and Ford Avenue. There's a little restaurant or diner. That's where we were. He called me from there, and then I got hit." Tonya stepped out of the car, staring at the bewildered man who looked at her. Tonya was visibly shaking, holding herself up against the vehicle. "Oh, my God. He's here."

About a hundred meters from the crash site, Jon stood by the side of the road, a broad grin on his face as he watched the events transpire. He waved mockingly before he got into a silver Prius and drove away in the opposite direction.

"Tonya, go home. Now! I'm on my way."

"My car..."

"Leave it. Take a taxi, but not back to your place. Go to Mom's instead. I'm sending officers out, and they'll be there in a few minutes. I'm going to pick up Shanice myself and bring her there. Tell Momma what happened and wait for me." The line went dead, and Tonya felt limp.

Jon chuckled to himself as he drove off. He didn't know Tonya would be in an accident, and he hoped she wasn't too badly injured. From the look of things, she would be fine. She was aware now; the whole family would know he had returned. They might not know what he wanted yet, but he hoped it would be enough to bring Nicholas out of hiding. He would have no choice but to protect his family.

Chapter
Forty Six

Nicholas never got phone calls. He had six phone numbers, three of which were accessible to him at all times, along with an untraceable burner phone. He had gotten it after he exposed the senator and Cosmo Reed. While they were no longer viable political or societal figures, they still had enough sway to ensure that the man who ousted them would be pursued. Nicholas had kept up with both men's activities, making sure he stayed one step ahead of them at every turn. The senator had ordered a private investigator to find him, and Cosmo had gone as far as reaching out to a bounty hunter, but he was unable to pay the rates. The phone in Nicholas' pocket rang, causing him to panic for a moment before he relaxed. Only one person had that number.

He didn't need to recognize the number that called—it was most likely from an unregistered number anyway. He'd told Sarah everything she needed to know to reach out to him, and that was what she was doing. She was going to discuss their meeting with the rest of the family and listen to what they had to say before reaching back out to Nicholas with the results. Her call was sooner than expected, considering they'd only discussed it the day before, making him wonder if they had come to a unanimous conclusion.

He would understand if they decided they didn't want to see him again. He had defined their lives and had made it a horrible way to live in more ways than one. Nicholas told himself that he would have to make do with whatever their resolve was and agree to it. But he knew that it would break him. There would be no reason for him to continue running from the police if his own family no longer wanted him. He would say goodbye to Sarah and surrender himself.

The ringing stopped, and the line went dead. He counted to twenty before calling back, a little trick he had learned during his days on the police force; it would throw off any potential listeners. They would be unable to track either of them down, but hearing what they discussed was just as important as where they were. Sarah picked up on the third ring before speaking, "Hello, is this Burger King?" She asked in an eerily convincing voice.

"Yes, ma'am, what can I get you?"

As Sarah read out a short order, Nicholas stared at his watch. Once they were in the clear, he cut her off mid-sentence. "We're clear."

"Jon found Tonya, and she was in an accident. She's fine, but he invited her to have lunch with him. She went looking for a story, but it turned out to be him. They're here with me now. Shanice and Tonya. There are officers outside, so we are safe, but if Jon is lurking after all these years... why now?"

Nicholas remained silent as emotions flooded him. Guilt for putting his family in danger. Regret for leaving them. Anger for not being able to stop Jon from coming back into their lives. He stopped himself as he realized he was squeezing the phone a little too tightly and was a few seconds away from crushing the twenty-dollar piece of plastic. "It doesn't matter why. What matters is that he is caught. Where is Thaddeus?"

"Investigating with the police. They're trying to track him down. Tonya managed to get a partial reading of the plate and model of the car he was driving. If they find it, maybe they'll be able to catch him and put him away for good."

"No, they won't. It will be a rental, and the name registered to it would be fake. If he spent all those years hiding and waiting until now to act, it could be for a few reasons. Either he finally got all he needed to come for my family, or he's reaching out on a limb. Either way, he needs to be stopped. The microwave—check underneath it. There's a number there. That's the next one you should call."

"It's still yours?"

"Yes, I put it there. Sorry, but we need it now. Find out where the car was rented from and tell me. Maybe I'll be able to track down something from my end."

"Alright." Sarah sniffled. "I'll call you once I find out."

"Hey, what about... did you talk to them about it? Did you tell them about me?" Nicholas asked, trying and failing to hide the desperation in his voice.

"I was going to tell Shanice first. She was so young when... you know. She still speaks highly of you. Tonya and Thaddeus have, well, different opinions. I'm sure I can reason with them, just not yet with this new situation. You can't come over now. The police..."

"I know, Sarah. It's ok. I'm going to end this. I'll make sure Jon is put back where he belongs, so just take care of yourself and the kids. It'll all be over soon, I promise."

Nicholas pulled up maps and searched for every car dealership in the state. He knew that Jon could pick one at random and be fine with it, but he had been on the case for a long time. Back when he was still an officer, Nicholas and his partner had spent countless nights pondering the serial killer's operational pattern. Most had considered him a spontaneous and sporadic man, but there was a pattern there, a method behind his madness.

He was a creature of habit, one which he tried to fight on occasion but couldn't resist in the long run. Nicholas concluded that Jon had some sort of OCD that made it compulsory for him to do certain things in precise ways. Once those ways were uncovered, it would be easy to predict his next move. Candice's notes were the reason he was caught in the first place. Anyone with a keen eye would be able to spot it, but only after spending a lot of time observing the man.

He marked out the three dealerships closest to the city and the house but then marked two of them off for being too obvious. The third one was the furthest away and did not have the same strict regulatory laws. Nicholas left the trailer, called home, and found a directory where he could look for their phone number. Before he located it, Sarah called back with the phone number and address of the dealership.

It took him two taxis and a bus ride, but he managed to make it there just a few minutes behind the police. Nicholas watched from a bench on the opposite side of the dealership and saw Thaddeus talking to a man who looked to be in charge. Almost ten minutes later, Thaddeus offered the man his card and a handshake before getting back in his car. As he kicked on the engine, Thaddeus turned his head to the left, staring across the road, right at Nicholas. Acting quickly, he turned his head to hide his face, acting as though he was deeply interested in one of the cars.

Nicholas watched as his son drove off, only a few meters from him. He could not bear to face him—the anger and rejection in the eyes of the boy still haunted him. The nightmare had returned, recurring in different forms, each one more horrific than the last. Nicholas knew he would have to confront his son someday, but this was not the time or place. He waited until the area was completely cleared of police officers before he went in, heading straight for the man Thaddeus had spoken to.

"Excuse me. I have some questions pertaining to one of your vehicles."

"You with the police? They just left," the man replied in a heavy mid-western accent.

"I'm not. Which is why I will be asking different questions." Nicholas pulled his gun, letting the man see it before he returned it to his waist. "Now, I don't want to hurt you, but I need you to cooperate with me. The man you rented that car to is an escaped convict responsible for a series of murders. The people he has set his sights on now are my family, and I'm going to do anything I can to protect them."

"The man wants your family?"

"Yes. Do you understand?"

The man pulled out a photo from his back pocket and unfolded it carefully. He kissed it once before he turned it around to let Nicholas see. It was a photo of the man, a woman, and two little girls. They looked so happy against the backdrop of a home in autumn. Nicholas pulled his gaze away from the photo and looked at the man, who nodded grimly. "I understand what a man has to do for family. I'll help you."

"Thank you. Now, what did you tell him?"

"Your son?"

Nicholas froze, staring at the man.

"Yeah, it's the stance, the voice, the cheekbones. You look just like him after a few years and some serious downtime. Why aren't you working with him? Listen, man, whatever it is, I don't want to know, but you need to get with family. Forget the past and everything. Don't let anything get in your way of being with them. Okay? You never know when it may be too late, so you gotta make something like Pepsi."

"Live for now," Nicholas said with a smile. "Tell me everything you told him."

"I'll tell you one even better. If he comes within a fifty-mile radius of this property, I'll be able to track him to his exact location. They called ahead, talking about the man and the plates. I ran a search. We got trackers in most of our vehicles, but they're really low-tech. We're just starting out, you know? So, we can track it to about a thousand meters of where the vehicle is, but that's the most accurate we can get once it's out of range."

"Can it be taken out?"

"With the proper tools, yeah. But if it were, we'd be alerted here 'cause the car would trigger a warning."

"Alright, where is it?"

"Beach Park."

Nicholas did a quick calculation in his head. Jon expected Tonya to tell her brother, who would be quick to jump on the investigation. Once the police were involved, they would try to track him down, and the car would be the obvious choice. Beach Park was an open area with hundreds of people and vehicles. Even if he were hiding there, it would take forever to canvas the whole area to find one man.

The car was most likely ditched there as a means to throw the police off the scent. But Nicholas knew how cops thought and how criminals would try to outsmart them. He knew it well because he had become one. Jon knew that Thaddeus would have come alone, and if Jon wanted to get his son alone, there were other ways he would have done it. All he had to do was find the pattern, and he would know what Jon's plan was so he could stop it.

"How did he pay?"

"Cash. Why?"

"I need to see the money. If it's what I think, then I might have another location in mind."

The man went back into his office, with Nicholas following casually behind him. He stood by a desk, waiting until the man returned with the vehicle's spare key and two hundred and fifty dollars in mint condition. They were mostly twenty-dollar bills, which had been stacked together and held by a rubber band. Nicholas picked through them one by one, looking at their serial numbers—as expected, they were all running similar digits.

He asked for a pen and scribbled the info on one of the notes, shoved it into his pocket. The dealership owner looked on in awe, and Nicholas offered him a knowing smile before looking up at the corners of the building. There was a single camera in the room, pointing directly at him. "Is that thing recording? If it is, I want to see if it has any images of him when he was in here. And I want all recordings of me deleted. I'm sorry to cause you so much trouble."

"No, no trouble at all. It's somehow exciting—I get to help you, and you get to save your family. I don't fully understand the situation, and I know it would put me in trouble if I have more information than I already do. You were never here, but the man you're looking for wasn't either. He never came inside. We have cameras outside, but they're just a deterrent. Our budget doesn't let us operate them. We have the man out at the gate, so the cars are somewhat safe here."

"Well, thank you. I appreciate your help," Nicholas added, shaking the man's hand. "I hope someday I'll be able to see you under better circumstances."

"I wish you and your family the best of luck."

Nicholas left the dealership and took the first taxi he saw. He did not have an exact location, so he just asked the man to ride into town and go in circles. As he did, Nicholas called a criminally-inclined acquaintance. When he and his partners had stolen diamonds, they needed to sell them and get the money into their hands quickly—well, one of them did. The diamonds were sold, and he was paid in laundered money.

A few weeks later, the police caught the man, but he never gave up their location. Nicholas realized that the man who handed him the laundered money was one of the few in a network of connected money launderers across the state and even across the country. He befriended one of them, and Nicholas knew the man would trace the bills or knew someone who could. Once he had that information, he would only be a few steps away from finding Jon.

Chapter Forty Seven

"Are they still out there?"

Tonya drew the back curtain and glanced out of the window at the patrol car parked outside. She could see the officers seated inside, their eyes roaming around the house, searching. Just the thought of what the officers were doing sent shivers down her spine. Her brother had said more officers would come but, for some reason, only the one vehicle had shown up. Tonya and her mother had walked up to the vehicle to confirm the presence of the officers before joining her younger sister inside.

"Yeah, they are," Tonya called back to Shanice, who sat on the couch with her legs bunched up against her chest.

Tonya looked down at her phone, at the message she'd just sent to Tim. He had assured her he was safe, but Tonya wasn't taking any chances.

She'd told him who they were dealing with and he agreed to stay over at her mother's place for safety reassurance. It wasn't how Tonya planned to spend her day, but fate had its own plans.

A simple phone call and an invitation to speak to a man about a story started this whole mess. Tonya should have declined, returned to her bed where Tim was waiting for her. She should've never gone back into work.

"Why would he come now?" Shanice had risen to her feet and was pacing back and forth across the room. "He's been out of prison this entire time."

"Sit down, Shanice." Tonya looked impatiently from her cellphone to the door. Her only wish was for the door to open followed by the sight of her brother and her fiancé. Only then would she be able to calm herself. The fact both men were out there with Jon Harkavy scared her to no end. "I need to think... Thaddeus is out there looking. Let him do his job while we stay here and watch over Momma. That's the plan."

"I know what Thad said," argued Shanice. "But I don't understand why Jon would suddenly come for us now."

Tonya grabbed a hold of her sister's shoulders and lowered her voice. "Shanice, listen to me—*it doesn't matter*. They're going to find him and put him away again. This time for good. The police will solve this and we won't have to deal with him anymore. We can't add any more stress to Momma than she's already going through."

"Don't worry. I helped myself."

Both girls turned to see their mother leaning against the staircase railing. Her slightly grayed hair accentuated her features—the wrinkles which had begun to sprout over the years, the wry smile which held nothing but the pain of losing a husband and a father. Sarah was in her fifties but somehow she looked ten years older.

"Momma," Shanice called.

"It's okay, girls. It's alright. I've been through this before. I was there when this bastard was caught the first time and if he thinks he can come back again, he has another thing coming. I'll be there when he's caught again. By the second generation of Carters."

Sarah smiled. Moving to the cabinet beside the small kitchen table, she pulled out a bottle of rum, popped the cork and took two swigs from the heavy bottle. As she sat down at the table, Shanice pulled two shot glasses from the cabinet—one for Tonya and another for their mother.

Sarah smiled to herself, seeing both her daughters under the same roof, working together. The sight brought her such joy.

"To put away bastards." Tonya raised her shot glass, smiling at her mother and sister.

Sarah gave a solemn nod and, with a knowing smile, raised her glass in agreement. She and Tonya downed their drinks while Shanice licked the rim of the bottle, drawing a laugh from all three of them.

Tonya's phone rang and her heart did a backflip. The caller ID showed it was Thaddeus. She picked up and put the phone on speaker.

"Tonya, how are you?" he asked. "How are Momma and Shan?"

"We're fine, baby. We're here," Sarah replied, a hint of positivity in her voice that left Tonya feeling slightly more hopeful.

"Good. I've got a squad car heading over to my place. They'll bring Ebony and the kids over. Everyone will be under protective custody, then. Tonya, you said Tim was coming?"

"Yeah," she replied. "I spoke to him before you called. He's coming."

"Good, good. You said you received a note with a number to call. Where is it?"

Tonya sent her mind back to the events of the last few hours. She'd used a burner phone she'd bought for occasions like this, where she didn't want her work and private life mixing. She remembered tossing the phone into her car before she went to meet Jon. That was the last she had seen of it.

"I left my burner phone in the car. The number should be in the call log. Any way you guys can trace it?"

Tonya heard her brother radio the station, asking who had been in charge of towing her vehicle away. When he had a name, he thanked the operator and returned to his sister. "I'll see what we can do. I'll be home this evening. Call me if you need anything or remember anything else."

"Alright. Stay safe out there and call us too," Momma said, reaching out to touch the phone as though the device were her son.

Tonya ended the call and Shanice went upstairs to fix up the rooms. Ebony and the kids would need somewhere to sleep. Later, Tonya joined Sarah in the kitchen to prepare a meal. Her mother joked about how she had wanted this for a long time, but not under the circumstances it was currently happening.

"And you just happened to have enough food for this many people on hand?" Tonya asked, waving a hand at the piles of groceries.

Sarah sighed as she chopped a stalk of celery, her demeanor changing, instantly. Tonya noticed and kept silent at first, wondering what else might be bothering her. She suspected the burden of today's events weighed on her mother, but there was more to it than that. There was something Sarah wasn't telling her. Tonya had learned to read her mother's behavior from a young age, in an attempt to understand the woman and ensure she never made her mother angry.

"What is it, Mom?"

The question caused a tear to fall. Sarah tried to hide it, but her voice wavered. "Nothing, honey."

"Mom, you're crying."

Sarah dropped the knife. When she turned around, her cheeks were flushed, her eyes teary, but she had a smile on her face. "It's the onions."

Both women looked at the table. There were no onions. Tonya walked up to her mother and pulled her into a hug. She felt the tension leave Sarah's shoulders as the tears fell freely.

"It's alright, Momma," Tonya said. "It's alright."

"I spoke with your father."

The words left Tonya feeling cold.

"A few weeks ago. He wants to meet," her mother continued. "With all of us, together. He wants to talk to everyone before he surrenders himself to the police."

"What?" Tonya's eyebrows had risen halfway up her forehead. "What's going on? Why didn't you tell—"

"Because… I didn't know how you'd react. Your father needs this, Tonya. Everything he's done, he's done to keep this family safe. He's always kept us safe, even if it didn't seem that way. Nicholas wants what's best for us. You can't be angry—"

Tonya didn't speak much about her father. The last memories she had with him were in the basement of a psychopath who had tried his weird experiment on her. Sarah must've thought Tonya hated her father, as everything had begun to go south after he had disobeyed orders and murdered the man, but Tonya didn't care. The man who had taken her had ruined so many other lives and, in her book at least, her father had done the world a favor.

"Mom, why didn't you tell us you met him? I mean… He could have allowed Barr to live, but I would be dead if he hadn't come after me. Dad saved my life and if meeting all of us again is what's going to save his, then *yeah*. We have to."

Tonya's phone rang on the kitchen counter. She excused herself from and took the call into another room. "Where are you, Tim?"

"Ten, maybe twenty minutes away. How're things going on there?"

"It's fine. We're fine. Thaddeus' kids and Ebony are coming over. It's going to be one big party."

"Really? Well, it's a full house then. I'll stop and get some snacks."

"No, don't. Mom's about as ready as she's ever been for an emergency family meetup. And, Tim… She's been in contact with my dad. After all this time, he reached out to her. He wants to see us."

The line was quiet for a moment, the only sounds Tonya could hear were that of the vehicles driving past him. Tim cleared his throat before he spoke. "Are you okay with that?"

"He's my father. I have to be okay." Tonya noticed a box partially hidden underneath the dresser in her mother's bedroom. "Look, babe, just hurry and get here."

"Alright, I'll be there in a bit."

After hanging up, Tonya pulled the box free of the dark jean cloth which had kept it hidden from view. It was a wooden box—strong and sturdy—and the top was open, allowing her to peek inside. It took Tonya a moment, but she soon recognized the contents. The box belonged to her father and was full of his personal effects.

Tonya imagined her mother having to go to the office to pick them up. Rummaging through the box, she found something which brought back memories. It was folded into four halves, with the edges creased tightly. Even before she had finished opening the folds, Tonya knew what she held. She had seen it a thousand times over until the day it broke and was taken down.

The family portrait.

She smiled, running her finger over young Shanice, who sat comfortably in Momma's arms. Tonya tried to isolate the similarities between the baby in the picture and the girl who was cleaning the spare room. It was a stretch, but the eyes were unmistakably hers. Thaddeus had a mischievous look etched into his face, like he had somewhere to be and wanted nothing more than for the photoshoot to be done. Sarah and Nicholas appeared young and happy. Sarah's eyes were alive, full of joy and hope for her family's future.

Tears welled up in Tonya's eyes. Eventually, she put everything back, leaving the photo on the table before wiping her eyes and heading back out into the living room. Shanice and Momma were in the kitchen. From the big smile that broke out across her face, Tonya could tell Shanice had agreed to see their father as well.

Now, all they needed to do was tell Thaddeus.

***

Tonya went outside to speak to the police officers and let them know Tim was coming so they wouldn't turn him away. Then, she went back to the front porch and waited for the black vehicle which belonged to the man she loved to arrive.

Light reflected into her face. She heard a car pull up but didn't have a chance to confirm who it was.

She never felt the bullet.

A brief flash came from the bushes opposite the house. Her body was dropping to the ground before she even knew what was happening.

Tim and the officers leaped out of their vehicles, rushing towards the porch. A scream erupted when Shanice exited the house and saw Tim leaning over Tonya's body.

The bullet had gone through the side of her head, killing her instantly. In the span of a few seconds, her heartbeat stilled. Right there, on the front steps of the family household, Tonya Carter passed away.

On the other side of the road, Jon Harkavy smiled to himself. He had hit his target with extreme precision. All he had to do now was wait for the man who had locked him up to come looking. He had killed his first-born daughter. Nicholas Carter would have to take the bait.

CLOSING CREDITS ————————

This book was inspired by my deceased sister Laqueta Williams whose untimely murder began my path and my mission on becoming a detective and providing justice to the voiceless.

ABOUT THE AUTHOR ──────────

Alphonso Williams Jr.'s childhood was immersed in positive values that have extended through adulthood. These values helped him overcome adversity while living in the inner city of Florida. Once he finished his military enlistment with an honorable discharge, Alphonso Williams Jr.' obtained a degree in Psychology after joining the police force in Florida. He has spent twenty years in dedicated service of law enforcement and received several accolades and awards.

During his early years as a police officer, Williams' sister was murdered. This event would be the turning point for Williams' career in law enforcement and his decision to pursue a detective's path, providing justice to the voiceless. As a detective, Williams investigated and solved high-profile murder, corruption, and government accountability cases. Along with a Master's in Public Administration, these achievements are the scaffold to his present position as detective supervisor in his current agency.

With these achievements and life experiences on his belt, Williams tells the story of law enforcement and crime from an African American police officer and detective's perspective. His persistence in mentoring a generation of detectives and law enforcement agents who help the voiceless has spurred this resolve.

Made in the USA
Columbia, SC
31 August 2021